Comparing long-term placements for young children in care

Comparing long-term placements for young children in care

The Care Pathways and Outcomes Study – Northern Ireland

Dominic McSherry,
Montserrat Fargas Malet
and Kerrylee Weatherall

Published by British Association
for Adoption & Fostering
(BAAF)
Saffron House
3rd Floor, 6–10 Kirby Street
London EC1N 8TS
www.baaf.org.uk

Charity registration 275689 (England and Wales)
and SC039337 (Scotland)

British Library Cataloguing in Publication Data
A catalogue record for this book is available
from the British Library

ISBN 978 1 907585 77 7

Project management by Shaila Shah, Publisher, BAAF
Designed by Helen Joubert Associates
Typeset by Avon DataSet Ltd, Bidford on Avon
Printed in Great Britain by TJ International
Trade distribution by Turnaround Publisher Services,
Unit 3, Olympia Trading Estate, Coburg Road,
London N22 6TZ

BAAF is the leading UK-wide membership
organisation for all those concerned with
adoption, fostering and child care issues.

Contents

Contents

List of tables

List of figures

Acknowledgements

All three phases of the Northern Ireland Care Pathways and Outcomes Study have been funded by the Northern Ireland Health and Social Care (HSC) Research and Development Division of the Public Health Agency. We are extremely grateful for this assistance, without which such a longitudinal study would not be possible. We would particularly like to thank the outgoing Assistant Director of Research and Development, Dr Michael Neely, for his continuous guidance and support throughout this period.

We are extremely grateful to all the parents, carers and children who agreed to participate in interviews with the research team. When developing the study, we were acutely aware that parents and carers might be reluctant to take part, for fear of stirring up old memories for the children, and perhaps unsettling them. The fact that so many agreed to take part is testament to their belief that research is important, and their desire to help in any way possible those who may be following in their footsteps was generous and admirable. We also want to highlight the courage of the children themselves, for agreeing to meet and talk to strangers about their lives. We were honoured, humbled and inspired by our encounters with these families.

We also want to thank all those professionals across the five Health and Social Care (HSC) Trusts in Northern Ireland who facilitated our access to the study population placement records and during the interview recruitment process; and to the Northern Ireland Guardian ad Litem Agency (NIGALA), particularly Ronnie Williamson and Declan McAllister, for providing additional data on the numbers and dates of adoption orders made.

Throughout the study, we were greatly supported by our professional advisory group: Pat Armstrong (Western HSC Trust), David Bickerstaff (HSC Board), Joan Coulter (Belfast HSC Trust), Karen Fox (solicitor), Priscilla McLoughlin (BAAF), Vivian McConvey (VOYPIC), Beth Neil (University of East Anglia), Frances Nicholson

(DHSSPS), John Pinkerton (QUB), Peter Reynolds (NIGALA), Dermot Slevin (Southern HSC Trust), and Karen Winter (QUB). We were also assisted by our parent and children advisory groups. This guidance was particularly important in the early stage of the study when we were developing our interview materials, helping ensure that they were age-appropriate and sensitive to the particular needs of these families. We are also indebted to the four children who took part in the pilot of the children's interview materials, and to those who assisted with our recruitment DVD, namely: John Devaney, Aideen Gildea and Meabh McSherry.

In addition to the authors of this book, a number of other researchers have played important roles in the development of this study over the last decade or so: Emma Larkin, Greg Kelly, Clive Robinson, Dirk Schubotz, Wendy Cousins and Marina Monteith. A number of colleagues from within the School of Sociology, Social Policy and Social Work in Queen's University Belfast also supported the research team during the interview period, where there was a requirement to have two people present during interviews with children, and we appreciate the support they gave. These were: Duana McArdle, Áine Aventin, Chaitali Das, Mandi MacDonald, Seaneen Sloan, Grace Kelly and also Christine McSherry. We were also assisted with the qualitative analysis of the interview data by Joanne Jordan (parent and carer interviews) and Colm Walsh (children's interviews). Furthermore, several of our colleagues in the School, in addition to Priscilla McLoughlin from BAAF and Greg Kelly, provided very helpful feedback on early drafts of the book chapters. These were: Davy Hayes, Mandi MacDonald, Trevor Spratt, Karen Winter and Kathy Higgins. We are deeply indebted to them all.

Finally, we would like to thank BAAF, the publishers, for providing the opportunity to share our findings with a national and international audience, and particular thanks go to Shaila Shah, BAAF's Director of Publications, for her patience, guidance and support in preparing the manuscript for publication.

Notes about the authors

Dominic McSherry is a Senior Research Fellow at the Institute of Child Care Research, in the School of Sociology, Social Policy and Social Work, Queen's University Belfast. Since obtaining his PhD in psychology in 1999, he has been working as a researcher in Queen's, focusing on foster care and adoption, and the interface between social work and the courts. He has been Principal Investigator on the Care Pathways and Outcomes Study since 2003. He is currently leading three other large scale studies: 'At home in care: children living with birth parents on a Care Order' (funded by HSC R&D Division, Public Health Agency); 'Exploring regional variations in long-term placements for looked after children and young people' (also funded by HSC R&D Division, Public Health Agency); and 'Mind your health: the physical and mental health of looked after children and young people in Northern Ireland' (funded by the Office of First Minister and Deputy First Minister – OFMDFM). He currently sits on BAAF's Research Group Advisory Committee.

Montserrat Fargas Malet is a Research Fellow in the Institute of Child Care Research at Queen's University Belfast. She has worked on the Care Pathways and Outcomes study, and has been involved in a range of other research studies, including a systematic review on the mental health of Northern Ireland's children and young people, and a study looking at children living with their birth parents on a Care Order. She is currently working on a study looking at regional variations in the placement of children in care in Northern Ireland. Before joining the Institute of Child Care Research, she worked for over two years in the School of Social Work, on a project looking at the effectiveness of services provided by community groups to those affected by the Troubles (i.e. Northern Irish political conflict).

Kerrylee Weatherall is a Principal Social Work Practitioner and Manager in the Belfast Health and Social Care Trust. Her social work experience includes working with children, young people and their families, and is focused on prevention, family support, child protection, looked after children services, and private and public law proceedings. She worked in the Institute of Child Care Research, Queen's University Belfast from 2008–11 as a Research Fellow on the Care Pathways and Outcomes Study and on a study examining social work assessments and care proceedings.

Foreword

One of the few advantages of growing old is the sense of history it affords. Having been involved in child care research for 50 years, I have seen ideas come and go, and in some cases the same things come around again as if new. When I set out in the 1960s, child care services were less than 20 years old but with the honeymoon period ending, they were beginning to face radical criticisms. One was that they were punitive, even for parents who faced difficulties through no fault of their own; another was that they offered an "all or nothing" approach with children either staying at home or removed to care. Their effectiveness was also starting to be questioned, especially in view of the extensive use of residential care and, in particular, residential nurseries. These establishments had become suspect following Bowlby's writings on infant attachment and Jack and Barbara Tizard's delineation of the care babies require; hence by the 1960s they were being phased out. Finally, there was a concern that with so much provision available, the system was "supply-led" and monolithic, pushing children into inflexible placements ill-equipped to meet their needs.

Apart from provision for infant care, there was little evidence available to support criticisms and it was possible for local authorities to pursue contrasting approaches without causing concern. In 1964, East Suffolk, for example, fostered nearly 80 per cent of its children compared with Worcester's less than 30 per cent. When I discussed this with the social workers in each department, I found that they simply agreed with the prevailing policies.

In the late 1960s, more research reports on foster and residential care began to appear and they revealed an unsatisfactory situation. Much foster care practice, such as the designation of foster homes as "open" and "closed", had no scientific basis and there was a widespread belief that it was possible to create a perfect residential regime.

Because of these uncertainties, in the late 1970s the Department of

Health inaugurated an extensive programme of research to inform the situation. This provided startling evidence about the selection of placements, the avenues children followed, the amount of movement and placement disruption and variations in important practice areas, such as reviews, schooling, health care and children's contact with birth families.

Despite the importance of the new findings, it was still the case that most of the studies were descriptive rather than analytic, being predominantly concerned with systemic processes and statistical correlations; thus their limitations were soon apparent. At an international child protection conference in Dublin in 1996, Sir Michael Rutter asked researchers to move from studies of risk associations to ones of risk processes; in short, linking children's developmental outcomes to what professionals were doing.

This, of course, is a tall order as dozens of factors can be influential in social situations and it is difficult to disentangle what is causing what, especially as many concepts have "meaning" to those involved and so affect individuals in different ways. But progress has been made and I think it is fair to say that there is now a better understanding of the relationship between needs, services and outcomes.

The combination of this new knowledge with explorations of children's wishes, evaluations of placements other than foster and residential care and the legal requirement for individuals to enjoy a family life and protection from abuse has contributed to a more sensitive approach to the care of separated children, even if it has made life more difficult for professionals.

Unfortunately, greater knowledge usually produces complexity and since those idealistic early days, views on what is needed for looked after children have become more circumscribed and the value of blanket policies has been questioned. For example, issues such as contact with birth families and "permanency" are now seen as neither intrinsically good nor bad; it all depends on the "who, what, why and where". This makes current child care practice quite different from that pertaining 30 years ago and light years away from the original children's departments. But a worry is that in widening the debate, concepts lose their connection to children's needs and take on a life of their own. Some even become a lynchpin of ideologies about what is good for children, the merits of the welfare state, dealing with feckless parents and responding to abusive behaviour.

So in the midst of this debate, new research that incorporates children's needs, care experiences and the long-term effects of different interventions, as well as measuring the impact of factors previously scanted, is especially welcome. Moreover, the facts that this is an extensive study and undertaken in Northern Ireland enable it to contribute in an increasingly politically devolved world to local, national and international banks of knowledge on the care of young children who for various reasons find themselves looked after away from home.

Roger Bullock
Fellow of the Centre for Social Policy, Social Research Unit, Dartington

April 2013

1 Introduction

The Care Pathways and Outcomes study

This book presents the findings of a longitudinal study, entitled Care Pathways and Outcomes, which has been tracking the placement profile of a population of children (n = 374) who were under the age of five and in public care in Northern Ireland on 31 March 2000. It also explores how sub-samples of these children adjusted to the placements provided for them, the background factors that influenced placement provision, and how they, and their parents/carers, coped across the different types of placement provided. Three phases of the study have been completed to date with the findings from Phase 3 being the focus of this book.

Phase 1 (2000–2003)

The study began in 2000 and focused on exploring the number and types of placements provided to a population of young children over a two-year period (2000–2002). It was a response to growing evidence and concerns in Northern Ireland (Social Services Inspectorate, 1998) about the numbers of placements being provided for children in care and frequent moves, the high level of breakdowns, children "drifting" in care and the importance of providing these children with some stability in their lives. Similar concerns had been raised and reflected in studies conducted in England (Rowe and Lambert, 1973; Rowe et al, 1989; Utting, 1997; Department of Health (DoH) – *Quality Protects*, 1998).

Placement histories for the study population (n = 374) up to 31 March 2002 were examined. This was made possible by the research team being given access to the Social Services' placement database known as the Social Services Client Administration and Retrieval Environment (SOSCARE). In addition, an extensive review was conducted of social work case files up to 2000, to establish a baseline of family characteristics and background factors for the study popula-tion. On the basis of these data, Event History Analysis models were developed that examined the predictive relationship between the children's background characteristics and their placement by 2002, with age of entry to care and geographic location being the strongest predictors of either being adopted or returning home to birth parents (McSherry *et al*, 2008; McSherry *et al*, 2010). It was also found that a high percentage of the study population had been adopted (18%) or were in prospective adoptive placements (7%) by 2002. This was surprising as earlier research that had focused on rates of adoption from care in Northern Ireland up to 2000 had suggested ambivalence within local authorities in Northern Ireland to pursue adoption as a permanent placement option for children in care (Kelly and McSherry, 2003).

The current study appears to have coincided with a marked transition in long-term placement practice for young children in care in Northern Ireland towards adoption. However, it was clear from comparisons of the placements being provided across the different Trusts that there were significant differences in the number of children being adopted, ranging from 70 per cent in one Trust to 10 per cent in another. This meant that the study could be seen to be a "naturalistic" experiment of sorts, in that it had the capacity to reflect variations in placement practice across Northern Ireland, and that a form of randomisation of the study sample had occurred as a result of the Trusts' differential approaches to placing children for adoption.

Phase 2 (2003–2006)

Research in England and Wales had begun to look at the types and outcomes of placements provided for young children in care, and how they were faring, in comparative terms, across different placement types, particularly foster care and adoption (Ward *et al*, 2003; Sinclair *et al*, 2005). The key question that was being addressed was: *does placement type have a bearing on children's outcomes?* Answering this question for our study population became the key focus for the Care Pathways and Outcomes study.

Phase 2 of the study focused on how the children were progressing in their placements, from their parents'/carers' perspectives, and also how these parents/carers were coping themselves. Consequently, a third study population placement profile was established (for 31 March 2004). A sub-sample of the children's parents/carers (adoptive parents of 51 children, long-term foster carers of 56 children, and birth parents of nine children) were interviewed and their experiences and views examined in relation to: Social Services' involvement in the child's life; stresses involved in caring for the child; how the child settled in the placement and at school; support services available to the family; and contact arrangements. In addition, parents/carers completed the Strengths and Difficulties Questionnaire (SDQ) (Goodman, 1997), and the Parenting Stress Index (PSI) (Abidin, 1990). Findings indicated that adopted children were doing marginally better than children in long-term foster care, and that both these groups of children were faring markedly better than those children returned to birth parents (McSherry *et al*, 2008; Fargas *et al*, 2010).

Phase 3 (2006–2010)

Phases 1 and 2 of this study indicated that adoption had become a major placement option for young children in care in Northern Ireland, alongside both kinship and foster care and returning to birth parents, and that children were faring differently depending on the placement type. However, these perspectives had been gleaned from parents/carers and not the children themselves. Consequently, Phase 3 of the study aimed to explore the *children's* perspectives of their lives across the different placement types, focusing on their own views and experiences. Children's views were sought on issues such as: family composition; closeness of relationships; attachment to carers/parents and peers; self-concept; and experience of school.

The two main aims of this phase were:

- to ascertain whether or not children (and their parents/carers) fared differently depending on the type of placement they lived in: adoption, long-term foster care, long-term kinship care, on residence order, or living with birth parents; and

- to identify differences (if any) within and between placement types, particularly in terms of what was working well and not so well, in order to help inform policy and influence practice regarding long-term care planning for young children in care in Northern Ireland, and further afield.

The relevance of the study

This study provides a platform for children, parents and carers to have their voices heard about their life experiences in relation to being in care, adoption, the use of residence orders, and living with birth parents after the child has been in care. It looks at the positive aspects, the challenges, and the extent to which these children and parents/carers feel that their needs are being met. This has practical relevance for social care and legal practitioners and policy makers, particularly those working with children in care, adopted children, or those who return home. It is also hoped that the work will contribute to research in respect of child development, functioning, and outcomes.

The legislative framework underpinning this study is the Adoption (Northern Ireland) Order 1987 and the Children (Northern Ireland) Order 1995. Consequently, although the study findings are of immediate and direct relevance to Northern Ireland, they will also have a significance elsewhere in the UK, given that the Children (NI) Order 1995 is closely aligned to the Children Act 1989 in England and Wales. Furthermore, this book reports on one of the very few longitudinal studies examining placements and outcomes for children in the care system in the UK.

The issues under discussion in this book are ubiquitous, dealing with themes such as: children's attachment to parents/carers to whom they are not biologically related; the development of children's self-concept in this context; how these children develop social relationships; and how they position themselves in terms of understanding their place in the "family". These issues transcend geographical and legislative boundaries, and as such, the findings should be relevant to an international audience.

The aims of the book

This book has three main aims.

- Firstly, it describes the placement patterns for a population of children (n = 374) who were under the age of five and in care in Northern Ireland on 31 March 2000, up until 31 March 2007.
- Secondly, it highlights the similarities and differences, across a range of coping indicators, between groups of these children who progressed along five different care pathways: adoption; long-term foster care; long-term kinship care; residence orders; and living with birth parents.
- Finally, it illustrates the importance of presenting the perspectives of children when attempting to answer questions regarding children's experiences, and shows how this can be enhanced through the application of participatory or activity-based data collection methods.

There is no other study, to date, on pathways and outcomes for young children in care in Northern Ireland. Thus, this book is designed to meet the needs of service providers by illustrating the longer-term impact on the lives of young children of decisions made regarding where they should live on a long-term basis. This is done through profiling the capacity of the different placement types to provide children with stability and to promote their health and wellbeing. The book is also important at an academic level, as it contibutes to the existing knowledge-base regarding the longer-term impact on children's lives of living on a long-term basis in different placement types (Ward *et al*, 2003; Sinclair *et al*, 2005; Biehal *et al*, 2010). This is particularly important in relation to understanding the capacity of these placements to promote positive outcomes for these children, in terms of security, stability and permanence.

Identifying the key issues

The research team identified a set of key issues that would allow the team to develop a comprehensive perspective on how the children were progressing. This was preceded by an extensive review of the relevant literature, consultation with research colleagues from Great Britain and further afield, and informed advice provided by the Institute of Child Care Research's (where the study is based) Scientific Advisory Group (SAG), and the Public Liaison Committee (PLG), in addition to the study's three dedicated advisory groups (professional, parent and children), as well as consultation with a range of practitioners working on the ground. The issues included: placement stability; attachment; self-concept; health; behaviour; education; parental/carer stress; contact with birth families; family communication; and support.

The remainder of this chapter highlights the extent to which these issues are relevant for understanding the lives of children who are adopted from care, live with kinship carers or foster carers, are placed on residence orders (primarily with former kinship and foster carers), or are returned to their birth parents, and concludes with a summary of the content of the forthcoming chapters.

Children in care: The Northern Irish context

When efforts to secure children's safety and wellbeing within their own families fail, the law in Northern Ireland makes provision for the responsible Health and Social Care (HSC) Trust (equivalent to local authorities in Great Britain), of which there are five in Northern Ireland, to share parental responsibility with the parents through a care order (Children Order 1995, Article 50). In these cases, children are placed in substitute care placements, including: kinship care, foster care and residential care (primarily for teenagers).

A child can also be accommodated by an HSC Trust on a voluntary basis. In such instances, birth parents retain full parental responsibility and may resume care of their child at any time. When reunification with the birth family is thought possible, children subject to care orders may be "placed" with their birth parents, pending the birth parents making satisfactory progress in terms of addressing the HSC Trust's concerns, with a consequent revocation of the care order. Some children also remain living with their birth parents while the HSC Trust makes an application for a care order through the courts, and on some occasions thereafter, even when a care order is granted.

Children may remain in kinship and foster care for a short period of time before returning home, or on a longer-term basis if the parents' difficulties remain unresolved. In some instances, kinship and foster carers may choose to apply to have the care order superseded by a residence order (Children Order 1995, Article 8), which effectively takes the child out of the care system and affords the carers shared parental responsibility with the birth parents. In effect, the shared parental responsibility held by the Trust when a care order is in place is transferred to the carers when a residence order is granted.

Outcomes for children in care

The concept of "outcome" is commonly applied within academia and the media as a means of reaching a value judgement on what the care system offers those children who are deemed to require it. The UK Government has expressed concern about the numbers of children and young people in the care system for whom outcomes could be described as poor. Children who are in care have been found to be: 10 times more likely to be excluded from school; 12 times more likely to leave school with no qualifications; four times more likely to be unemployed; 60 times more likely to join the ranks of the homeless; 50 times more likely to be sent to prison; and their own children are 66 times more likely to need public care than the children of those who have not been in care (UK Joint Working Party on Foster Care, 1999; Social Exclusion Unit, 2003; Department of Health, Social Services and Public Safety (DHSSPS), 2006). They are also more likely to have physical and mental health problems, and emotional and behavioural difficulties (McCann et al, 1996; Ward et al, 2002; Meltzer, 2003; McCarthy et al, 2003; Dixon, 2007). Further, high proportions of children in the care system have been found to have low self-esteem and self-concept (Gil and Bogart, 1982; Hicks and Nixon, 1989; Ackerman and Dozier, 2005). Similar findings have been reported in the USA (Courtney and Barth, 1996; Courtney *et al*, 2001; Pecora *et al*, 2003; Casey Family Services, 2005). In Northern Ireland, 10 per cent of children in care were cautioned or convicted of an offence in 2008, compared to one per cent of all children (DHSSPS, 2009a), whilst 30 per cent of children in custody and 23 per cent of the adult prison population have spent time in care (Centre for Social Justice, 2008).

In educational terms, almost a quarter of children in care in 2010 had been covered by a statement of Special Educational Needs (SEN), compared with four per cent of the general school population in Northern Ireland. Furthermore, one in every 100 looked after children had been permanently excluded from school in 2009/10, compared with one in every 10,000 children in the general school population; 10 per cent had been suspended, compared with two per cent of the general school population; and 64 per cent of looked after children eligible to sit these exams (excluding those covered by a SEN) attained at least one GCSE/GNVQ at grades A–G, compared with 99 per cent of the general school population (DHSSPS, 2012).

The concept of "outcome", when comparing how children in care progress relative to their non-care peers, is problematic. At simple face value, the statistics present a very negative picture of the care system. However, a difficulty is that they typically compare children who have been in care with the general population of children, rather than with children from similar backgrounds who have not been in care. Another issue often overlooked is the fact that the care population is not a homogeneous group. At one end of the spectrum, there are children who enter care at a very young age and remain in stable long-term placements until adulthood and beyond, whilst at the other end, some children only enter the care system as teenagers as a result of deterioration in their behaviour that renders them beyond parental control. Consequently, on an arbitrary outcome measure such as behavioural adjustment, the score for the recently entered teenager is less likely to be related to their experiences of the care system than it would be for the child who had remained in a long-term stable foster placement. Furthermore, the score for the newly-entered teenager would be more likely to be reflective of problematic behaviour, and it would be unfair on the care system to suggest that this poor behavioural profile reflected the experience of being in care. Minty (1999, p. 997) commented that 'several longitudinal studies indicate that the outcomes for long-term foster care are generally much better than current professional prejudice suggests', and it has been recognised that a significant proportion of children who have been in the care system go on to experience rewarding and fulfilling lives (Festinger, 1983; Kufeldt et al, 1995; Dumaret et al, 1997; Schofield, 2002; Allen, 2003; Jackson et al, 2005; Biehal et al, 2010; Turner and Macdonald, 2011).

Adoption as a "solution" to the "problems" of care

For children unable to return to their birth parents, the search for stability and a sense of belonging to a family is a major goal of child welfare policy-makers and practitioners around the world (Thoburn, 2007). Since the 1980s, domestic adoption of children from care has become a major long-term placement policy initiative across the different countries of the UK (McSherry et al, 2010), a policy shared with the USA and Canada. However, no other country in Europe has a policy that places adoption as a central part of the strategy for children in the care system (Selman, 2010). Furthermore, across many countries in Europe, Africa, Australia and New Zealand, widespread domestic adoption of children from care without the consent of the birth parents, as occurs in the UK, would not be legislatively possible. Consequently, in places where adoption is not an option, foster care is used to provide a substitute family for these children, from infancy to adolescence (Thoburn, 2007). For example, in Germany, Denmark, Norway and Sweden, fewer children enter care when young, compared with the UK, but they are more likely to spend longer or remain until adulthood in care, thus increasing the proportions of older children in care (Thoburn, 2007).

In this context, the adoption of children from care in the UK can be seen, to some degree, as a social experiment, in that it was more of a social policy, rather than a research-driven initiative. The substantial research evidence regarding outcomes for adopted children that existed at the time was primarily related to children who had experienced traditional adoption or had been adopted from an institution; there was no significant research base on outcomes for children who were adopted from care.

The adoption of children from care is extremely controversial, involving the permanent severing of legal ties between children and their birth parents. Therefore, comparative research that examines the long-term impact upon children and their adoptive parents of adoption from care, relative to other forms of long-term placement provision, is vital. Rushton (2004, p. 94) commented that 'the consequences of adoption for very young children who were admitted to care following neglectful or abusive parenting is under-researched', and earlier stated that 'an important question is not just how adoptions turn out, but how they compare with other placement plans' (Rushton, 2003, p. 5). Seeking to provide answers to this type of question is a central goal of the Care Pathways and Outcomes study.

The contemporary research base suggests that adoption delivers better outcomes than long-term foster care. The use of the term "outcome" when comparing groups of children who enter the care system but follow different care trajectories or pathways, is less controversial, because some effort has been made to distinguish between different types of care experience, and comparison is not with standardised non-care peers, but with children who have relatively similar backgrounds and early childhood experiences. Triseliotis (2002, p. 31) noted that 'compared with long-term foster care, adoption still provides higher levels of emotional security, a stronger sense of belonging, and a more enduring base in life for those who cannot live with their birth parents'. Sinclair *et al* (2005) reported that adopted children were doing better on most outcome variables, although not dramatically so. They attributed this, in part, to the feeling of belonging to a family, which adoptive placements generate in children. They argued that the 'difference between adoption and long-term fostering is partly symbolic. Foster carers are not parents, while adoptive carers are' (p. 103). Yet, research by Schofield (2002, p. 271) highlights that some children who spend their lives with foster carers do consider them to be their 'real parents', in much the same way that adopted children view their adoptive parents. Rushton (2004, p. 95) also noted that 'despite deficiencies in the foster care system, some children and young people do, nevertheless, find a family for life through fostering'.

These findings have been supported more recently by Biehal *et al* (2010). Theirs is an important study, in comparative terms, for the current study, as it is one of only a handful of longitudinal studies that has been tracking a cohort of children through the care system, in this instance in England. The most recent phase of the study was overseen by Biehal and colleagues (2010), and was a continuation of the work of Sinclair and colleagues (2005) at the University of York. This primarily involved a parent/carer survey of 196 children adopted by strangers or foster carers, or in long-term foster care, and interviews with 37 children and their parents/carers. These were drawn from the original York sample of 596 children who were fostered in seven English local authorities in January 1998. This study revealed that children who were settled in long-term foster care viewed their carers as 'parental figures' (p. 6) and felt a strong sense of belonging to the foster family.

Returning home from care

Although there has been a growth in interest and research over the last decade in the lives of children who remain in foster care or are adopted, the experience of those children who return home after a period in care had received relatively little attention (Bullock *et al*, 1998) until more recently (Biehal, 2006; Farmer *et al*, 2011; Thoburn *et al*, 2012). Research that has managed to incorporate the experiences of these children (Aldgate and Bradley, 1999; Cleaver, 2000; Selwyn *et al*, 2003; Skuse and Ward, 2003; Sinclair *et al*, 2005) has highlighted two related methodological issues: firstly, the difficulty of attempting to recruit these "hard-to-reach" children, and secondly, the importance of trying to achieve this.

Although often described as an almost impossible task, Skuse and Ward (2003) managed to interview 39 per cent (n = 49) of their sample of children who had returned home at some point during the tracking period of their study (which examined children's own perspectives of care and accommodation). The study provided a worrying account of the lives of rehabilitated children, which was typified by a lack of formal support. Older children tended not to remain at home for long, with multiple transitions between different relatives being commonplace. The study raised questions concerning the emphasis placed on having children returned home, the extent to which these placements are supported when the child does return home, and the appropriateness of defining return-home placements as permanent. Similarly, research from Sweden has indicated that children who enter care for more than a few weeks, and then return home to their birth parents, do less well than children who remain in long-term stable care or are adopted (Vinnerljung *et al*, 2010).

More recently, Farmer *et al* (2011) looked specifically at what makes reunification work. They examined the patterns and outcomes of returning home through a two-year follow-up of 180 children in care, aged up to 14 years. All these children had been returned home from care in six local authorities in England during a one-year period. They found that returns that were subject to scrutiny by the Courts were more likely to succeed, and that the concerns that had led to care had often not been addressed. They recommended more targeted work with children with behavioural and emotional problems during their placement and greater consistency in arranging tailored support and intervention packages for children and their parents to support them when the child returned home from care.

Achieving placement stability

Having a stable and permanent home is important in terms of a child's ability to develop positive attachment relationships with a parent or carer. Continuity of attachments in early childhood predicts better peer relationships, fewer behavioural problems in later childhood and adolescence, healthier relationships, and better outcomes throughout life (Rutter, 1995; Aldgate and Jones, 2005).

In terms of comparing stability across the different types of placement, Thoburn (1991) argued that, when other variables are held constant, there was no difference in breakdown rates between children placed for adoption and those placed in "permanent" foster families. Furthermore, Triseliotis (2002) reported a diminishing of the differences in disruption rates between adoption and long-term foster care as older and more difficult children are adopted. However, Selwyn and Quinton (2004) reported quite substantial differences between the two. They followed 130 children who had a "should be placed for adoption" decision as the care plan, but 46 of them were not adopted but placed in long-term foster care. At follow-up, 46 per cent of the foster placements had disrupted compared to 17 per cent of the adoptive placements. However, although these two groups of children came from similar abusive backgrounds, the fostered children were older when they first entered care and when the decision was made, and were also more likely to have learning difficulties and health problems. This might explain to some degree the increased rate of placement breakdown for these children. Other research continues to suggest that children in long-term foster care remain at risk of either placement moves or placement breakdown, certainly more so than those in adoptive placements (Ward *et al*, 2003; Wilson *et al*, 2004; Sellick *et al*, 2004; Sinclair, 2005). For example, Sinclair (2005, p. 157) noted that in most instances 'long-term foster care does not offer a secure family for life'. More recently, Biehal *et al* (2010) found that, despite the fact that children in long-term foster care had as strong a sense of belonging to their families as adopted children, disruption rates for these children continued to compare unfavourably with those for adopted children.

Numerous Government initiatives (*Quality Protects*, DoH, 1999; *Choice Protects*, DfES, 2002; and *Every Child Matters*, DfES, 2003) have been launched to help ensure better life outcomes for children in care, which begs the question why the main thrust of the research findings continue to suggest that long-term foster placements are at greater risk of breakdown than adoptive placements. One argument is that current foster care structures do not encourage the commitment of the foster carer to the child, and vice versa, that will see them through the inevitable crises that they face. The alternative argument is that the focus on adoption as the "holy grail" has seen the status of, and the investment in, foster care and alternative forms of long-term family placement diminish. Rushton (2004, p.91) argued that 'advancing adoption as the preferred placement choice is driven not only by child-welfare imperatives, but also by the need to reduce state expenditure on the in-care population. Furthermore, to favour adoption, it is argued, may also turn alternatives like long-term foster care and residential care into second-class options, although good quality placements of this kind may be the first choice for some children'. Similarly, Sinclair (2005, p. 17) noted 'a lack of attention to long-term foster care as opposed to the more highly valued adoption'.

Children's attachments

Anyone familiar with the processes involved in seeking care orders for vulnerable children, and in planning for their long-term placement, will appreciate how commonly the issue of a child's attachment to birth parents and current carers, and their capacity to attach to new long-term carers, is raised as a central issue of concern, often requiring expert clinical assessment. Attachment, i.e. the ability to form secure and lasting relationships to a caregiver, is widely viewed as the bedrock upon which all future interpersonal relationships are founded (Bowlby, 1951, 1969, 1973; Belsky and Cassidy, 1994; Rutter, 1995; Aldgate and Jones, 2005). Security of attachment refers to the degree to which a child has internalised experiences based upon continuous exposure to significant others who are perceived as trust-worthy, available, sensitive, and loving. The child requires a secure base to establish positive relationships, and this can be detrimentally affected by serial-attachment experiences, while frequent changes of caregivers may be painful and anxiety-provoking for the child (Thompson, 1998; Schofield and Beek, 2006). Emotional availability and consistency are extremely important in promoting healthy development (Iwaniec, 1995), and the emotional security derived from attachment-relationships (reflected by the child's confidence in the availability, familiarity, and responsiveness of attachment figures) is central to the development of emotional wellbeing (Bowlby, 1969).

Parental attachment

Some children in care experience a number of placements with different foster carers and may experience these changes as relationship losses early in their lives. This, in turn, may 'affect their ability to form a secure attachment relationship with their primary caregiver' (Cole, 2005, p. 44). Despite these concerns, numerous research studies have found that the majority of children in care are able to form satisfactory attachment relationships with their new foster or adoptive parents (Rushton, 2003; Kaniuk et al, 2004; McSherry et al, 2008). Research that has concentrated on the minority of children who do not develop satisfactory attachments with their new caregivers highlights a range of precipitating factors, such as: a history of multiple abuse and frequent moves in foster care (Groze and Rosenthal, 1993); active rejection by birth parents; and multiple child behavioural and emotional problems (Rushton et al, 2003).

Peer attachments

The concept of attachment refers to the nature of the relationships with significant others or a stable loving bond with either parents or peers (Ainsworth, 1989). Throughout adolescence, children rely less on parents as attachment figures, as their relationships with peers become increasingly important when seeking comfort in times of stress (Laible et al, 2004). Laible et al (2004) found that 'both parent and peer attachment were related to adolescent self-esteem, although the nature of the relationship was different for each variable' (p. 711). Furthermore, research conducted by Nelis and Rae (2009) suggested that adolescents who were securely attached to their peers were significantly less depressed and anxious than those who were insecurely attached.

Children's self-concept

Children who have been abused or neglected, like many of those who enter the care system, are more likely to have poor self-esteem and self-concept because of feelings of incompetence and lack of support and encouragement from parents (Fischer and Ayoub, 1994; Harter, 1998; Kim and Cicchetti, 2009). Conversely, those who receive affection, acceptance, safety, and assistance from their parents are more likely to show higher levels of self-esteem and self-concept (Peterson *et al*, 1983; Barnes and Farrell, 1992; Roberts and Bengtson, 1993; Kim and Cicchetti, 2003; DeHart *et al*, 2006).

High proportions of children in the care system have been found to have low self-esteem (Ackerman and Dozier, 2005), in part due to their early experiences of abuse and neglect (Schofield, 2002) but also because of the 'negative stereotypes inflicted on them by society' (Martin and Jackson, 2002, p. 126). Fostered children have been found to show lower levels of self-esteem than non-fostered samples (Gil and Bogart, 1982; Hicks and Nixon, 1989; Kaufman and Cicchetti, 1989), although other studies have found no difference (Lyman and Bird, 1996; Flynn *et al*, 2004). In a study of 96 foster families with a foster child and a birth child, the self-esteem of foster children appeared to be more affected by support and conflict processes in the foster family than was the self-esteem of birth children in the same family (Denuwelaere and Bracke, 2007). It has been argued that 'foster parents can have a positive and lasting effect on children's self-esteem' (Luke and Coyne, 2008, p. 403). In fact, some studies have revealed improvements in foster children's self-esteem and self-concept when their carers offered them acceptance, security, and sensitive parenting (Ackerman and Dozier, 2005; Schofield and Beek, 2005).

The self-esteem of adopted children has also been empirically examined. In a series of meta-analyses, Juffer and van IJzendoorn (2007) found no difference in self-esteem between adoptees (N = 10,977) and non-adopted comparisons (N = 33,862) across 88 studies. This was equally true for international, domestic and transracial adoptees. In a study seeking the perspectives of eleven-year-old adopted children (some adopted as babies in the UK, and some adopted at slightly older ages from Romania), Beckett *et al* (2008) found that 'the ease with which children can talk about adoption does appear to be associated with higher self-esteem and the individual child's difficulties, as well as family composition' (p. 29).

Children's health

The relationship between health and social inequalities is well documented (Leon and Walt, 2001; Wilkinson and Pickett, 2006; Marmot, 2010) in that inequalities in social conditions are associated with poor health for particular vulnerable social groups. Both nationally and internationally, children in care are considered one such group (Mather, 2010). They are largely drawn from families who experience considerable social disadvantage and deprivation (Bamford and Wolkind, 1988; Bradshaw and Millar, 1991; McSherry *et al*, 2008; 2010). Most of those who enter care have experienced abuse or neglect (DoH, 2009), which may have adverse consequences for their cognitive development, educational attainment, self-efficacy, capacity to form attachments, and social competencies (Tanner and Turney, 2003).

Physical health
Research evidence suggests that children in care have a greater degree of physical health problems and risks than their peers (Williams *et al*, 2001; Ward *et al*, 2002; Hill and Thompson, 2003; Leslie *et al*, 2003; Mooney *et al*, 2009). Compared with children of the same age and social status who live with their birth parents, children in care are more likely to have incomplete immunisations; lower health surveillance; worse dental health; poorer nutrition; to make unhealthier lifestyle choices (Mather, 2010; Williams *et al*, 2001), and may leave care with unidentified physical health needs (Hill and Watkins, 2003). A longitudinal study of children in care in England (Skuse and Ward, 2003) found that 52 per cent had a health problem which required outpatient treatment, with 26 per cent having more than one problem requiring treatment. The study estimated that 15 per cent of children were likely to have required treatment from a specialist. Similarly, in

Wales, Williams *et al* (2001) found that the 'overall health care of children who have been established in care for more than six months is significantly worse than for those living in their own homes, particularly with regard to emotional and behavioural health, and health promotion' (p. 280). However, it was also found that children in care were more likely to have had a recent hearing or eye sight test, and to report less physical ill health overall, than children living at home with their birth parents.

These health problems might be caused by early abuse and neglect, or poor parenting, but there may also be a deterioration of the child's health while in care (Gallagher, 1999). In fact, a study that focused on statutory health assessments for children in care in England suggested that the system might be failing to address identified health problems, since nearly 'half of all health recommendations had not been acted on by the time of the follow-up review' (Hill and Watkins, 2003, p. 10). It has also been noted that there is 'an absence of accurate, up-to-date data concerning children's health needs and their access to health care on social services case files' (Ward *et al*, 2002, p. 20). This is often due to frequent changes in social workers and children's placement moves. In addition, 'there is poor access to health records or liaison between health professionals' (Anderson *et al*, 2004, p. 31).

Mental health

In the 1990s, a few studies (McCann *et al*, 1996; Dimigen *et al*, 1999) attempted to explore the mental health of children in care. These were hampered to some extent by small sample size, geographical area, and the lack of comparison groups in the general population. However, the studies did highlight the high level of need experienced by these children on entry to care and when living in foster and residential placements. In 2000 and 2004, Meltzer and colleagues conducted the child and adolescent mental health study in Great Britain, and in 2003 conducted the first national survey of the mental health needs of looked after children in England, with surveys following for Wales and Scotland (Meltzer *et al*, 2003, 2004a; 2004b).

Meltzer *et al* (2003) found that as many as 36 per cent, 46 per cent and 44 per cent of children respectively in care in England, Wales, and Scotland had conduct disorders compared with five per cent, six per cent and four per cent of children in private households. As many as 11 per cent, six per cent and 14 per cent respectively had emotional disorders compared with three per cent, two per cent and four per cent of children in private households. In addition, 11 per cent, 12 per cent and 11 per cent of these children were found to have hyperkinetic disorders (ADHD) compared with three per cent, two per cent and one per cent of children in private households (Meltzer *et al*, 2003, 2004a, 2004b). In addition, it was found that 45 per cent of 5–17-year-old children in care had a mental health disorder, compared to 10 per cent of the general population (Meltzer *et al*, 2003). The rate of mental disorder for 5–10-year-olds in care was over five times higher than that for the general population (42 per cent compared to 8 per cent), whilst for those children aged 11–17 years, the rate was four times higher (49 per cent compared to 11 per cent). These older children were also seven times more likely to have conduct disorders. Children in residential care were much more likely to have a mental disorder than those in foster care, or placed with family or friends (72 per cent compared with 40 per cent and 32 per cent). They were also more likely to have other problems, with over 75 per cent having at least one physical complaint, while in addition they were twice as likely as children with no mental disorder to have difficulties with reading, mathematics and spelling. They were also twice as likely to play truant and four times more likely not to spend time with friends.

More recently, researchers have attempted to compare the mental health profile of children in care with that of children from a range of socio-economic backgrounds. The British epidemiological study undertaken by Ford *et al* (2007) compared the mental health of children in care with that of children living in deprived and non-deprived private households. They found that children in care had a significantly higher prevalence for most psychiatric disorders, after controlling for age and sex, in comparison to all children from private households, and importantly, from an equitable comparison perspective, to the most disadvantaged children from private households. The percentage of children scoring in the normal range on the six SDQ sub-scales was nine per cent of the sample of children in care, in contrast with 41 per cent of the disadvantaged children and 53 per cent of the non-deprived sample (ibid).

Children's behaviour

SDQ and children in care

Significant majorities of children in foster care have been found to fall within the borderline or abnormal range on the SDQ "total difficulties" score based on parent/carer reports. This has been found to include as many as up to half (Dunne and Kettler, 2008; Egelund and Lausten, 2009) and as much as three-quarters (Milburn et al, 2008) of the populations under investigation, suggesting that these difficulties may be having a significant impact on these children's lives. Research has also indicated that children in care experience some, or significant, difficulties in all of the subscales of the SDQ. For example, Whyte and Campbell (2008) found that 56 per cent of Northern Irish carers, 39 per cent of teachers, and 30 per cent of children aged 11 and older considered that there were significant difficulties in all or some of the domains of the SDQ. Another Northern Irish study found that children in care had higher levels of emotional symptoms, conduct problems, hyperactivity/inattention, and peer relationship problems, and fewer prosocial behaviours, relative to age-appropriate norms for parent, teacher and self-reports (Teggart and Menary, 2005). Millward et al (2006) found that children in care scored significantly higher than a non-care sample on conduct problems, emotional problems (anxiety and depression), hyperactivity, and problems with peer relationships. Other research has indicated that children in care score more frequently within the pathological range especially for hyper-activity and conduct problems (Egelund and Lausten, 2009) and are more likely to score within the abnormal and borderline range on the SDQ prosocial behaviour scale (Dunne and Kettler, 2008).

Behavioural outcomes for adopted children

While a body of evidence suggests that children in care are particularly vulnerable to experiencing physical health and complex behavioural and emotional problems, less is known about the prevalence of these difficulties for children who have been adopted from care. This is particularly pertinent given the increased use of adoption for a broader range of children, including older children and those with multiple needs. Initial evidence suggests that children adopted later (aged 10 or above) are more at risk of disrupted placements (DoH, 1999), with an early study by Fratter *et al* (1991) suggesting that they share an equal risk of placement breakdown as those of the same age in "permanent" foster care. A growing body of clinical and anecdotal evidence also suggests that a significant number of adoptive parents and foster carers of older-placed children are facing major relationship and behavioural difficulties, particularly during mid-to-late childhood and adolescence (Howe and Fearnley, 2003). More recently, Biehal *et al* (2010) found that just over one-third of the children in their sample, who were either adopted or in stable long-term foster care, scored in the clinical range for behavioural and emotional difficulties, as measured by the SDQ, and that there were no significant differences between these two groups on this measure.

Children's education

Children in care may experience disruption to their schooling due to multiple placement moves, which can impact adversely on the development of social relations and may lead to slow academic achievement (Courtney *et al*, 2004). Multiple placements may deter the process of special education provision, and furthermore, disabilities may go undetected and services not provided (Trout, 2007). Research has found that children who experience cognitive delay and placement instability (Courtney *et al*, 2004) are more at risk of poor academic performance. Other studies have reviewed problem behaviours of children and young people known to child welfare services and found that, when reviewing the academic status of children with emotional and behavioural disorders (EBD), 91 per cent of the sample

21

was academically deficient and did not perform at age or grade level (Trout *et al*, 2003).

Similarly, Crozier and Barth (2005) found that adolescents who were known to child welfare services, due to alleged maltreatment, scored below average on cognitive functioning and academic achievement. Trout *et al* (2007) conducted a literature review of 29 published research studies on the academic and school functioning behaviours of students in care from 1940–2006 and evaluated these to assess academic and school functioning, school performance, and the quality of the reported research. It was found that children in care were at risk of both short- and long-term failure at school. It was also noted that intervention programmes focusing on the mental health, family functioning, and behaviour of these children should also include academic functioning in order to better understand their needs, and to aid the design of services to improve the short- and long-term educational outcomes of this population.

Longitudinal studies have indicated that the IQ levels of adopted children become more similar to that of their birth parents as they get older (Fulker *et al*, 1988; Plomin *et al*, 1997), and that the correlation between the adopted child and their adoptive parents' IQ appears much lower than the correlation with their birth parents (McGue *et al*, 1993; Plomin *et al*, 1997). In a meta-analysis of 62 studies examining whether the cognitive development of adopted children differed from that of children in institutionalised care, in the birth family, or compared to their non-adopted "environmental siblings" or peers, Juffer *et al* (2005) found that adopted children scored higher on IQ tests than their siblings or peers who remained with their birth families, and that their school performance was better. They also did not differ from their non-adopted environmental peers or siblings in IQ levels, nor in their school performance, particularly in relation to language ability. It was also found that although the percentage of adopted children who needed special education for learning problems was twice as large as that for non-adopted children, they did better than their birth siblings or peers who were in 'poor institutions or deprived families' (p. 310).

Parent/carer stress

It is widely accepted that stress in parenthood is to be expected and is part and parcel of the 'costs and rewards of children' (Nomaguchi and Milkie, 2003), and that the presence of parental stress will not inevitably lead to negative consequences, such as disruption and trauma for children. According to Abidin (1992), parental stress can have a positive influence up to a certain point, after which it becomes problematic. If stress is experienced within the confines of boundaries, without it leading to negative consequences, then it can be a source of stimulation and an opportunity for growth. In contrast, stressed-out parents who are irritable, uncommunicative, critical and harsh in their parenting style are more likely to cause problematic behaviour in their children, which in turn results in further parental stress, thus creating a vicious circle (Webster-Stratton, 1990).

Bearing in mind the stresses of "normal" parenting, those parents or carers of children who have past experiences of the care system, or who remain within the care system, are faced with greater parental challenges than the norm. Research evidence consistently demonstrates that children in care have higher emotional disturbance than the general population (Meltzer et al, 2003). Yet, there is an expectation that when children come into care, their new care placement will 'provide compensatory experiences of care that enable their positive development' (Morgan and Baron, 2011). Given the previous experiences of these children, parents/carers are tasked with providing a substitute nurturing and safe family home for children who typically have medical and health problems, dysfunctional attachments, academic and cognitive problems, and behavioural and psychiatric disorders (Carbone et al, 2007). At the same time, they are expected to manage relationships with birth family members, their own family tensions, the risk of placement disruption, the potential for complaints or allegations, and social work involvement (Wilson et al, 2000). Relatively few studies have explored parental stress on parents and carers who have themselves experienced or are experiencing the care system (Quinton et al, 1998; Bird et al, 2002; Judge, 2004; Lipsombe et al, 2004; Schofield and Beek, 2005; Wilson,

2006; Morgan and Baron, 2011). Moreover, examining and comparing parental stress across different types of care placement is an under-researched topic in the literature.

Contact with birth families

The similarities and differences in relation to contact with birth families have been explored between different types of placements for children in care, in particular adoption, foster care, kinship care, and residential care (Bilson and Barker, 1995; Neil *et al*, 2003; Neil and Howe, 2004; Farmer, 2010).

Contact in foster care

In the late 1980s and early 1990s, contact with birth families was assumed to be valuable for children in foster care, and some benefits were attributed to it, such as: facilitating the child's return home (Millham *et al*, 1986); preventing breakdowns (Berridge and Cleaver, 1987); and having a positive impact on the child's behavioural and emotional wellbeing (Berridge and Cleaver, 1987; Hess and Proch, 1988; Thoburn and Rowe, 1991). Nevertheless, according to Quinton and colleagues (1997, 1999), these aspects were never fully corroborated by robust scientific evidence, and recent research (Schofield *et al*, 2000; Macaskill, 2002; Sinclair *et al*, 2005; MacDonald and McSherry, 2011) has revealed that 'contact can be detrimental as well as beneficial for children' (Sen, 2010, p. 2).

On the one hand, a variety of challenges and problems have been reported in relation to contact with birth families, including:

- foster carers' difficulties in handling aggressive or violent birth parents (Wilson *et al*, 2000);
- practical problems, such as the extent of commuting involved, and the amount of time children spend in cars travelling with multiple strangers, or the unsuitability of the environment/venues provided for visits (e.g. child protection offices) (Kenrick, 2009; Humphreys and Kiraly, 2011);
- the unreliability of birth family members (e.g. failing to turn up or

being consistently late), which often causes disappointment, distress, feelings of being rejected and upset to children, and inconvenience to foster families (Moyers et al, 2006);

- placing children at risk of physical or sexual abuse during contact (Selwyn, 2004; Sinclair et al, 2004; Moyers et al, 2006);
- children (particularly infants) being rendered unable to have established routines and the consequent discontinuity of care, which may lead to high levels of stress and anxiety, and might jeopardise the child's development in the long-term (Kenrick, 2009; Humphreys and Kiraly, 2011; Schofield and Simmons, 2011);
- the triggering of "loyalty conflicts" for children (Leathers, 2003), thereby undermining the influence of foster carers and replaying negative relationships (i.e. entrenched, unresolved attachment difficulties), which in turn might cause the deterioration of children's emotional wellbeing (Moyers et al, 2006) and conduct; and
- ultimately, these issues may contribute to placement instability or disruption (Wilson et al, 2000; Macaskill, 2002; Sinclair et al, 2004, 2005; Loxterkamp, 2009).

On the other hand, it has been argued that contact with birth families can be valuable and beneficial for children. For instance, Moyers et al (2006) found that, although the majority of the foster children in their study experienced significant and persistent problems in their contact with birth family members, 'in the cases where social workers took action, changes usually resulted in definite improvements for the young people and their placements' (p. 557). They also argued that contact with other relatives, such as grandparents or cousins, could have a positive impact on children. Similarly, in their study of 58 children in long-term foster care, Schofield et al (2000) found that despite contact being problematic for most of them, the four children who had no contact were amongst the group of children experiencing more difficulties. An even more positive picture was presented in Cleaver's (2000) study in which sustained contact with the birth mother was found to be among the factors positively associated with the child's adequate adjustment to their foster placement.

Foster carers seem to display both positive and negative attitudes towards contact (Wilson and Sinclair, 2004); thus, while some reported being satisfied with contact arrangements and managed to establish good working relationships with birth parent/s and relatives (Oke et al, 2012), others felt that contact left them dealing with the child's distress and disappointment (if the relative failed to turn up) or placed a further burden on them in terms of transportation and other arrangements (Triseliotis et al, 2000; Sen and Broadhurst, 2011). Moreover, many perceived support and practical help to be vital if contact was to succeed (Oke et al, 2012).

Comparing contact in kinship and foster care

Some studies have compared kinship and foster care in relation to contact with birth family, and these have revealed some differences between the two types of placement. One of the main differences is that kinship carers have been found to experience more difficulties in terms of the relationship they have with the birth parents. Sykes and colleagues (2002), in a qualitative study of 20 kinship care placements, found 'a high degree of tension among the families of kinship carers. In only three out of the 20 cases was there no evidence of conflict between carers and birth family' (p. 44). Contact visits were notably difficult to manage and control, and sometimes these difficulties were found to affect the children. In another study conducted in Spain, kinship carers found contact more challenging than foster carers (Palacios and Jiménez, 2009). More recently, in a study in England, Farmer (2010) found that over half of the kinship carers sampled (54%) had difficult relationships with the children's birth parents or other birth relatives, compared with a much smaller percentage (16%) of foster carers.

Furthermore, children in kinship care often have more frequent and unsupervised contact with birth parents (Rowe et al, 1984; Berrick et al, 1994; Palacios and Jiménez, 2009) than those in foster care. For instance, in Farmer's (2010) study, kinship and foster placements differed in terms of the supervision of contact visits: kinship carers supervised contact in 43 per cent of placements, with 25 per cent supervised by social workers; whereas in foster placements, carers supervised contact in only 16 per cent of placements, with social workers undertaking this role in 55 per cent of these placements. Contact supervision was found to be of vital importance to the stability of kinship care placements and it was observed that when contact was supervised either by social work staff or the carers themselves, there were significantly fewer disruptions in kinship care than in foster care.

Contact in adoption

In the UK, as the number of domestic adoptions of children in care has steadily increased, there has also been a move towards more post-adoption contact (Ryburn, 1998). Lowe and Murch (1999) found that 83 per cent of the 226 adoptive families included in their postal survey had some type of contact with one or more of the children's birth relatives. This rise in contact has been primarily driven by concerns about the consequences of closed adoption, in particular, its potential to exacerbate feelings of loss and separation, and cause anxiety in the child and worry about family members, and has a detrimental effect in helping the child develop a positive sense of self-identity (Neil, 2010). The most commonly used contact arrangement is "letterbox contact", an "indirect" form of contact which consists of a regular exchange of letters, cards and photographs between adoptive parents and birth relatives mediated by the adoption agency (Neil, 2002; McSherry *et al,* 2008).

A plethora of research studies over the last decade or so have been investigating contact arrangements for adopted children, particularly focusing on: information exchange (Logan and Smith, 1999); the perspectives of children (Thomas *et al,* 1999); face-to-face contact arrangements between adoptive and birth families, and an assessment of contributory factors and obstacles in successful contact (Logan and Smith, 1999); the impact of contact on families (Macaskill, 2002); decision-making in contact arrangements and the attitudes of professionals (Harris and Lindsey, 2002; Rushton, 2003); and the impact of contact on adopters' sense of parenthood (MacDonald and McSherry, 2011, 2013).

Children's perspectives on contact

'One noticeable gap in the literature is the scant attention being paid to the meaning and experience for the child of ongoing contact with the birth parent(s)' (Harris and Lindsey, 2002, p. 148).

Dance and Rushton (2005, p. 18) commented that 'although a considerable amount of research has been conducted on young people who have been placed for adoption and those living in long-term foster care, hearing the views of those young people directly is rare'. Indeed, children's perspectives on contact have not been sought until relatively recently. Those studies that include the children's own views have revealed the importance that most children in care give to contact and maintaining their links with their birth families (Macaskill, 2002; Mendenhall et al, 2004; Mullan et al, 2007; Sen and Broadhurst, 2011). For instance, in Sinclair et al's (2005) study of foster placements in England, it was found that most children appeared to want contact with their birth families (sometimes with particular family members and not others) and often more contact than they were getting, although according to their foster carers, nearly six out of ten children experienced distress after the visits. Furthermore, in studies of children in kinship care, their most common wish was to have more contact with their birth parents (Aldgate and McIntosh, 2006; Aldgate, 2009).

In another study that sought the views of foster carers, children and social workers, Moyers et al (2006) highlighted the importance for children in care of being able to talk about their past and their birth family with their carers or others; this was more likely to be the case when children had beneficial contact. They also found that 22 per cent of the children in their sample were upset because of the lack of contact with someone important to them, usually their mother, siblings, or their father. However, some children in kinship care have talked about feeling disappointed or "let down" by birth parents, while others have expressed issues of "divided loyalties" (Burgess et al, 2010).

Thomas *et al* (1999) interviewed 41 children, aged between eight and 15, who were adopted when they were five years old or over and had previously been in care. Most of them (n = 38, 93%) talked about contact, although only 24 (59%) were having direct or indirect contact with birth family members, whilst 26 (63%) had no contact with their birth parents, with seven children stating that they would have liked to have some form of contact with one or both of their birth parents. The study also revealed that some children did not appear to understand why it was not possible either to have contact or have more contact with their birth families, and some had not been given the opportunity to discuss their wishes and feelings about contact with their adoptive families or any other significant adult.

The scope and coverage of this book

This book has 13 chapters.

Chapter 1: Introduction

This provides a summary of the book and its structure, and places the Care Pathways and Outcomes study within a contemporary research and policy context, within Northern Ireland, across the UK, and internationally, in relation to the long-term placement of children in care. It also highlights the unique contribution that findings from the study can make to the existing knowledge-base regarding how best to ensure that young children in care enter placements that provide stability and promote their health and wellbeing.

Chapter 2: Methodology

This chapter details the study methodology and the innovative aspects of recruitment and data collection. For example:

- the research team developed a DVD that was sent to potential participating families, along with information sheets for parents/ carers and children;
- two interactive activities were developed by the research team to facilitate the applications of two standardised measures; and

- the research team also developed a storybook, termed the "me-book", which acted as a catalyst for discussion during a semi-structured interview with the children about their lives.

Chapter 3: The children and their placements

Chapter 3 describes the placement profile for the study population (n = 374 children) on 31 March 2007, and explores a range of factors that were related to the type of placements provided. It also compares the capacity of the different placements to provide the children with stability. Finally, the chapter profiles the children and families who took part in the interview phase of the study. In total, 135 families were approached to participate in interviews, and 77 families were recruited, with parents/carers and children being interviewed. The placements included:

- adoption (n = 18)
- long-term foster care (n = 19)
- long-term kinship care (n = 13)
- on a residence order (n = 15)
- living with birth parents (n = 12)

Chapters 3–12 conclude with a summary of key findings, which are further discussed in Chapter 13.

Chapter 4: Children's attachments

This chapter explores issues of attachment, in terms of the children's relationships with their parents/carers and peers, from the perspectives of both the children and their parents/carers. These issues emerged from the quantitative analysis of the Inventory of Parent and Peer Attachment – Revised for children (IPPA-R) (Gullone and Robinson, 2005) that was completed by the children, and the qualitative analysis of the interviews with children and parents/carers. The semi-structured interview schedule with parents had sections on attachment of the child towards them and other family members; while the "me-book" contained sections that looked at their family and the level of closeness to family members; feelings towards their family and the wishes they had for them; and whether they would like to remain living with their parents/carers when they were older. Quantitative and qualitative analyses focus upon comparisons of children within and between the different placement types.

Chapter 5: Children's self-concept

Chapter 5 explores and compares children's self-concept within and between the five different placement types. These findings emerged from the quantitative analysis of the Piers-Harris Children's Self-Concept Scale (Piers and Hertzberg, 2002) completed by the children, and the qualitative analysis of the interviews with the children. Children were asked specifically about their level of life satisfaction, as well as their feelings and wishes, when completing the "me-book".

Chapter 6: Children's health

This chapter focuses on children's physical and emotional/psychological health. The interviews with the children and the parents/carers touched upon the subject of health, in terms of understanding the child's health needs, worries in relation to the child's health, the services received to meet those needs, and satisfaction with these services.

Chapter 7: Children's behaviour

Chapter 7 examines and compares children's behaviour within and between the five different placement types. It presents the findings that emerged from the quantitative analysis of the Strengths and Difficulties Questionnaire (SDQ) (Goodman, 1997) that was completed by the children's parents/carers, and the qualitative analysis of the section of the interviews with the parents/carers focusing on behaviour, as well as the observations of the research team during the interviews.

Chapter 8: Children's education

This chapter explores children's educational achievements and difficulties; schooling needs and supports; children's experiences of school; parents/carers' attitudes and views on education; and children's and parents/carers' future expectations. The findings reported derive from the quantitative analysis of the questionnaire completed by parents/carers focusing on school; the British Picture Vocabulary Scale (Dunn *et al*, 1997) completed by children; and the qualitative analysis of the interviews with children and parents/carers.

Chapter 9: Parent/carer stress

Chapter 9 examines the level of parenting/carer stress within and between the different placement types. It reports on the findings of the quantitative analysis of the Parenting Stress Index (PSI) (Abidin, 1995) that was completed by parents/carers.

Chapter 10: Contact with birth families

This chapter explores contact with birth family members and previous carers, including the level and quality of contact arrangements, being either direct face-to-face contact visits, or phone, digital (i.e. skype, e-mails, social networking sites) and post-box contact; the attitudes of the parents/carers in relation to contact; and children's feelings towards their birth family and contact with them. This information was derived from interviews with both the children and their parents/carers. Comparisons are made in terms of the quality and type of contact arrangements that the children have within and between the five different placement types.

Chapter 11: Family communication

Chapter 11 examines the level and quality of communication between the children and their parents/carers, including the level of difficulty that children and parents/carers experience when talking about feelings and worries, or sensitive issues regarding the birth family; and with whom the children discuss this type of subject. Communication was one of the topics discussed in the interviews with the parents/

carers, and was indirectly referred to in the interviews with the children, as well as being one of the dimensions in the IPPA-R.

Chapter 12: Social Services' involvement and social support

The first part of this chapter explores the relationship the parents/carers and the children themselves had with Social Services. This includes their feelings and involvement in statutory Looked After Children (LAC) review meetings and other processes, their personal relationships with social workers, and their different experiences of the formalities of the care system. The second part looks at the extent and quality of the social networks for the children and families, with a particular focus on the social supports parents/carers receive when caring for the children. These findings were derived from the qualitative analysis of the interviews with the parents/carers.

Chapter 13: Discussion and conclusion

Chapter 13 draws together the key findings of the study. It presents a picture of how these children are progressing, and compares them with others who followed both similar and different pathways through care. Differences and similarities within and between the groups of children in the different care pathways are explored, across the range of quantitative and qualitative measures employed. This allows for a multi-informed perspective to be developed as to the relative capacity of the different placement options to provide stability and positive wellbeing for children who enter care at an early age.

Conclusion

This chapter has reviewed themes that are the fabric and building blocks of childhood wellbeing, and has reflected on what the research tells us about the extent to which the different types of placement facilitate this sense of wellbeing for children who enter care at an early age. Much of the research suggests that the likelihood of children in care reaching their full potential is limited. However, other research that focuses on children who is provided with long-term stable placements reveals a more positive perspective. Furthermore, the prevailing opinion on long-term placement continues to perpetuate the notion of adoption as the "gold standard". Yet, Rushton (2004) flagged up the fact that there was a lack of longitudinal research that compared outcomes from adoptions with other long-term placement types. It was also suggested that 'although no studies have made detailed and direct comparisons of these high-quality, stable foster care environments with adoptions, differences in adjustment during the placement are not likely to be pronounced' (Rushton, 2004, p. 95). The current study allows for this perspective to be developed, and does so with the presentation of its findings across a range of key issues from Chapters 3 to 12.

2 Methodology

Introduction

Phase 3 of the Care Pathways and Outcomes study focused on obtaining children's own accounts of their lives and experiences, and of their placements in adoption, long-term kinship care, long-term foster care, being subject to residence order, and living with birth parents (including on a care order). A range of issues were explored with the children, including family composition; closeness of relationships; their sense of security and attachment to carers/parents and peers; self-concept; school; their sense of belonging; and future aspirations. In addition, and for a second time, the study provided an in-depth examination of parent/carer perspectives on how these children were faring, with a particular focus on the child's behaviour, attachment, formal and informal supports, and contact arrangements. This chapter sets out the methodology that was used to enable the research team to address these key issues, with a particular focus on the background to the study; rationale; methodological and ethical issues and challenges; research techniques and instruments; and data analyses.

Terminology

The terms "placement" and "pathway" are commonly used throughout this book. "Pathway" is a representation of the current "placement" for the child, i.e. adopted, in foster care, kinship care, on residence order, or living with birth parents, in addition to their placement history up to that point in time. Consequently, a "pathway" will include children with a range of placement histories. For example, one child on the adoption pathway at one point in time may have been placed as a very young baby with prospective adopters, while another child may have been in several foster placements before being placed with adoptive parents. The one thing that locates both these children in the adoption "pathway" is the nature of the "placement" they are in currently.

The study design

Phase 3 of the study was based on the same sample that had been studied in Phases 1 and 2, i.e. a population of children (n = 374) who were under the age of five and in care on 31 March 2000 in Northern Ireland. As had been the case in the two previous phases, a SOSCARE download was obtained from Social Services and this provided placement data for the full study population on 31 March 2007, which supplemented previous placement profiles that had been obtained in 2000, 2002 and 2004. This also enabled interview sub-samples to be specified for the five placement types that were the focus of investigation.

Mixed-method design: Balancing qualitative and quantitative analyses

Both quantitative and qualitative data were collected from the children and their parents/carers, i.e. a mixed-method design. Collecting both types of data from the same sample was deemed critical so that they could be linked in the analysis. This required ensuring that the sample selected was not too large to be overly cumbersome for qualitative analysis, but also not so small that appropriate inferential comparative statistical analyses would not be possible. Therefore, to balance both elements of the design, a target of 15 cases per placement type was established, giving an overall target sample of 75 cases (across the five different placement types), with each case representing one child and their parents/carers. It was considered that 15 cases would provide adequate scope for in-depth qualitative analysis while at the same time allowing for the appropriate use of inferential statistics for comparative analysis, namely Analysis of Variance (ANOVA).

Sample selection

When the placement data were analysed for 31 March 2007, the study population was found to be living in five different types of placement: adoption, foster care, kinship care, on residence orders, and with birth parents. It was decided that the proposed interviews should attempt to reflect the perspectives of children and parents/carers across all placement types. It was also considered that, where possible, children and families should be recruited from those families where the parents/carers had participated in Phase 2 of the study, as this would enhance the capacity of the study for longitudinal analysis, particularly the repetition of standardised measures.

Adoption group – Of the 51 adoptive children whose parents were interviewed in the previous phase of the study, 30 children who remained in placement by 2007 were selected for recruitment. This group was selected randomly, although it was deemed necessary to have an even distribution of children who were adopted by their foster carers (n = 15) and by strangers (n = 15). Consequently, the selection process involved designating cases to one or other of these groups until there were 15 cases in each.

Long-term foster care group – Of the 56 children whose foster carers were interviewed during Phase 2 of the study, 24 remained in the same long-term foster placement in 2007, with the remainder being adopted, returned home, or placed with kinship carers. All 24 children who remained in the same foster placement were selected for recruitment.

Long-term kinship care group – In Phase 2 of the study, the foster care group had included both kinship and foster carers, although only five were kinship carers. Additional recruitment was therefore required from the study population where carers had not been previously interviewed. By 2007, there were 30 children in kinship care (in addition to the five where carers had previously been interviewed). All 30 were selected for recruitment.

Residence order group – This was the first time during the study that any focus had been given to examining the situation for children subject to a residence order. By 2007, residence orders had been granted in respect of 21 children living with former kinship and foster carers. All were selected for recruitment.

Birth parent group – The placement analysis indicated that on 31 March 2007, 30 children were living with their birth parents with a care order either rescinded or continuing. The parents of eight of these children had been interviewed in the previous phase of the study, and all 30 were selected for recruitment.

Overall, this gave an initial sample of 135 children selected for recruitment, with an expectation of 75 children/young people (15 in each group) and their parents/carers agreeing to participate.

Recruitment procedure

An initial letter asking parents/carers if they would be willing to receive an invitation pack for the study was written by the research team and sent by the relevant HSC Trust to be forwarded to the 135 families selected for recruitment. A passive consent approach was initially used and the letter informed parents/carers that they should ring a specified representative in the HSC Trust if they did not consent to the research team receiving their contact details. If parents/carers did consent to the research team receiving their contact details from the HSC Trust, they were advised to do nothing and the invitation pack was forwarded to them. It was also noted that consenting to receive the invitation pack would not be construed as consenting to participate in the study. The initial letter also included reference to a £50 shopping voucher that would be provided to participating families in recognition of the time and effort that would be required to participate in two visits to the family home from the research team.

After a two-week period, the representatives in each of the five HSC Trusts were contacted, and contact details forwarded to the research team of those parents/carers who had not contacted the HSC

Trust to opt-out of the study at that point in time. Those families who had not opted out were sent an invitation pack containing information leaflets for children and their parents/carers; reports from the previous phases of the study; and a DVD for children that introduced the researchers and explained what would be involved if they chose to participate (this can be viewed at: www.qub.ac.uk/cpo). At this point, an active consent approached was used. If agreeable to participate in the study, parents/carers were asked to call a freephone number within a two-week period so that a first interview could be scheduled. Where parents/carers did not contact the research team within the two-week period, direct calls were made by the research team to enquire as to whether or not they had received the invitation pack and if they were willing to participate in the study.

Data collection

Data were collected using qualitative and quantitative methods with the children and their parents/carers. Interviews took place in the family home. The fieldwork was organised to minimise disruption to the child's everyday life, and therefore appointments were arranged after the child's school day, other than during periods of school holiday. There were two visits to each family (or more if there was more than one child from the study population). Each interview lasted approximately one hour. During each visit, parents/carers and children were reassured of confidentiality, and their willingness to participate was re-affirmed. The interviews with the parent/carer and child took place at the same time in separate rooms in their home.

On the first visit, the parents/carers and children were introduced to the study, and informed consent to participate was sought from both. Parents/carers completed the Strengths and Difficulties Questionnaire (SDQ) (Goodman, 1997) and the Parenting Stress Index-Short Form (PSI/SF) (Abidin, 1990), as well as a short background questionnaire on the placement. Children completed the Piers-Harris Self-Concept Scale 2 (Piers and Hertzberg, 2002), the Inventory of Parent and Peer Attachment – Revised (IPPA-R) for children (Gullone and Robinson, 2005), and the British Picture Vocabulary Scale –

Second Edition (BPVS = II) (Dunn *et al*, 1997). The children completed the IPPA by playing a board game, and the Piers-Harris using a post-box game, both of which were developed by the research team (and are discussed in more detail later).

On the second visit, parents took part in a semi-structured interview. The children also engaged in a semi-structured interview, centred on the completion of a booklet covering key aspects of the child's life, the "me-book", which was also developed by the research team (and is discussed in more detail later).

Instruments

A range of quantitative and qualitative measures were used.

Quantitative measures

As mentioned above, children completed three quantitative measures: the Inventory of Parent and Peer Attachment – Revised version for children (IPPA-R), the Piers-Harris Children's Self-Concept Scale 2, and the British Picture Vocabulary Scale. Research in this area conducted in England had suggested that children's attachment relationships and self-concept may be determined by the nature of the long-term placement in which they were living (Sinclair *et al*, 2005). These conclusions had been derived from an analysis of qualitative interview data. Although qualitative analysis does allow for comment upon the extent to which data is reflective of theory, the research team felt it would reduce the potential for subjectivity if these issues were examined quantitatively. Hence the decision to use the first two measures identified.

The Inventory of Parent and Peer Attachment – Revised version for children (IPPA-R) (Gullone and Robinson, 2005):
The original IPPA (Armsden and Greenberg, 1987) was developed to measure the positive and negative affective and cognitive dimensions of adolescents' relationships with their parents and close friends and how well these figures serve as sources of psychological security. The IPPA-R is appropriate for use with young people aged between 9

and 11 years. Gullone and Robinson (2005) provide support for the reliability and validity of the revised measure. It contains two scales: 28 items assessing parent attachment and 25 items assessing peer attachment. Respondents are required to rate the degree to which each item is true for them on a three-point scale: "always true", "sometimes true", or "never true". The items in each of the two scales cluster into three factors:

- trust – the degree of mutual understanding and respect in the attachment relationship;
- communication – the extent and quality of spoken communication; and
- alienation – feelings of anger and interpersonal alienation.

This measure was administered using a board game and stickers, an activity created by the research team. The child was asked to place either: green (indicating an "always true" response), blue (indicating a "sometimes true" response) or red (indicating a "never true" response) stickers for each of the statements read out by the researcher, on numbered circles on a large poster, with each circle representing a question on the measure.

The Piers-Harris Self-Concept Scale 2 (PH-2) (Piers and Herzberg, 2002):
This standardised self-report questionnaire, which is a modification of the 1984 Piers-Harris Children's Self-concept Scale, examines self-concept in young people aged 7–18. It is based on the child's own perceptions about themselves rather than the observations of parents or teachers. It is composed of 60 items and yields a general measure of the respondent's overall self-concept, but also includes six domain scales:

- Physical appearance and attributes – measures a child's appraisal of her/his physical appearance, as well as attributes, such as leadership and the ability to express ideas (e.g. 'My looks bother me', 'I have a pleasant face');

- Intellectual and school status – represents the child's self-assessment of intellectual abilities and academic performance. It also covers general satisfaction with school and future expectations about achievement (e.g. 'I am smart', 'I am an important member of my class');
- Happiness and satisfaction – assesses general feelings of happiness and satisfaction with life (e.g. 'I am cheerful', 'I am a good person');
- Freedom from anxiety – assesses anxiety and dysphoric mood. Individual items tap a variety of specific emotions, including worry, nervousness, shyness, sadness, and fear (e.g. 'I feel left out of things', 'I am often afraid');
- Behavioural adjustment – represents the child's admission or denial of problematic behaviour in home or school settings (e.g. 'I am well behaved in school', 'I behave badly at home'); and
- Popularity – represents a child's evaluation of his/her social functioning. The items tap perceived popularity, the ability to make friends, and inclusion in activities such as games and sports (e.g. 'I have many friends', 'It is hard for me to make friends').

In addition, two validity scales identify biased responding and the tendency to answer randomly. Children complete the 60-item scale by responding yes or no to the statements. It is widely used and has good reliability and validity (Jeske, 1985; Piers, 1984; Piers and Herzberg, 2002). The measure was administered using a post-box system developed by the research team, where the child was asked to put the statements written on cards into either a "yes" box or a "no" box.

Interpretation of scores on the Piers-Harris total self-concept measure are in the following range: very low ($\leq$2% of population); low (3–14%); low average (15–28%); average (29–71%); high average (72–83%); high (84–97%); and very high ($\geq$98%). Whilst on the different domains of the measure, the range is as follows: very low ($\leq$2%); low (3–14%); low average (15-28%); average (29–71%); and above average ($\leq$72%). Given the size of the comparison groups in this study, it was considered more appropriate for the display of results to re-categorise the total self-concept range from seven to three dimensions. These are: low (combining very low, low and low average scores, $\leq$2–28%);

average (representing the original average range, 29 – 71%); and high (combining high average, high and very high scores, 72 – ≥98%). Similarly, the domains range was re-categorised from five to three dimensions. These are: low (combining very low, low and low average, ≤2 – 28%); average (representing the original average range, 29–71%); and high (representing the original above average range, ≥72%).

The British Picture Vocabulary Scale – Second Edition (BPVS-II) (Dunn *et al*, 1997):
This is a test designed to assess receptive vocabulary in children aged 3–16, and shows the extent of their English vocabulary acquisition. The scale may be viewed as a screening test of scholastic aptitude (verbal ability or verbal intelligence). While not a perfect indicator, vocabulary has been found to be a reliable index of school success and vocabulary sub-tests have been found to be among the most important contributors to comprehensive tests of intelligence. The scale employs a multiple-choice approach, where children are presented with four simple black and white illustrations on a page and the task is to select the picture considered to best illustrate the meaning of the target word that is presented orally by the researcher.

Parents and carers also completed a short questionnaire about the placement, the child and themselves, and two quantitative measures, which had also been used in the previous phase of the study: the SDQ, and the PSI/SF.

Parent/carer questionnaire:
This was a brief questionnaire developed by the research team, containing general questions in relation to the placement and characteristics of the child, as well as some questions regarding how the child was performing at school. The questionnaire was administered by the researcher face-to-face with the parents/carers, and questions were read aloud by the researcher.

The Strengths and Difficulties Questionnaire – SDQ (Goodman, 1997): This measure was contained in the above-mentioned questionnaire. It is a commonly used behavioural screening questionnaire for assessing psychological morbidity in children and adolescents, as perceived by their parents/carers. It is composed of 25 items divided into five scales of five items each, including:

- emotional symptoms;
- conduct problems;
- hyperactivity/inattention;
- peer relationship problems; and
- prosocial behaviour.

A total difficulties score is based on the combined scores of each of the scales, except the prosocial scale. The scores can be classified as normal, borderline or abnormal. Approximately 10 per cent of a community sample scores within the abnormal band on any given score, with a further 10 per cent in the borderline band.

The SDQ has adequate discriminant and predictive validity (Goodman, 1997; Goodman and Scott, 1999). It correlates highly with the Rutter Questionnaires (Goodman, 1997) and with the Child Behaviour Checklist, although it was considered more sensitive in detecting inattention and hyperactivity, and equally effective in detecting internalising and externalising problems (Goodman and Scott, 1999). The reliability and validity of the SDQ make it a useful brief measure of the adjustment and psychopathology of children and adolescents (Goodman, 2001).

The Parenting Stress Index – Short form – PSI/SF (Abidin, 1990): This is a measure for stress in the parent–child relationship. It contains 36 items divided into four sub-scales:

- Defensive responding – assesses the extent to which the respondent attempts to minimise indications of problems or stress in the parent–child relationship and to present a favourable impression of themselves;

- Parental distress – determines the distress an individual is experiencing in his or her role as a parent, as a function of personal factors related to parenting, such as impaired sense of parenting competence; stresses associated with the restrictions placed on other life roles; conflict with the child's other parent; lack of social supports; and presence of depression;
- Parent–child dysfunctional interaction – represents parent/carer perception that their child does not meet their expectations and that the parent-child interaction is not rewarding; and
- Difficult child – indicates parent/carer perceptions of child difficulty based on child characteristics including temperament, defiance, compliance and degree to which the child's behaviour is demanding.

The measure provides a total stress score in addition to a score for each of the sub-scales. The normal range of scores is within the 15th to the 80th percentiles. Abnormally high scores are considered to be those at or above the 85th percentile. The PSI/SF was administered by a researcher. Each item was read out to the participants who then indicated their preferred response, which could be either strongly agree, agree, not sure, disagree, or strongly disagree.

Qualitative measures
Parents/carers and children took part in a semi-structured interview.

The children's me-book:
This instrument was developed by the research team to structure the interview with the child. It was a "task–based" (Punch, 2002) tool that allowed children to express their own views, according to their level of ability. Each page referred to a particular topic and involved an activity, such as drawing, using stickers or circling pictures. Each topic or question was broad enough to allow the child to talk freely about a particularly issue, thus giving them a certain degree of control over the interview. It acted as a stimulus for dialogue, and provided children with time to think about what they wanted to say. The "me-book" addressed the following issues:

- family membership;
- degree of closeness to individual family members and friends;
- people important in the child's life;
- family activities;
- school (what they like and do not like);
- hobbies and spare time;
- expectations for the future (what the child would like to do when they grow up and who the child would like to live with when they grow up);
- feelings (about the present, past and future);
- wishes;
- life satisfaction; and
- health.

Other issues, such as contact, were approached indirectly, when talking about family membership and family activities. The interview was audio-recorded and transcribed, with the permission of the child.

The parent/carer semi-structured interview:
The interview with parents/carers was audio-recorded and transcribed, with the permission of the participant/s. Interviews were conducted with one or two parents/carers. The interview focused on the following issues:

- how the placement had progressed (including current worries or issues);
- attachment and bonding;
- the child's behaviour;
- contact with birth family or previous carers;
- supports;
- involvement with Social Services;
- the child's relationship with other family members;
- family activities;
- school and the child's peer relationships;
- the child's health;

- communication with the child; and
- feelings and expectations regarding the child's future.

Furthermore, observations were noted immediately after each visit, by the researchers present. These were analysed together with the transcripts of the interviews with the children and parents/carers.

Fieldwork

As specified earlier, 135 children were selected for recruitment, with an expectation of 75 children (15 in each placement type), and their parents/carers, agreeing to participate. Table 2.1 below illustrates the number of interviews that were conducted.

Table 2.1
Families recruited for interview

Care placement	Selected for recruitment	Recruited	% of recruitment
Adopted	30	18	60
Foster care	24	19	79
Kinship care	30	13	43
Residence order	21	15	71
Birth parent/s	30	12	40
Total	**135**	**77**	**57**

Table 2.1 indicates that 77 children (and their parent/carer) were recruited, with an overall success rate of 57 per cent. This met the pre-specified recruitment target of 75. However, not all placement groups reached the target of 15, whilst a couple exceeded it. There were a number of reasons why 58 (43%) families that were initially approached did not participate in the research. These are specified in Table 2.2 below. All interviews were conducted between March 2009 and January 2010, when the children were aged between 9 and 14 years old.

Table 2.2
Reason for non-participation

Care placement

Reason for non-participation	Adopted (n = 30)	Foster care (n = 34)	Kinship care (n = 30)	Residence order (n = 21)	Birth parent (n = 30)
Opt-out after initial letter from Trust	3		4	1	1
No current address	2		4	4	8
No answer to telephone call					3
Declined interview over telephone	4	3	5	1	6
Unable to locate telephone number	1		1		
Interview arranged but later cancelled	1	1	2		
Placement breakdown	1	1	1		
Total	**12**	**5**	**17**	**6**	**18**

There were a number of occasions when it was not possible to complete the full interview with the family (n = 9). Reasons for incomplete interviews included the following.

- The adoptive parents of one child felt that the child would be too shy to be interviewed, and agreed only to be interviewed themselves (on occasions where this happened across all placement types, the parent components of the two scheduled interviews were combined into one interview).
- For one child who had been in a long-term foster placement when the population placement profile had been specified on 31 March

2007, the placement had just broken down. The foster carers agreed to be interviewed to give a perspective on how the placement had progressed and the factors that may have contributed to the breakdown. For another child, the foster placement broke down just after the first interview. However, the foster mother took part in the second interview to give a perspective on the issues that led to the placement breaking down. For two other children in foster care, the foster carers declined to take part in the second interview.

- For one child, who had been in a long-term kinship placement when the population placement profile had been specified in 2007, there had been a recent return to the birth parent/s. The kinship carers agreed to be interviewed to give a perspective on how the child had been getting on, and to discuss any issues concerning the child's return to birth parent/s.

- One child who was on a residence order suffered from profound learning difficulties that rendered communication with the researcher impossible. However, it was still possible to gain a perspective on the child's life from the carers.

- For one child who was living with only the birth mother, the latter declined to take part in the second interview. For another child who was living with the birth mother, the latter did not want the child to be involved, as they would have no memory of being in care, and she did not want to unsettle the child.

Analysis

Quantitative analysis

Quantitative data from all the measures and questionnaires (administered to the parents/carers and the children) were input in SPSS for Windows, version 15.0 (SPSS INC., Chicago, 2006).

The form of analysis applied was one-way Analysis of Variance (ANOVA), which allowed for a comparison of the extent of difference in mean scores between the different placement groups across the range of measures applied with parents/carers and children. In terms of post-hoc analysis between the different groups, Tukey's HSD (honestly significant difference) test was applied. Most researchers tend to assess the power of their statistical tests using $\pi = 0.80$ (alpha = 0.05, two-tailed) as a standard for adequacy. The SAS Institute (1999) advised that 'to achieve a minimum of 80 per cent power (in a one-way ANOVA), 11 units per groups would be needed'. The numbers within the five pathway groups in this study were: 19 (foster care), 18 (adoption), 15 (residence order), 13 (kinship care), and 12 (birth parents). These figures meet the unit-threshold specified by the SAS Institute (1999) for 80 per cent power. Furthermore, this study utilised five cells (pathway groups), which would also increase statistical power.

It can also be seen that the study sample is representative of the pathway groups within the total study population (n = 374):

- the 15 children recruited on residence order represent 71 per cent of all children on residence order for the total study population in 2007 (n = 21);
- the 13 children recruited in kinship care represent 43 per cent of all children in kinship care (n = 30);
- the 12 children recruited living with birth parents represent 40 per cent of all children with birth parents (n = 30);
- the 19 children recruited in foster care represent 25 per cent of all children in foster care (n = 75); and
- the 18 adopted children recruited represent 13 per cent of all children that had been adopted (n = 140) for the total population by 2007.

Qualitative analysis

The interviews with the children and their parents/carers were audio-recorded with their permission, transcribed and analysed through a process of framework analysis, developed by the National Centre for Social Research (Ritchie and Spencer, 1994), and specifically geared towards generating policy and practice-orientated findings. Furthermore, some aspects of the analysis were supported by managing the data on the computer package NVivo.

Framework analysis is a content analysis method that involves summarising and classifying data within a (given) thematic framework. In the case of the interviews conducted for this study, this framework was derived from the content of the semi-structured interview guides for the children (the "me-book") and parents/carers. In this way, the large body of data furnished by the interviews could be organised in ways that immediately "made sense" to the research team and could be effectively translated into recommendations for these children.

The process of analysis involved the following steps. An initial *familiarisation* with the data involved repeated readings of the transcripts until familiarity was achieved with them in their entirety. A subsequent *thematic analysis* focused on the development of a coding scheme; in essence, this scheme followed the content of the questions asked. The process of applying these codes to the entire dataset in a systematic way is known as *indexing*, and represents the third stage of framework analysis. This was achieved by going through the interviews one-by-one, assigning relevant thematic codes to extracts of the interview data and thus producing a fully coded interview.

The fourth and final step involved the production of the final analytic framework. This was achieved in two stages, producing two complementary bodies of findings. Firstly, the interviews were analysed on a group-by-group basis, by comparing relevant interviews with each other, according to each of the designated themes. The comparative process was facilitated by a process of *charting*, which involved drawing up tables for each of the pathway groups that tabulated relevant individual interview codes under each of the issues or themes. In this way a number of stand-alone *group* analyses were developed. In the second stage, a fully inclusive or integrated analysis, which compared all pathway groups according to each of the themes, was undertaken. In this way a number of stand-alone *thematic* analyses were developed. This comparative analysis highlighted patterns within the data and thus provided the research team with an insight into the degree and nature of similarity and differences across groups in relation to each of the issues.

Methodological considerations: innovative methodology with children

There is growing recognition that the views of children need to be brought more to the centre of the research process (Thomas *et al*, 1999; Gilligan, 2000; Gilbertson and Barber, 2002; Skuse and Ward, 2003, Clarke, 2005). Speaking to children directly acknowledges their right to express their views on all matters concerning them, as laid down in Article 12 of the United Nations Convention on the Rights of the Child (UNCRC, 1989). Until relatively recently, children's views about their lives and experiences tended to be overlooked, and research was primarily carried out *on* children, rather than *with* children or *for* children (Mayall, 2000; O'Kane, 2000; Darbyshire *et al*, 2005). In the mid-1980s, a new approach to researching children emerged (James and Prout, 1990), which recognised children's competence and agency, and aimed to explore their own explanations of their lives (Valentine, 1997). From this perspective, children were depicted as knowing *something else*, rather than *something less* (Matthews and Limb, 1999).This new approach introduced a method-ological shift, involving the emergence of innovative, "task-based" (Punch, 2002) research methodologies, the adaptation of more traditional methods (e.g. observation and questionnaires), and the use of multi-method approaches.

Embracing this methodological shift, in Phase 3 of the Care Pathways and Outcomes study, the research team was keen to develop interview techniques that moved beyond the use of face-to-face interviews with children. Thus, as described previously, a number of innovative and novel techniques were created to facilitate data collection. These were:

Board and post-box activities

The decision to use quantitative instruments with the children presented challenges. For example, some children might find reading and writing difficult. Where this was the case, questions would have to be read aloud by the researcher, to ensure, as best as possible, that these were understood. The problem with this approach was that the questions specified in the IPPA-R and Piers-Harris questionnaires could raise potentially sensitive issues for children, which could make them feel uncomfortable verbalising their responses during interview. These issues were overcome, however, by developing two activities, involving a board and a post-box system, facilitating the completion of the instruments (these can be viewed at: www.qub.ac.uk/cpo).

According to the four children with whom these materials were piloted (two in adoption, two in foster care – neither from the study population), these activities added an element of fun to the process of data collection and the less formal nature of the interactions allowed the children to relax, and to deflect any discomfort that emanated from the sensitive nature of some of the questions, into the activity itself. The activities appeared to provide a "protective cover" which enabled the children to express themselves freely.

A "me-book"

When interviewing children, it was considered that a standard interview with a stranger might be uncomfortable, particularly as it was likely that the interview would be dealing with sensitive issues for the child. With this in mind, the research team developed a "me-book" to facilitate the semi-structured interviews with the children (downloadable at: www.qub.ac.uk/cpo). The "me-book" took the children through a series of topics, and they were asked to comment on the information contained on each page. As with the board and post-box activities, this tool decreased the intensity of the interview by allowing the child and the researcher to move their focus from each other to the "me-book". This acted as a stimulus for discussion.

Ethical considerations

Two separate ethical applications were made to the Office for Research Ethics Committees in Northern Ireland (ORECNI) in relation to this phase of the study. The first was made regarding the SOSCARE download that was required to specify the placement profile for the population on 31 March 2007, which, in turn, allowed for the identification of the interview sub-sample. The second focused on the issues pertinent to the interviews with children and their parents/ carers. Both applications received favourable outcomes.

One unanticipated requirement that emerged from the second ORECNI application was for two researchers to conduct the interviews with the child, whilst another simultaneously carried out the interview with the parents/carers. The original plan had been for two researchers to visit each family, with one interviewing the parents/carers, and the other the child. The requirement to have three researchers per visit created some resource and logistical pressures for the study. However, in hindsight, the researchers did appreciate the value of having two researchers for the child interviews, both in terms of ensuring protection for the child and the researcher, and allowing for observational notes to be taken by the second researcher.

Strengths and limitations of the study

The Care Pathways and Outcomes study has a number of strengths and limitations.

Strengths

The study has uniquely been able to follow a population of young children from early placement in the care system, across a range of different placement options. It has also been able to gather data that allow for a longitudinal perspective on changes within and between different placement types to be established and also cross-sectional data that allow for comparisons of how the children and their parents/ carers are faring across the different placements and at different points in their developmental trajectory.

In addition, it also presents the often unheard perspective of the children, which provides an insight into how they view their life experiences and how they are coping. Having this information enables policy-makers and practitioners to inform care planning regarding the long-term placement of young children in care, and to develop the necessary support packages, both to ensure that these children achieve their full potential, and that their parents/carers are adequately and appropriately supported.

Limitations

One limitation may be the numbers of children and parents/carers who were interviewed. Although the numbers in each comparison group were sufficient for one-way ANOVA, larger numbers of children and parents/carers would have increased the statistical power of the quantitative analysis. However, this needed to be balanced in relation to three other competing sample selection drivers: first, the qualitative requirements of the study that necessitated a reduction in participant numbers; second, the resource implications of conducting a greater number of interviews; and third, the difficulty that is commonly experienced in this type of research in terms of gaining access to "hard-to-reach" families to conduct interviews.

Secondly, although 135 families were identified to participate in the study, with a target participation of 75, and achieving 77, the research team had no control over which children and their parents/carers would decide to participate. Table 2.2 indicates that although non-participation was due in some instances to technical difficulties in the recruitment process (no current address – n = 18, no answer to telephone calls – n = 3, and the HSC Trust being unable to locate telephone number – n = 2), there were a number of cases where the families had directly declined to participate (opting out after receiving initial recruitment letter – n = 9, declining interview during telephone conversation with researchers – n = 19, interview arranged but later cancelled – n = 4, and recent placement breakdown – n = 3).

It is not clear why these families did not want to participate (although efforts were made, unsuccessfully, to identify these reasons) and it might be argued that they represent those families that were experiencing particular difficulties, thus skewing our sample towards those families where there may have been fewer difficulties. Yet, the findings that are presented in this book clearly indicate that the families that did agree to participate in the study were themselves experiencing a range of difficulties. Furthermore, if it is argued that the study has not included the views and experiences of those children and parents/carers who were really struggling, then this suggests that where we do highlight the challenges being faced across the placement types, it is likely that this is an underestimation of the problems being experienced.

Another possible limitation of the study is that it is based in one small geographical area, Northern Ireland; the smallest of the two jurisdictions in Ireland and of the four jurisdictions in the UK, making it difficult to generalise to national and international populations. However, a counter argument might be that Northern Ireland and the rest of the UK, particularly England and Wales, have very similar legislative frameworks and long-term placement options, thus providing a context for research outputs in any one jurisdiction to be relevant to the other. At the international level, it could also be argued that, irrespective of location, the issues facing children and parents/carers, where children have been provided with alternative long-term carers and placements, are universal, and that any in-depth examination of key issues for children and their parents/carers will be universally informative.

3   The children and their placements

The children's placements

The placement profile for this population of children had been specified for 31 March 2000, 2002, and 2004 (McSherry *et al*, 2010). The third phase of the study allowed for the placement profile to be specified for a fourth time, on 31 March 2007. Profiling was primarily based on SOSCARE placement downloads provided by the HSC Trusts, in addition to cross-referencing of legal status for the population, which was provided by the Northern Ireland Guardian *ad Litem* Agency (NIGALA). In Table 3.1 below, the placement profiles for the study population in 2000, 2002, 2004, and 2007 are detailed, with this being illustrated graphically in Figure 3.1.

Table 3.1
Population placement profiles 2000–2007 (%)

Placement	2000	2002	2004	2007	n
Adopted	0	18	38	42	156
Birth parents	14	22	24	21	75
Foster care	61	41	22	20	75
Kinship care	10	11	9	8	32
Residence order	0	1	4	6	22
Prospective adoption	13	7	3	3	11
Assessment unit	2	0	0	0	4

It can be seen from Figure 3.1 that there was a major decline in the percentage of young children in foster care across the seven years, dropping from 61 per cent in 2000 to 20 per cent in 2007, with this

Figure 3.1
Placement profiles between 2000 and 2007

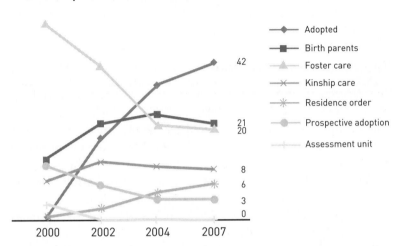

being mostly accounted for by the rise in proportion of children being adopted (from 0% in 2000 to 42% in 2007). However, a slowing in the rate of adoption is apparent as the children get older, particularly between 2004 (38%) and 2007 (42%). There was also a steady rise in the proportion of children living with their birth parents between 2000 (14%) and 2002 (22%), with this then levelling out to some degree between 2002 and 2007 (at around 20%). Finally, there was a relatively small, but steady, proportion of children living in kinship care (10% in 2000 and 9% in 2007), and a lesser proportion of children placed on residence orders, with a small increase between 2000 (0%) and 2007 (6%).

Care pathways

The range of placements presented in Table 3.1, and illustrated in Figure 3.1, can be categorised as representing five care "pathways" for this group of children, i.e. adoption (combining children adopted and in pre-adoptive placements), long-term foster care, long-term kinship care, on residence order, and living with birth parents.

Figure 3.2
Population care pathways at 31 March 2007

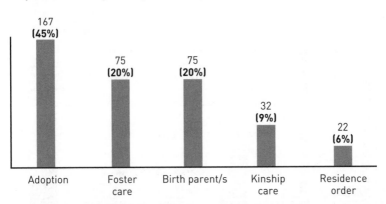

Figure 3.2 illustrates the distribution of the study population across these five care pathways in 2007 and shows that almost half the study population had been adopted or were living with prospective adoptive parents by 2007. This is quite a significant finding given that, prior to 2000, very few children were being adopted from care in Northern Ireland (Kelly and Coulter, 1997; Kelly and McSherry, 2002).

Characteristics of the children on the different pathways

Previous analyses, which examined the relationship between a range of background factors and the children's care pathway by 2004, indicated that there was a significant association between the type of care pathway and the area in Northern Ireland where the children were living in 2000, the age at which they first entered care, and the length of time that they had been in care when the study commenced (McSherry *et al*, 2010). These continued to be the key factors in understanding the distribution of the study population across the five care pathways in 2007, as illustrated in Figures 3.3–3.5.

There was a significant relationship between the child's care pathway in 2007 and the HSC Trust area they were living in (chi-square test, significant at p = .00, df = 8). Figure 3.3 illustrates the extent of

Figure 3.3
2007 care pathway by HSC Trust across Northern Ireland (%)

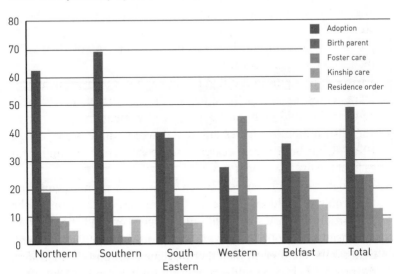

regional variation in care pathway across the five HSC Trusts and the overall percentage distribution for the total population. In terms of adoption, the rate for the total population by 2007 was 45 per cent. However, this ranged considerably from high levels in both the Northern (63%) and Southern (69%) HSC Trusts, to lower levels in the South Eastern (39%), Belfast (39%) and Western (25%) HSC Trusts. The percentage of children on the foster care pathway was almost the converse of the adoption pathway, with 20 per cent of the total population being represented on this pathway in 2007, but with this varying dramatically from 43 per cent in the Western HSC Trust, to nine per cent in the Northern and six per cent in the Southern HSC Trusts.

In relation to the birth parent pathway, although this represented the care pathway for 20 per cent of the total population in 2007, it ranged from 36 per cent in the South Eastern HSC Trust to 14 per cent in the Western. For the kinship care pathway, this represented nine per cent of the total population, ranging from 14 per cent in the

Figure 3.4
2007 care pathway by age child first entered care (%)

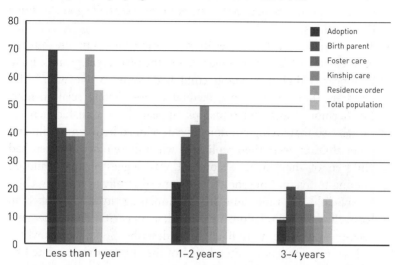

Western HSC Trust to two per cent in the Southern. There was also some variation in the use of residence orders, representing six per cent of the total population, but ranging from 10 per cent in the Belfast HSC Trust to three per cent in the Northern Trust.

In addition, as shown in Figure 3.3, there was marked variation in the percentage of children who remained in care by 2007. If one considers that adoption, living with birth parents, and the use of residence orders are effectively routes out of the care system (although it is acknowledged that some children live with birth parents on a care order), very few children remained in care in the Southern (8%), Northern (16%) and South Eastern (20%) HSC Trusts by 2007, compared with the Western (57%) and Belfast (34%) HSC Trusts.

There was a significant relationship between care pathways and age at entry to care (chi-square test, significant at $p = .00$, $df = 8$). Although 54 per cent of the total population was less than one year old when they first entered care, this is not reflective of the extent of variation that existed between the different pathways (see Figure 3.4).

Figure 3.5
2007 care pathway by time in care at census (31 March 2000) (%)

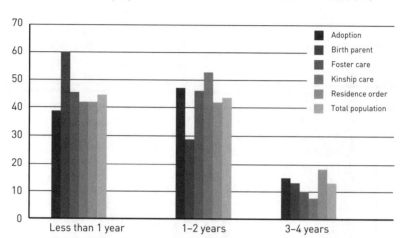

Considerably high percentages of children on both the adoption (69%) and residence order (67%) care pathways were less than one year old when they came into care, compared with those on the foster care (38%), kinship care (38%), and birth parent (41%) care pathways. Furthermore, where children were aged between three and four years old when they first entered care, there were marked declines in the percentage of children who followed the adoption (8%), residence order (10%), and kinship care (13%) pathways, compared to the birth parent (23%) and foster care (20%) pathways.

Care pathway and time in care at census were significantly related (chi-square test, significant at p = .05, df = 8). As indicated in Figure 3.5, although 44 per cent of the total population had been in care for less than one year at the time of the census, this ranged considerably from 60 per cent of those who followed the birth parent pathway, to between 38 and 45 per cent for the other four care pathways. Further, there were higher percentages of children who followed the adoption (17%) and residence order (18%) care pathways, who had been in care for between three to four years at census, compared with those who followed the kinship care (6%), foster care (9%) and birth parent (13%) pathways.

Pathway stability

As highlighted in Chapter 1, a key issue that needs to be addressed when trying to understand the comparative strengths and weaknesses of the range of long-term placements provided to young children in care, is an assessment of the extent to which the various placements have the capacity to persist, often referred to as placement stability. Table 3.2 examines the placements for the study population in 2007 (combining adopted and prospective adoption) and looks at the percentage of those children that were in the same placement in 2002 and 2004, as they were in 2007. Figure 3.6 looks at those children who were in the same placement between 2002 and 2004 (n = 330), and then illustrates the percentage of those children that were in the same placement (i.e. with the same carers) by 2007, i.e. reflecting a comparative perspective on placement change between 2004 and 2007.

Table 3.2 shows that this population of children experienced a high level of placement stability between 2002 and 2007, ranging from 91 per cent of those children in birth parent and residence order placements being in the same placement at the two time intervals, to 69 per cent of those in foster care. Between 2004 and 2007, the stability level was even higher, ranging from 99 per cent of those in birth parents placements in 2007 in the same placement as they were in 2004, to 83 per cent of foster care placements.

Table 3.2
Comparing placement stability between 2002/04 and 2007 (%)

Care pathway 2007	Same placement 2002 %	Same placement 2004 %	Total no.
Birth parent	91	99	75
Adoption	89	98	167
Kinship care	78	97	32
Foster care	69	83	75
RO	91	91	22
Total	**85**	**94**	**371**

Figure 3.6
Comparing placement stability in long-term placements 2002–2007 (n = 330, %)

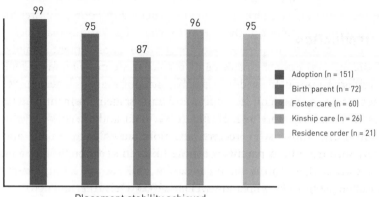

Placement stability achieved

Figure 3.6 illustrates that, in terms of capacity to remain stable in the longer-term, adoptive placements had the greatest level of stability (99%) between 2002 and 2007, closely followed by kinship care (96%), residence order (95%), and birth parent (95%) placements. The least stable long-term placements were in foster care (87%), although they still had a very high overall level of stability.

The interview sub-groups

As specified in Chapter 2, a sample of children and their parents/ carers was interviewed in each of the five care placements: adoption (n = 18), foster care (n = 19), kinship care (n = 13), residence order (n = 15), and living with birth parent/s (n = 12). These sub-groups were generally representative of the larger groups in the total population and this is reflected in Table 3.3.

As specified in Chapter 2, these children were selected on the basis of their placement on 31 March 2007. Given that the interview phase did not commence until March 2009, there were a number of children who had moved placement in the intervening period. Placements had

Table 3.3
Interview sub-group characteristics

Variable	Adoption	Foster care	Care placement Kinship care	Residence order	Birth parents
Mean age entered placement (mths)	20	48	41	17	54
Mean length of time in placement at interview (yrs/mths)	10 yrs 1 mth (min 7 yrs 8 mths, max 13 yrs 9 mths)	8 yrs 5 mths (min 2 yrs 6 mths, max 13 yrs 3 mths)	8 yrs 11 mths (min 2 yrs 8 mths, max 11 yrs 1 mth)	10 yrs 3 mths (min 7 yrs, max 12 yrs 8 mths)	8 yrs 3 mths (min 3 yrs, max 13 yrs 10 mths)
Entered care under one year old %	89%	17%	25%	57%	18%
In care 3–4 years at census %	41%	23%	0%	21%	9%
Total (n = 72)	**18**	**16**	**12**	**14**	**12**

broken down for three children who were in separate foster placements in 2007 and these children were in new foster placements in
2009. In one case, it was not possible to interview the child in the new
placement, but the previous foster carers agreed to be interviewed. In
the remaining two cases, the child and foster carers were interviewed
in the new placement. Furthermore, one child who had been in a
kinship placement in 2007 was living with birth parent/s in 2009. It
was not possible to arrange an interview with the child and the birth
parent/s, but the previous kinship carers agreed to be interviewed.

This research is focused primarily upon children across a range of
long-term placements. As such, all quantitative analysis focused solely
on those children who had not changed placement since the placement
profile was specified in 31 March 2007 (n = 72), with the exception of
one child (on residence order) who had profound learning difficulties,
and for whom it was not possible to gather any quantitative data.
However, all qualitative data gathered from children and parent/s
where there had been a placement change since 2007 (n = 4), and
including that gathered from the carers of the one child with profound
disabilities, is included within the overall qualitative analysis, given
the importance of understanding issues around sustaining long-term
placements for young children in care and adopted from care.

Summary of main findings

- Although rates of adoption for children in care were low prior to
  2000, almost half (45%) of the study population had been adopted
  by March 2007.
- There was significant regional variation in the use of different placements for young children in care across Northern Ireland.
- Children were significantly more likely to be adopted if they entered
  care under the age of one. However, a small proportion of children
  (8%) who entered care aged three to four were adopted.
- The longer children had been in care the less likely it was that they
  returned to birth parents. There also appeared to be a critical threshold for returning home, with approximately 20 per cent of the

population returning home up to the threshold, and very few returning after that point. It was also found that placements for those who did return home were very stable, with very few returning to care.

- Very high levels of placement stability between 2002 and 2007 were provided by adoption (99%), kinship care (96%), birth parents (95%), and residence order (95%). Although lower than the other four placement types, foster care also provided a high degree of stability (87%). However, it needs to be borne in mind that these children were in early adolescence.

4 Children's attachments

Introduction

For several decades, professional decision-making by social services and within the courts in the UK regarding the future of children about whom there were serious child protection and welfare concerns, has mainly been dominated by consideration of one theoretical perspective: the attachment model (Bowlby, 1951, 1969; Ainsworth *et al*, 1978; Rutter, 1995). The importance of stability for children in care, and its implications for the development of secure attachment, was and continues to be a strong driving force behind efforts to have such children adopted, to ensure that they do not "drift" in care (Rowe and Lambert, 1973), and to avoid the insecure limbo that a childhood spent in care would offer. However, others argue that care can actually provide children with the same degree of stability and engender the same strength of attachment relationship with carers as might be expected in adoption, provided foster care is adequately resourced and carers and children properly supported (Schofield, 2002; Biehal *et al*, 2010). This chapter presents a comparison of the attachments that the children in this study developed with their parents/carers and peers, across the different placement types, with the findings essentially testing assumptions regarding adoption and foster care as highlighted above.

Attachment is addressed on the basis of the findings that emerged from the quantitative analysis of the Inventory of Parent and Peer Attachment – Revised for children (IPPA-R) (Gullone and Robinson, 2005) completed by the children, together with qualitative analysis of interviews conducted with children and parents/carers.

The parent/carer semi-structured interview covered a range of circumstances that may be deemed pertinent to understanding the nature and development of children's attachments with their parents/carers, including: the settling in period; the child being temporarily left alone; the child's response to the parent/carer leaving the family home; meeting strangers; behaviour in new situations; signs of affection; relationship with other family members; and developments in attachment security. Furthermore, the qualitative analysis allowed for a separation of the adoption group into two further sub-groups: those children who had been adopted by former foster carers (n = 9) and those by strangers (n = 8), and reflects Biehal *et al*'s (2010) depiction of these two distinct forms of adoption. In the current study, the terms "foster adoption" and "stranger adoption" are used. However, the size of the adoption group did not support this type of separation when applying comparative inferential statistical analysis for the IPPA-R. This was also the case in relation to the other quantitative measures applied in this study, i.e. the PSI, SDQ, Piers-Harris, and BPVS; these are examined in the following chapters.

The "me-book" that formed the basis of the interview with the children examined their views about their family and the level of closeness to family members; feelings towards their family and wishes for them; as well as whether or not they would like to continue living with their parents/carers.

In the analysis of these data, reference will be made to a "majority" or a "minority" of parents/carers. This refers not to the majority or minority of parents/carers in the different pathway groups, but to the majority or minority of parents/carers who reflected upon a particular issue, as not all parents/carers commented on each of the issues raised with them. Throughout this and the following chapters, the children are referred to by pseudonym to ease the presentation of the findings.

The children's attachment to their parents/carers and peers

In addition to allowing for the depiction of overall parent and peer attachment scores, Armsden and Greenberg (1987) established a system for categorising scores on the IPPA as indicative of either low or high security. This was based upon a re-categorisation of scores across the Trust, Communication and Alienation domains (these were combined to produce the parent and peer attachment scores), as low, medium or high scores. These categories were created by dividing the range of the children's scores into three equal segments. Certain combinations of these scores across the different domains were considered to be indicative of either low or high security of attachment.

This categorisation system was applied in the current study and it was found that only five children had scores that indicated low security of attachment with parents/carers. These were: Abbie (stranger adoption); Alexandra (with birth parents); Liam (foster care); Sarah (residence order); and Jo (residence order). No children in the foster adoption or kinship care groups received a low security of attachment on the IPPA-R. This indicated that the vast majority of children in the sample were securely attached to their parents/carers, irrespective of placement type.

The figures in this chapter compare the children in the five placement groups for both parent and peer attachment across the three dimensions of the IPPA-R (Trust, Communication and Alienation). In order to examine any variations in the strength of attachment to parents/carers within and across the different groups of children, the low, medium and high categories of the Trust, Communication and Alienation dimensions that were initially used to establish low or high security, are displayed for illustrative purposes. Furthermore, although the overall attachment (both parent and peer) scores did not contribute to the estimation of low or high security, the range of the children's scores for overall attachment were also divided into three groups and the children assigned to one of these groups on the basis of their score. The distribution of the children's scores for parental and peer attachment, both within and between the five groups, are also displayed. While completing the parent section of the measure, the children were reminded that these questions were focused on the parents or carers with whom they currently lived.

One-way ANOVA indicated that there was no significant variation in mean score between the five pathway groups for attachment to parent/carer. Additionally, post-hoc Tukey HSD tests indicated that there were no significant mean differences between any of the five care pathway groups. Although the differences in mean scores were not significant, Figure 4.1 indicates that scores for attachment to parent/

Figure 4.1

Care pathway mean scores for IPPA–R on "attachment to parent/ carer"

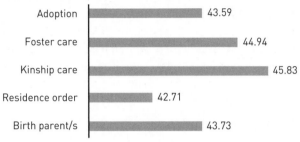

carer were higher for children in the foster and kinship care groups than in adoption, whilst mean score was lowest in the residence order group. On this dimension of the IPPA–R, higher scores are indicative of a more positive relationship with parents/carers.

Figure 4.2

Care pathways by IPPA–R attachment to parent/carer on the low/ medium/high score range (n)

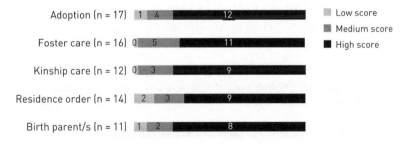

Figure 4.2 highlights the lack of variation in distribution of low, medium and high parent/carer attachment scores between the five groups. For all the pathway groups, it can be seen that most children scored highly in terms of attachment to their parent/carer, with only a small number in each of the groups having a low score.

Figure 4.3
Care pathway mean scores for IPPA–R parent sub-scale – Trust

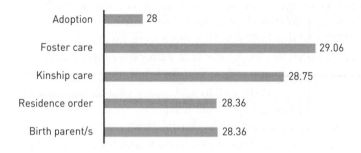

Trust: On this dimension (see Figure 4.3), higher scores are indicative of a more positive relationship with parents/carers. One-way ANOVA indicated that there was no significant variation in mean score between the five pathway groups for parental trust. Furthermore, post-hoc Tukey HSD tests indicated that there were no significant mean differences between any of the five care pathway groups. Although the differences between mean scores were not significant, the adoption group had the lowest mean score for parent/carer Trust, with the foster and kinship care groups showing the highest scores.

Figure 4.4 illustrates the lack of variation in distribution of low, medium and high scores on the parent/carer trust dimension, between the five pathway groups. It can be seen that the vast majority of

Figure 4.4
Care pathways by IPPA–R parent sub-scale – Trust on the low/ medium/high score range (n)

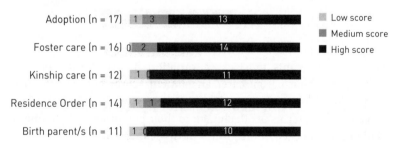

Figure 4.5
**Care pathway mean scores for IPPA–R parent sub-scale –
Communication**

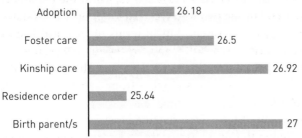

children in each of the pathway groups score highly for parent/carer trust, with the adoption group showing the lowest proportion of children scoring highly (reflecting the lower mean score presented in Figure 4.3).

Communication: On this dimension (see Figure 4.5), higher scores are indicative of a more positive relationship with parents/carers. One-way ANOVA indicated that there was no significant variation in mean score between the five pathway groups for parental communication. Additionally, post-hoc Tukey HSD tests indicated that there were no significant mean differences between any of the five care pathway groups. Despite the lack of significant difference, mean scores were highest for children in the kinship care and birth parent groups, and lowest in the residence order group. It can also be seen that mean scores were lower for the adoption group than both the foster and kinship care groups.

Figure 4.6 illustrates a very similar pattern of scores for communication across the different pathway groups. With the exception of the residence order group, over half the children across the pathway groups scored highly in terms of communication with parents/carers, with the proportion being greatest in the foster care group. The residence order group had the smallest proportion of children with high scores on this dimension.

Figure 4.6
Care pathways by IPPA–R parent sub-scale – Communication – on the low/medium/high score range (n)

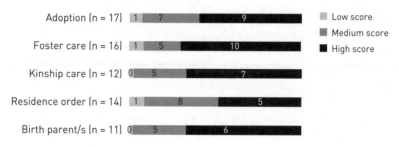

Figure 4.7
Care pathway mean scores for IPPA–R parent sub-scale – Alienation

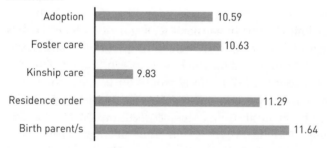

Alienation: On this dimension, higher scores are indicative of a more negative relationship with parents/carers. One-way ANOVA indicated that there was no significant variation in mean score between the five pathway groups for parental alienation. Furthermore, post-hoc Tukey HSD tests indicated that there were no significant mean differences between any of the five care pathway groups. Despite the lack of significant difference, the children in the kinship care group had the lowest mean score (with low scores indicating that the children did not feel alienated by parents/carers), whilst children in the birth parent group had the highest mean score, with children in the residence order group having the second highest score. Mean scores

Figure 4.8
Care pathways by IPPA–R parent sub-scale – Alienation – on the low/medium/high score range (n)

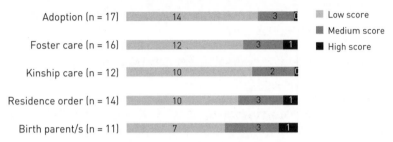

for alienation by parents/carers were very similar for the adoption and foster care groups (Figure 4.7).

The pattern of distribution of low, medium and high scores on the alienation dimension was very similar across the different pathway groups (Figure 4.8). The vast majority of children in each group had low scores, with the birth parent group having the smallest proportion.

In relation to peer attachment, unlike parental attachment, there were several children across the different pathway groups with low security scores (n = 12, 17%). These are represented in Figure 4.9. The residence order and kinship care groups had the largest proportion of children with high security of attachment to peers, with similar proportions of children in the birth parent/s, foster care, and adoption groups demonstrating low security of attachment to peers.

Figure 4.9
Care pathways by IPPA–R – Security of peer attachment (n)

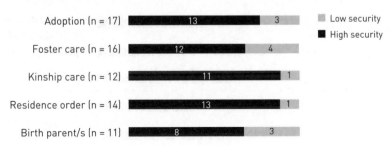

Figure 4.10
Care pathway mean scores for IPPA–R – Peer attachment

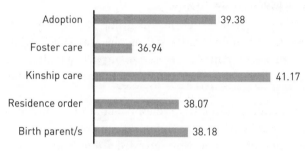

Adoption	39.38
Foster care	36.94
Kinship care	41.17
Residence order	38.07
Birth parent/s	38.18

Peer attachment: On this dimension, higher scores are indicative of a more positive relationship with peers. One-way ANOVA indicated that there was no significant variation in mean score between the five pathway groups for peer attachment. Additionally, post-hoc Tukey HSD tests indicated that there were no significant mean differences between any of the five care pathway groups. The children in the kinship care group had the highest mean score, with those in the foster care group having the lowest. Furthermore, the mean score for the kinship care group was higher than for the adoption group.

There was some variation in the distribution of low, medium, and high scores between the five pathway groups in terms of peer attachment (Figure 4.11). The pattern of distribution is very similar for the residence order, adoption, foster care, and birth parent/s

Figure 4.11
Care pathways by IPPA–R – Peer attachment – on the low/medium/ high score range (n)

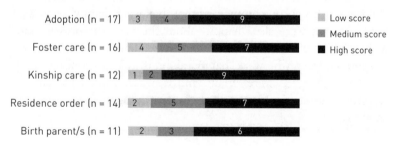

	Low score	Medium score	High score
Adoption (n = 17)	3	4	9
Foster care (n = 16)	4	5	7
Kinship care (n = 12)	1	2	9
Residence order (n = 14)	2	5	7
Birth parent/s (n = 11)	2	3	6

groups, with around half the children in each group having a high score for peer attachment. However, three-quarters of the children in the kinship care group had high scores on this domain.

Figure 4.12
Care pathway mean scores for IPPA-R peer sub-scale – Trust

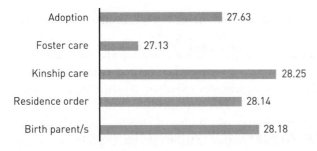

Trust: On this dimension, higher scores are indicative of a more positive relationship with peers. One-way ANOVA indicated that there was no significant variation in mean score between the five pathway groups for peer trust. Additionally, post-hoc Tukey HSD tests indicated that there were no significant mean differences between any of the five care pathway groups. However, the mean score for the children in the foster group was lower than for any other group.

As can be seen from Figure 4.13, there was some variation in the distribution of low, medium and high scores between the various pathway groups in relation to peer trust. Most children in each of the groups scored highly for peer trust, but the proportion was highest in the residence order group. Only a small proportion of children across the groups had low scores on this dimension.

Figure 4.13
Care pathways by IPPA–R peer sub-scale – Trust – on the low/ medium/high score range (n)

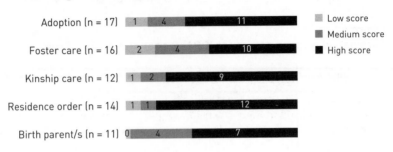

Figure 4.14
Care pathway mean scores for IPPA–R peer sub-scale – Communication

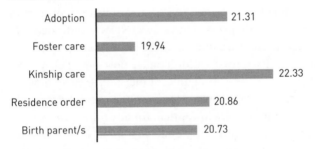

Communication: On this dimension, higher scores are indicative of a more positive relationship with peers. One-way ANOVA indicated that there was no significant variation in mean score between the five pathway groups for peer communication. Furthermore, post-hoc Tukey HSD tests indicated that there were no significant mean differences between any of the five care pathway groups. However, there were some differences in mean score, with the largest difference between the foster and kinship care groups. It can also be observed that the mean score for the kinship care group was higher than for the adoption group.

As was the case in relation to the peer attachment dimension, with

Figure 4.15
Care pathways by IPPA–R peer sub-scale – Communication – on the low/medium/high score range (n)

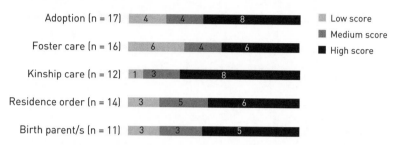

the exception of the kinship care group, the distribution in low, medium and high scores was very similar across all of the groups, with a relatively even distribution of each of these scores (Figure 4.15). However, the kinship care group had the largest proportion of children with high scores.

Figure 4.16
Care pathway mean scores for IPPA–R peer sub-scale – Alienation

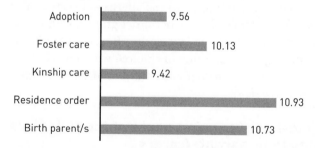

Alienation: On this dimension, higher scores are indicative of a more negative relationship with peers. One-way ANOVA indicated that there was no significant variation in mean score between the five pathway groups for peer alienation. Additionally, post-hoc Tukey HSD tests indicated that there were no significant mean differences between any of the five care pathway groups. However, Figure 4.16 highlights a difference between the lower mean score for the kinship

Figure 4.17
Care pathways by IPPA–R peer sub-scale – Alienation – on the low/ medium to high score range (n)

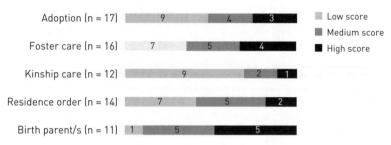
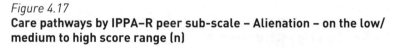

and the higher scores for the residence order and birth parent groups. It also illustrates that the mean score for the adoption group was lower than for the foster care group, but higher than the kinship care group. Both the residence order and birth parent/s groups had the highest peer alienation mean scores.

A degree of variation was found between the different pathway groups in terms of the distribution of low, medium and high scores on the peer alienation dimension (Figure 4.17). Patterns were very similar for the adoption, foster care and residence order groups, with half of the children in these groups having low scores. However, the kinship care group had the highest proportion of children with low scores on this dimension, while only a small proportion of children in the birth parent group had a low score.

Using the "me-book" to gain a sense of the children's attachment to their parents/carers

Asking the children to specify who they considered to be in their family provided an opportunity to explore the extent to which children living in placement with non-biological parents/carers con- sidered birth relatives to be part of their family. This was also useful in terms of understanding how boundaries of family membership were negotiated by children living with relatives, i.e. in kinship care and sometimes on residence order. Exploring this issue further, with questions about who the children felt was most important to them in their family and to whom they felt closest, allowed the researchers to examine the relative strength of these relationships, particularly in instances where non-biological parents and carers, and members of their wider family circle, in addition to birth family relatives, were included in the child's conceptualisation of their family. Offering an imaginary "three wishes" was included to provide children not living with birth family an opportunity to disclose future hopes in relation to birth family members. Finally, asking the children to specify where they would like to live when they were 16 (or when they had the choice to decide) enabled an exploration of the extent to which the children considered their placement to be permanent, and if their current family was the one that would support them through to early adulthood. This also revealed whether those children not living with birth family were contemplating living with them in the future.

The birth parent group

As might be expected, the concept of family for those children living with birth parents was centred solely on immediate and extended birth family. In many cases, the households in which children resided appeared to be transient, with people coming and going, siblings temporarily living in other homes, or extended family members living in their homes for periods of time. The majority of these children (n = 7) specified only their birth parents in terms of who was most important and closest to them. Other children specified either cousins as both most important and closest, a female sibling as most important, while an uncle and mother's boyfriend were also included for closeness.

Four of the birth parents had indicated some concerns regarding their child's attachments; however, of these, three had a high IPPA-R parental attachment score, with only one having a score in the medium range, suggesting these concerns may have been misplaced. Seven of the 10 children stated that they wanted to live with their parents when they were 16 or older, whereas two said they wanted to live on their own, and two were not sure. Of these two, Alexandra was the only child in the birth parent group to have a low IPPA score, and to have received a low security of parental attachment rating. This appears to be reflected by her identifying her cousin as the person in her family who was closest and most important to her.

Nina specified her father as the person who was most important and closest to her, and indicated that she wanted to live with him when she was 16 and older, although she had been living with her mother for the last four years, since returning from foster care at the age of 10. In addition, although she displayed a high IPPA score for parental attachment, her mother had raised some concerns about her attachment.

When specifying their three wishes, none of the children in the birth parent group suggested that they did not want to be living with their birth parents, or that they wanted to be living with anyone else.

The foster adoptive group

Of the nine children in foster adoptive placements, the majority (n = 5) considered birth relatives to be part of their family. For two of these children, a birth family member was included in their depictions of who was most important to them (Justin – birth father) or closest (Bridget – birth parents). These were also the only two children in this group who specified that they wanted to live with their birth parents when they were 16, and that one of their wishes was to live with their birth parents (none of the other children in this group referred to their birth family in their three wishes). In Justin's case, he had regular contact with his birth father and had a very strong connection to his birth family. Bridget, however, had never lived with her birth parents, or had any contact with them:

Researcher: *First of all, if you had one wish for your family what do you think it would be?*

Bridget: [Writes in "me-book"] *To live with my birth mummy.*

Despite both Justin and Bridget appearing to have strong connections to their birth family, they both scored in the high range on the IPPA in terms of their attachment to their adoptive parents.

For the four children who did not refer to any birth family member in their family, their adoptive parents were deemed to be the most important people in their lives, with other adoptive family members identified as people to whom they were closest. In terms of the whole group, four children wanted to live with their adoptive parents when they were 16 and beyond, whilst John wanted to live on his own, and Laura and Amy were not sure where they wanted to live.

The stranger adoptive group

Two of the eight children in this group (siblings Claire and Morgan) specified birth relatives as being in their family:

Researcher (R): *And Morgan? Why would Morgan be important to you?*

Claire (C): *Because she's my sister and I've been with her for ages.*

R: *What do you mean?*

C: *Uhm, we have been . . . we used to be with [birth mother].*

R: *Right. So you've always been with Morgan?*

C: *Yeah.*

R: *Is [birth mother] part of your family then?*

C: *She sort of is.*

R: *She sort of is?*

C: *Yeah, she is.*

Although they did not include birth relatives as part of their family, Tracy, Rory and Charlie referred to them, but were clear that they were actually not in their family (see interview extracts below).

Tracy (T): *What do you do about the birth mum?*

Researcher (R): *Well, it's really who you consider to be in your family.*

T: *She's not in my family* [nervous laugh].

Rory (Ro): *What's that one?*

Researcher (R): *Birth father.*

Ro: *Mmm, I don't understand that.*

R: *Okay, well some children would be born and then they would go and live with someone else, so they would have a birth father.*

Ro: *If you were adopted?*

R: *Yeah, that could be the case, but it's not unless you consider that person to be in your family.*

Ro: *I've never seen them . . . what's that?*

R: *A birth mother . . . So would there be a birth father and a birth mother?*

Ro: *I don't even know them, if they're dead, I don't know, I've never met them before.*

R: *Okay, so do you consider them in your family?*

Ro: *No . . . I've got pictures of them but I've never seen them . . . But I'd rather be in this family I'm in now.*

Researcher (R): *Ok, so well, that is quite a lot* [referring to the number of people Charlie circled as being in his family]. *Is there anybody there that you would consider to be in your family that you haven't included in the circle?*

Charlie (C): *Well, I might have used to include that* [pointing at "Birth mum"].

R: *You might have used to include your birth mum in your family . . . Why would that have been a "used to"?*

C: *Well, I just got used to this being my family.*

R: *Right, okay. So there is a birth mum, do you know your birth mum?*

C: *Yeah, she is called [birth mother].*

R: *And would you see her often?*

C: *No, not really . . . I am allowed to see her when I am 16 and at my brother's wedding.*

R: *And you are going to see her at your brother's wedding and you would like to see her?*

C: *Yeah.*

R: *Okay, but do you consider her to be part of your family?*

C: *No, I don't consider her and I call her [birth mother, indicating that he calls her by her first name].*

Despite the fact that there was reference to birth relatives being in the family and discussion of birth relatives when constructing their family in the me-book, none of the children in this group referred to any birth family member in their three wishes. In terms of who was most important to them in their family and to whom they felt closest, only in Ciara's case was this exclusively the adoptive parents. In all other cases, the adoptive parents were mentioned in addition to other adoptive family members.

Three children (Ciaron, Claire and Morgan) stated that they wanted to live with their adoptive parents when they were 16 years old and beyond, three wanted to live on their own (Abbie, Rory and Charlie), one with friends (Ciara) and one with boyfriend/husband and children (Tracy). It was pointed out to Tracy that this was about where she wanted to live when she was 16, and not when she was an adult, but she still maintained that this would be with a boyfriend and children.

Although Abbie's adoptive mother had believed her to be securely attached, she was the only child in this group to receive a low IPPA score for parental attachment and to receive a low security of parental attachment rating. She was one of the three children who had specified that they wanted to live on their own when they were 16. She was also the oldest in the group when she was first placed with her adoptive parents, at almost six-and-a-half years old, and had mild learning difficulties.

The foster care group

In relation to who the children considered to be in their family, a majority of children in this group included members of both the foster and birth family (n = 9), as Connor explained:

Researcher (R): *Well, is there anybody else in your family?*

Connor (C): *There's . . . mum.*

C: *Should I just write one?* [Writes "1" in the pin of "Mum"] . . . *What about the foster parent? Oh, there's foster mum there.*

R: *There's foster mum, would that be the same? Would you say mum is like foster mum?*

C: *No, it's just foster mum* [Writes "1" in the pin of "Foster mum"].

R: *So that would be a different mum?*

C: *Yeah, mum that I'm living with.*

R: *So would your foster mum be the most important to you or your birth mum, or both of them?*

C: *Uhm . . . I don't know.*

R: *That's okay.*

C: *Uhm . . . just . . .* [Writes "foster mum", in addition to having written "mum" previously]

R: *So both of them?*

C: *Yeah.*

R: *And why are they important to you?*

C: *Uhm*... [Writes in "me-book" 'because foster mum looks after me and other mum is part of my family'].

Three children did not consider their birth parents as part of their family, but included their birth siblings instead, as explained by Martin:

Researcher (R): *So you've circled mum, two sisters and dad, and so what about your sisters? Do they live here?*

Martin (M): *Yeah, they're here.*

R: *What do you call them?*

M: [Names two sisters.] *Does it have to be your actual sister?*

R: *Are they both your actual sisters?*

M: *No, one of them is.*

R: *One of them? Who's the other one then?*

M: [Name] *is my real sister and* [name] *is like stepsister or whatever it's called.*

R: *Okay. So* [name] *lives here with you and* [name]. *What age are* [name] *and* [name]?

M: [Name] *is 13 and* [name] *is 15.*

R: *And* [name] *is your stepsister?*

M: *I like referring to her as my sister 'cos I don't wanna know my real mum.*

R: *You don't want to. And is your real mum* [sister's name]'s *mum?*

M: *No.*

R: *No?*

M: *My real mum is* [birth mother].

R: *And do you see* [birth mother] *much?*

M: *No, I don't wanna see her.*

R: *You don't see her at all . . . and would you consider her to be in your family?*

M: *No.*

R: *No. So that mum* [which had been circled in the "me-book"] *is your foster mum, is it?*

M: *Do I have to write that down?*

R: *No. It's just who you would call Mum.*

M: *Oh, my foster mum* [Writes "1" in the pin of "Foster mum"].

For two children, only birth relatives were specified as being in their family, no foster family member was included, whilst the reverse was true for Dylan, who only included foster family members in his family, with no reference to any birth relative.

Of the nine children who described their family as consisting of foster and birth relatives, four specified their foster carers as the most important and closest to them; two identified both their foster and birth mothers as most important and closest; two specified the whole family as equally important and close; whilst one felt that his birth brother (with whom he was placed) was the most important and closest person for him. Three children included both foster and birth relatives in their family, but only birth siblings. For these three, foster carers were depicted as closest, but birth siblings were considered most important by two. Two children did not include any foster family member in their family. Patrick identified his older (non-resident) birth brother as most important and closest, while Liam considered his birth mother to be most important and closest to him. This is interesting given that Liam was the only child in this group who received a low security of parent/carer attachment on the IPPA, thereby suggesting that his primary attachment relationship remained with his birth mother. For Dylan, who did not include any birth relative in his family, his foster carers and foster sister were identified for both importance and closeness.

The vast majority of these children stated that they wanted to live with their foster carers when they were 16 or older, with two children stating that they wanted to live with friends, and Patrick on his own. In addition, two children commented that they would like greater contact with birth relatives, particularly siblings, in their three wishes.

Although Liam received a low security rating, no children in this group had an IPPA–R score for parental attachment in the low range, and all foster carers stated that they felt the children were securely attached to them, with only four suggesting some concerns in this regard. Two of those had IPPA scores for parental attachment in the medium range, with the other two in the high range. Of these four, only Patrick did not want to live with his foster carers when he was 16, preferring to live on his own. Both Patrick and James identified a particular birth brother as most important and closest to them.

The kinship care group

As might be expected, the vast majority of children in this group included members of their immediate kinship placement and other birth relatives in their family. Only in Orlaith's case were members of the immediate kinship family referred to exclusively as family, to the exclusion of birth parents, siblings and other relatives. In Áine's case, only birth siblings were included alongside immediate kinship placement members, as representing family, again with birth parents being excluded:

Researcher (R): *So you have a granny and a granddad but they've . . . passed on?*

Orlaith (O): *Yeah, I still have a granddad but I wouldn't really count him as my granddad. He's like in my . . . mum's side, in the birth mum's side.*

[Completing the family page in the "me-book", Áine circles "Mum" and writes "1" in its pin]

Researcher (R): *And would that be* [kinship carer]*?*

Áine (Á): *Yeah.*

R: *Yeah? Very good.*

Á: *And what about if I don't like the . . . birth daddy and the birth mother, do I have to . . .* (referring to including them in the family)?

R: *Only if you consider them to be in your family. Do you consider them to be in your family?*

Á: *No.*

Both these children had high IPPA parent/carer attachment scores, were deemed to be securely attached by their carers, did not express any wishes regarding their birth family, and wanted to live with their kinship carers at age 16 and older. In terms of who was most important and who was closest to them, a mixture of immediate kinship and wider birth family members were mentioned, but the kinship carers predominated for both.

Most of the children in this group stated that they wanted to live with their kinship carers when aged 16 and beyond, with three wanting to live on their own or with friends. Only Rebecca stated that she wanted to live with her birth mother, and also used her three wishes to express a desire to see more of her birth mother. One other child in this group (Marie) mentioned her birth family members in her three wishes:

Researcher (R): *So first of all, what would you wish for your family if you had a wish for them?*

Marie (M): *Uhm, I don't know. It would either be that they didn't die or they all wised up.*

R: *In what way do you mean wise up?*

M: *Like my mummy and daddy stopped drinking and they got me back and all and they would have a better life.*

Rebecca and Marie were the oldest in the kinship group when placed with their kinship carers, at nine and seven respectively. Most of the other children were under three when they were first placed. All of the children, with the exception of Tierna, were deemed to be securely attached by their kinship carers and none registered a low score on the IPPA for parent/carer attachment, with three having scores in the medium range. Two of these, Áine and Marie, were amongst the three who had wanted to live alone or with friends at 16.

Residence order group

For the vast majority of children, both individuals from the immediate residence order placement and the wider birth family were included in their depiction of their family. For three children, only those living within the immediate residence order placement were considered family, with birth relatives being excluded. In each of these three cases, the residence order had been granted to former foster carers, who were referred to as "mum and dad" by each. All three had been placed with their carers before the age of six months. Where the residence order had been granted to former kinship carers (n = 6), all children considered wider birth family members to be in their family. They also tended to refer to their carers as "aunt", "uncle", "grandmother" etc., rather than using parental terms such as "mum and dad". This pattern was found to be much more common for those children living with former foster carers.

In terms of importance, invariably the residence order carers were cited as most important, with other residence order placement and birth family members also included for closeness. A challenge highlighted by Nicole, Kirsten, and Ryan (see interview extracts below respectively) was negotiating how to refer to their residence order carers and birth parents, so as not to cause offence to either. The children were trying to make sense of, and find some way of explaining or defining, the relationships they had within the residence order placement and within their wider birth family:

Researcher (R): *And who do they* [birth brothers] *live with?*

Kirsten (K): [Residence order carer's daughter].

R: *Who's* [Residence order carer's daughter]*?*

K: *I don't know. I know where she's . . . well, she's my mum's* (residence order carer) *daughter. She's* [residence order carer] *daughter but I call her, I don't know what I call her* [laughs].

Researcher: *So, anybody else here* [to be included in the family page of the "me-book"]*?*

Nicole (N): *I don't get this though, where it says, like, birth mother?*

R: *Well, we are doing this book with lots of different children who have had lots of different experiences so we try to put everybody in . . . Some kids are in foster care, for example, and they might call the foster mum, mum or foster mum, but they might see their parents every week and they would call the parent they see, you know their birth parent, the parent who gave birth to them, they might say aye, that's my birth parent and this is my foster mum . . . What about you?*

N: *I don't know . . . mmm, well, I call my daddy* [birth father] *but I wouldn't call my mummy* [birth mother, indicating that she would not call her by her first name]*, I don't know why, just . . . I don't like say it to their faces.*

R: *Well, would you see* [birth mother]*?*

N: *See her? No, not really. But I think my mummy's* (paternal aunt with residence order) *going to organise a visit for her because it's around Christmas.*

R: *Would that normally happen? Would* [birth mother] *be part of those visits at Christmas time?*

N: *Well, I used to see her every three months and now just, I don't really see her but I don't really mind either.*

R: *Would* [birth mother] *say when she wants to see you, or would you say when you want to see her, what way does it work?*

N: *She would like, say, she would phone up and say, 'Can I see Nicole?' But then my mummy* [kinship carer] *would say it's up to me. And then I wouldn't know what to say . . .*

N: *She* (birth mother) *like tries to, like, make me say "mummy", but whenever I was younger I said to her, 'I'll call you mummy and I'll call mummy* [name of aunt with residence order], *"mum", but it just ended up me calling my mummy (aunt) "mummy" . . . I said to her once, I'll have to ask my mummy about something, and she said* [name of aunt with residence order]. *Just said to me* [name of aunt with residence order] *. . . it's kind of annoying though.*

R: *Annoying?*

N: *Hmm. I don't see her, so I don't really class her as my proper mummy.*

R: *But would you consider* [birth mother] *to be in your family?*

N: *Well, if someone said to me, 'Who's in your family?' I would just say the* [surname of aunt with residence order]. *I don't know whether I should have done that.*

Ryan (Ry): *Well, she is not really a foster sister because we got, like, a residence order, well Mum got, like, a residence order I think or something.*

Researcher (R): *Right, okay.*

Ry: *It's, like, the same for me or something. I don't know anything about it like.*

R: *And do you call her your foster sister or do you call her your sister?*

Ry: *Sister.*

Jo and Sarah received a low IPPA parent/carer attachment score, and received low security of attachment to carer ratings, although both were deemed to be securely attached by their carers. In relation to whom they wanted to live with on reaching 16, Jo stated he wanted to live on his own, while Sarah wanted to live with friends. Both these children were living with former foster carers, rather than kinship carers. Three children had medium IPPA–R parent/carer attachment scores, and all three were living with former foster carers, rather than kinship carers.

Only Luke referred to the birth family in his three wishes:

Researcher: *So, what do you think you would wish for your family?*

Luke: *To have my mum back.*

In terms of whom they would like to live with when they were 16 and older, most of the children named their residence order carers, two children wanted to live with friends, Caoimghin wanted to live on his own, and two children stated that they did not know.

Parent/carer perspectives on the children's attachment to them settling in

Birth parents

Of all six groups of parent/carers, it was the children placed with birth parents who seemed to have had the greatest difficulty settling in. About half of these parents described their child as having no problems settling (back) into their care while others acknowledged at least some difficulties. Although they talked about their child as not having problems settling in, a further two parents described behaviour that suggested at least some degree of stress or anxiety, for example, having repeated nightmares or bedwetting. A variety of possible reasons for the child's problematic transition was suggested, including lack of continuity or repeated moves in foster care; adverse and psychologically damaging experiences while in the care of another birth parent; or enjoyment of excessive freedom when in the care of other family members. Joseph's parent attributed his difficulty in settling in to recurring placement breakdowns and moves:

I think it was because of all the different foster homes he was at. First one was for a year and then he had two, a short-term one and then another short-term and then the last one about six months before [he] came home.

Only Caomhan's parent reflected on why they thought their child had settled relatively unproblematically, highlighting the importance of the frequency of contact visits in the run-up to his permanent return.

Foster adoptive parents

The majority of foster adoptive parents (n = 8) considered that their child had settled (relatively) easily/(very) well. Of those who suggested possible reasons, all made an explicit link with their child's placement with them at a young age (either a few weeks old or young toddler), as Karl's adoptive parent commented:

He was only a few weeks old so . . . he didn't have to adapt so much to our family.

Those whose child had experienced a more problematic settling in (n = 3) identified a range of reasons. Bridget's adoptive parent focused on the 14 placements she had in the space of two-and-a-half years, as well as the initial contact with the birth mother which, when ceased, they believed had allowed her to settle. Joey's adoptive parents highlighted their son's autism and associated aggression, which had been gradually diminishing as mutual understanding between them developed. Amy's adoptive mother described her daughter's extreme stress and anxiety, which eased over time, as her sense of security grew.

Stranger adoptive parents

The vast majority of stranger adoptive parents (n = 8) considered that their child had settled easily/(very) well. Several reasons were proffered, including that adoption brought with it an end to contact with birth parents and had occurred at a (very) young age. According to Tracy's adoptive mother, her settling in had taken longer because of her initial intense feelings of loss in relation to her foster carers.

Tracey's adoptive mother was aware of the strong bond that existed between them, and consequently facilitated post-adoption contact. However, in hindsight she considered that this contact had militated against her daughter's settling in to her new family.

Foster carers

It was the children of foster carers who seemed to have had the easiest of transitions, as the vast majority of carers (n = 14) considered that the child had settled (very) well and quickly. For Trevor's foster mother, the ease with which he had settled was surprising, given the fact that he came to her at a relatively late age (10 years old), having been at his previous foster placement since the age of three. Although Tony's placement had broken down just prior to the interview, his previous foster mother described him as settling very easily, with the problems that led to the breakdown of the placement emerging much later. The most frequently mentioned reasons for unproblematic settling in were relatively young age (typically a young child/toddler) when first placed with them; prior contact in the lead up to the placement; presence of the child's birth sibling (also fostered in the same placement); other similarly aged birth grandchildren in close proximity; and placement in the local area to enable established relationships to be maintained. As stated by Dylan's foster carer:

He came out and he was just beaming . . . he was used to street life in [name of city].

Although their foster child was considered to have settled well, three foster carers described the process as having taken some time. Reasons identified were: an abusive/troubled early childhood and multiple placements that had contributed to a sense of insecurity. Two carers described more problematic settling in experiences. Jack's foster mother attributed these difficulties to the child's hyperactivity, but felt that the process was helped by the presence of Jack's birth brother, who was also fostered by her. Martin's foster mother attributed his difficulties to ongoing profound behavioural problems, caused by brain damage sustained in utero.

Kinship carers

The majority of kinship carers (n = 6) also reported that settling in had gone well or very well. Explanations for the ease of the transition focused on the timing of the child's placement with them at a relatively young age; the presence of other related children (cousins/older birth siblings) in the family; and the significance of existing familial relationships in ensuring mutual understanding and support, as Maggie's carer pointed out:

> I think she's more settled with the family members because she can go to any one of them. If she was fostered with strangers it would be a totally different situation.

Two kinship carers reported more problematic settling in processes. In the case of Tierna, initial disturbed behaviour had gradually diminished, although excessive anger could still be displayed. David's kinship carer accounted for difficulties on the grounds of continuing contact with his birth mother, as well as the child's inability to understand why he could not live with his birth mother:

> His mammy used to come and visit him and then she would have went and he didn't understand why he couldn't go along with his mammy and stay with his mammy.

Residence order carers

The majority of residence order carers (n = 10) also described their child as having settled well/very well into family life. Where explanations were offered as to why this had been the case (n = 6), without exception, all highlighted that their child had come to them as a baby and had no recollection of any other life. Only two residence order carers talked about more problematic settling in, caused by distress at being removed from either birth parents or long-term foster carers with whom significant attachments had developed. Nicole's carer explained this in terms of her attachment to her previous foster carers:

> Probably it was a big thing for her to . . . move to a different

family . . . She would have known that [previous foster carers] really as her family . . . So as far as she was concerned . . . there was a big big change to her system.

Felt security

Birth parents

Across all six groups of parents/carers, it was the birth parents who felt their children had the most mixed experiences concerning felt security. Thus, although the majority of birth parents (n = 7) described their child as feeling secure, there were higher numbers in this group (n = 4) who described behaviour they believed to indicate a degree of ongoing insecurity. In essence, this behaviour involved clinginess, with the child fretting at their parent's temporary absence, and/or ensuring they remained in their presence as much as possible. Although such behaviour was considered to have diminished over time, for the majority of children, it continued to some degree, as Nina's parent explained:

> *But she seems to need her own surroundings . . . she's a wee bit clingy to me if she knows I'm going somewhere . . . she'd cling on to my arm as if to say 'I'm coming'.*

Three of these four birth parents described a consequent felt responsibility to maximise their child's sense of security, including a degree of over-protectiveness, acknowledged as potentially detrimental to the child in the longer-term. In addition, although they did not identify behavioural indications of insecurity as such, two other birth parents highlighted issues that were likely to mitigate against their child feeling totally secure: these were a fear of the parent being admitted to hospital because of ongoing mental health problems; and living with an alcoholic parent which might lead to their being removed by Social Services again, a situation which had been common in the child's early life. Aidan's birth mother recalled her son's concern and uneasiness:

*I'm worried, Mum, in case you have to go into hospital again,'
and I says, 'Well, there's no worrying, I'll not be getting into
hospital again'. They were changing my antidepressants.*

Only Jim's mother stated outright that she considered her son to be
insecure, which she attributed to earlier adverse experiences in the
care of his father and saw as having compromised Jim's confidence in
the permanency of his return to her care. However, her concerns were
not reflected in his high security of parental attachment rating on the
IPPA–R and his high score for overall parental attachment. Conversely, Alexandra's mother felt that she was securely attached but the
child received a low security for parental attachment rating on the
IPPA–R.

In terms of the child feeling secure when left on their own, the
majority of birth parents who commented (n = 4) described their
child as comfortable in this situation. Ronan and Joseph's parents
were unable to leave their child alone in the house; for Ronan's
mother, the concern was his behavioural issues (learning difficulties)
which meant that he could not be trusted not to harm himself. Joseph's
mother reported that he refused to be left alone in the house, even
when offered the opportunity; she understood this reluctance as
another indication of his insecurities. Although the majority of birth
parents highlighted acceptance of being left alone for short periods of
time, this did not equate, necessarily, with total contentment. Thus,
both Jim and Niall's parents described being questioned by them
about their planned whereabouts and length of absence or being
content with being left on their own in the house only in quite specific
circumstances, e.g. when the parent was "nipping" to the local shop.
Aidan's parent described an almost polar opposite set of circumstances
in that he agitated to be left on his own significantly beyond what the
parent was comfortable with, although this was interpreted as a
teenager's typical push for independence.

The majority of birth parents (n = 4) described their child as
behaving much as they would expect on their departure and return
from a short time away, that is, they might ask about where they were

going/had been and/or give them a hug or a kiss. Joseph and Niall's birth parents went slightly further, to suggest that their children's behaviour on their return demonstrated to them that they were relieved to have them back. Aidan and Nina's parents contrasted their children's current behaviour, essentially a relative decline in displays of open affection on the departure or return of the parent, to how they had behaved as younger children, when more overt displays were common. Ronan's mother commented on her son's occasional misbehaviour when in the care of a babysitter, describing him as "playing up" on her return as a way of avoiding punishment.

Several birth parents talked about their own insecurities, which affected their approach to raising their child. For example, Aidan's mother described deep-seated fears concerning her child's safety to the extent that she was extremely reluctant to allow him to be on his own for any length of time, no matter how short. Ashley's mother stressed how she had only been separated from her child once in ten years. She was reluctant to leave her in the care of anyone else, in case she would feel "abandoned". Emma's father acknowledged his reluctance to allow her to have sleepovers at friends' houses, describing himself as "over-protective"; so much had happened in her life that he was pre-occupied with ensuring her safety. In this context, it would seem that some birth parents had been significantly affected by their past experiences (e.g. of their child's placement in care and their own role in this), which contributed to their relative "over-protection" of their child.

Foster adoptive parents

All foster adoptive parents described their child as feeling secure. The most frequently mentioned behavioural indicator of (developing) security was their child being comfortable with his/her own company and being content to be (left) on their own for short periods of time (n = 4). These adoptive parents offered two main reasons underpinning their child's felt security. Firstly, three parents felt that being adopted, as distinct from being fostered, promoted felt security, as it provided definitive reassurance regarding the stability of their placement.

Secondly, four parents believed that being placed at a young age facilitated attachment, understanding, care and attention over the long term. Amongst those adoptive parents who addressed the specific issue of the child having previously been fostered by them prior to adoption, views on the potential impact of this on their child's sense of security were mixed. Three adoptive parents considered that fostering had served to effectively "pave the way" for the development of their child's sense of security/attachment, as stated by John's adoptive parent:

> I think it makes him more secure . . . once he knew that he was staying and was not moving anywhere else you know . . . he knew there was no chance of him getting moved on again.

Conversely, Danny's adoptive mother suggested that her son attached to them whilst being fostered as he had no awareness of the differences between being fostered and adopted. Despite their assessment of their child as essentially secure, three previous foster adoptive parents acknowledged lingering insecurities, demonstrated by behaviours such as ongoing wariness of social workers; associating them with being moved against the child's will; a need to know precisely the parents' whereabouts at all times; and clinginess and the child's need to be with their parents and looking to them for constant reassurance.

Despite all foster adoptive parents describing their child as secure, for three children, being left alone, however temporarily, was problematic. Joey felt extremely averse to being left on his own even for short periods of time no matter how short the physical distance between himself and others. Due to Justin's Foetal Alcohol Syndrome (FAS) and consequent impulsivity, he could not be left on his own, whilst Steve's adoptive mother described him as prepared to be away from them, but only if he knew precisely where they were and that he could return to them quickly if necessary.

The majority of foster adoptive parents (n = 6) described their child as behaving much as they would expect on their departure or return from a short time away, citing indications of behaviour similar to those of the birth parents. For Laura's adoptive mother, her daughter's response was unpredictable and considered difficult. Depending on her mood at the time, she could either kiss her mother hello/goodbye or completely ignore her.

Stranger adoptive parents

Although all stranger adoptive parents who commented (n = 7) described their child as feeling secure, Paul's adoptive mother described his dislike of being left on his own in the house for any length of time and his consequent need for company. In addition, Claire's adoptive mother thought that Claire's lack of emotional response to her and her husband's departure/return was concerning and related this to her ongoing suspicions about her cognitive/developmental problems, including an inability to form attachments. No concerns were highlighted by Abbie's adoptive parents despite her having received a low security of parental attachment rating on the IPPA–R.

A number of reasons underpinning feelings of security for these children were offered. Of these, the most frequently mentioned was that of early adoption, in that the child was placed with them as a baby (n = 4) resulting in the child growing up always knowing the family as "theirs".

Other reasons mentioned were having a birth sibling also adopted; specific unanticipated events that had served to cement the parent–child relationship; positive past childhood experiences that had contributed to their child's perceived emotional stability; and the presence of birth children to provide company and spontaneous support. Notwithstanding their assessment of their child as secure, Charlie and Paul's adoptive parents described behaviour that, to them, indicated lingering insecurities; while Charlie insisted on sleeping in his parent's bedroom, Paul was anxious about being left on his own in the house, even for short periods of time.

Foster carers

All foster carers who commented on this issue (n = 13) described their foster child as feeling secure. The majority also described them as being content to be left on their own for (brief) periods of time; and all those who mentioned the issue (n = 12) described their foster child as behaving much as they would expect on their departure and/or return from a short time away, citing indications of behaviour similar to those of the other groups.

Various behavioural indicators of (developing) security were given, including the contrast drawn between their child's current openness and outgoing personality with their previous "clinginess" (n = 2), and between their child's current acceptance of being left alone for brief periods of time with past anxieties (n = 3); enhanced carer–child communication (n = 2); regular overt statements from the child concerning his/her love for/commitment to the foster carer (n = 2); and stated wish to be called by the foster carer's surname. Suggested reasons underpinning felt security were the child's placement at a young age; repeated reassurances to the child that he/she was now in their permanent home and would not be sent away again; and the presence of other birth siblings, as reflected by Connor's foster mother:

> *[Connor's older birth brother] was here for a couple of years before . . . I thought I'd put the two of them together to see what happens, because after all, they only had each other . . . Connor seemed to be unsettled at the time ... but he was glad to see his brother and to be with him . . . It helped in a way that he didn't have anybody else . . . which was good in a way that he had somebody that he could call his own brother.*

Despite their assessment of their children as secure, some foster carers (n = 4) described what could be considered behavioural indicators of lingering insecurity. For instance, Patrick's foster carer talked about his attention-seeking, including his threats to leave home and to self-harm, as well as his fear of becoming separated from her when out together. She advised that she never left him alone, describing him as "a compulsive thief" whom she felt unable to trust not to steal something. Both James and Pol's (siblings), and Martin's foster carers described their children's clinginess and emotional dependence on them. Libby and Mary's foster carers explicitly discussed the issue of being fostered, as distinct from being adopted, in terms of how this might impact on their child's ability to attach and feel secure. Both considered that their foster child was no less attached because they had not been adopted. In this context, Libby's foster carer talked about how she always described her two foster children as being adopted, as this was how she thought of them, and she wanted to avoid being considered as somehow less bonded to them because they were "only" fostered. In contrast to the other carers in this group, Liam's carer highlighted no concerns despite him receiving a low security of carer attachment rating on the IPPA–R.

Kinship carers

The only other group that included children described as insecure by their carers was the kinship care group, although only in relation to one child, Tierna. However, neither she nor any of the other children in this group received a low security of attachment to carer rating on the IPPA–R, and Tierna was rated as having high security and received a high score for overall parental attachment. An example given by her carer of Tierna's insecurity was that she was uncomfortable being left alone in the house, irrespective for how short a time. Tierna's insecurity was explained by her knowledge that her siblings had been returned to her birth mother, something she was adamant she did not want for herself. Otherwise, all other kinship carers considered that their child felt secure/very secure. This sense of felt security was most often associated with the fact that the child was being cared for by relatives and, consequently, their carers experienced similar feelings for them as their own birth children, as stated by Joanne's carer:

> Because family is very important to Maggie . . . for example, she will say to me, 'Which one of [kinship carers] do I look like? . . . this is my family' . . . Or she might say, 'How did you pick my name?'

The only other explanation offered for the child's felt security focused on the importance of reassurance regarding the permanency of their placement, as Marie's carer pointed out:

So we said to her about the first year she was here . . . look Marie, you'll never be moved from here. I know we'll have arguments . . . but unless it's something really really bad . . . or something would happen maybe to us . . . you'll never be moved from here unless you want to go yourself, obviously.

The majority of kinship carers (n = 6) described their child as behaving much as they would expect on their departure and/or return from a short time away. Maggie's grandparents talked about her as accepting the need to go to respite care occasionally, referring to her happiness and relief on returning to them. The situation with Tierna was more complicated in that her response to being separated depended on her mood at the time; if in a bad mood, she would simply watch her carers leave and not speak. Typically, she demonstrated that she was glad to see them on her return.

Residence order carers

All Residence order carers who commented (n = 12) described their child as feeling secure and as behaving much as they would expect on their departure or return from a short time away, citing indications of behaviour similar to those mentioned by other parents/carers. Other indications of (developing) felt security were provided. In order of frequency, these were their child had voluntarily changed the surname they used or insisted that on using the carers' surname; typically in the context of seeing themselves as adopted/part of the family (n = 5); regular conversations that made clear their child's sense of belonging and attachment to the carer (n = 2); and increasingly enhanced carer–child communication (n = 1). Explanations offered concerning the positive development of their child's sense of security and attachment were the importance of their child being with them from a young age; protection of their child from information likely to jeopardise felt security; being brought up with birth siblings and by a birth family member; and the birth parents' withdrawal from contact which was seen as facilitating the development of the child's emotional attachment to carers.

Indirectly, Nicole's carers prioritised the importance of age in facilitating felt security when they suggested that the problems they had experienced with her were largely borne from the fact that she had come to them at a relatively late age (six years old).

Notwithstanding their assessment of the child as secure, Jonny, Kirsten and Jo's carers identified what could be considered as indications of lingering insecurities. Jonny's carers talked about him as "jealous" of other children coming into the house, describing territorial behaviour designed to impress upon others that this was his home. Kirsten's carer talked about the fact that, when visiting her birth mother, Kirsten was clearly anxious to be reunited with them. Similarly, Jo's carer described him as unhappy and anxious when on his own, even when somebody else was in the house. This was the only instance where a parent/carer had identified a concern regarding the child's security of attachment for one of the five children who received a low security of parent/carer attachment rating on the IPPA–R.

Children's behaviour when meeting strangers

Birth parents
The majority of birth parents (n = 5) described what they considered to be "normal" or "typical" behaviour when their child met with strangers. They described their child as being somewhat shy and reserved, sometimes awkward, but never overly so, and certainly not acquiescent or overly-familiar. Jim and Ronan's birth parents suggested that their behaviour was "abnormal", in the sense of their being overly compliant/overly-familiar with strangers, to the point that both were considered liable to place themselves in danger if not protected from so doing. In Ronan's case, the child had diagnosed learning difficulties.

Foster adoptive parents
Most foster adoptive parents (n = 5) recalled their child displaying behaviours similar to that described by birth parents, when meeting with strangers. The parents of the remaining four children considered

their child's behaviour to be atypical to a greater or lesser degree, as they had a range of behavioural problems. Although Joey conversed with strangers in a well-mannered way, he invariably disclosed sensitive and personal information to them, which his parents associated with his Autistic Spectrum Disorder (ASD). Laura's adoptive mother worried about her over-friendliness and flirtatious behaviour with strangers, something she attributed to her daughter's recently acquired friendships with older girls. Justin's adoptive mother described him as over-friendly, talking to anybody and everybody and disclosing personal information tactlessly (associated with FAS). In contrast, Steve's adoptive mother described him as extremely wary of strangers and lacking confidence to such an extent that he would avoid interaction (also FAS).

Stranger adoptive parents
The majority of stranger adoptive parents (n = 6) also felt that when meeting strangers, their children showed "normal" or "typical" behaviours, similar to those described by birth parents and foster adoptive parents. However, Claire and Paul's adoptive parents described what they considered to be somewhat "abnormal" behaviour, in that both their children were overly wary, inclined to withdraw into themselves, and unwilling to interact. Although this was the perception of Claire's adoptive mother, Claire was pleasant to the researchers and engaged well during the interview.

Foster, kinship and residence order carers
The majority of foster, kinship carers and residence order carers considered the child's behaviour on meeting strangers to be perfectly normal and similar to that described by the other parents/carers. David's aunt described him as too trusting of people, tending to be friendly with strangers, but not in ways that caused her concern. Two foster carers described more atypical behaviour. Patrick's foster mother described him as being extremely shy with strangers, often either hiding or covering his face, something she put down to very low self-esteem. Conversely, James's foster mother described him as overly friendly with strangers, and expressed worry about his behaviour

(James was diagnosed with Attention Deficit Hyperactivity Disorder - ADHD). Gary's residence order carer was the only one in this group to identify more problematic behaviour, highlighting his propensity to wander off on his own when out shopping, and to talk to strangers with no appreciation of the dangers involved (associated with FAS).

Children's behaviour in new situations

Birth parents

There was an even split between birth parents (n = 4) who considered their child's behaviour as unproblematic, in that they had coped well with new and different situations, and those who recognised their child's attitude/response as more circumspect (n = 4). Amongst parents who considered their child to cope well with new situations, the most frequent example provided was their child's relatively unproblematic settling into secondary school. Of those who did not, Jim and Ronan (diagnosed with learning difficulties) were described as particularly "vigilant", asking questions and wanting to remain close to them when in an unknown environment. Nina was described as wary of new environments, to the point where she actively avoided them, preferring the security of familiar surroundings. Joseph's mother highlighted how he would tend to become quiet and to comfort eat when faced with change.

Foster adoptive parents

A minority of foster adoptive parents (n = 3) described their child's behaviour as typical or normal in that they might be a little apprehensive, but not overly so, and would be quite able and willing to participate, perhaps with a little reassurance from themselves/others. A majority (n = 5) described their child as finding the prospect of new situations somewhat more challenging/anxiety-provoking but, usually, still able to participate. For three of these, the central issue was their child's cognitive/behavioural limitations, likely to make them apprehensive/anxious about new situations, and typically requiring concerted explanation/reassurance.

Stranger adoptive parents

Amongst stranger adoptive parents, there was an almost 50/50 split between those whose children's behaviour was described as essentially "to be expected", and those children whose behaviour was considered more problematic. Ciara and Ciaron's adoptive parents described their children's behaviour in new situations as typical or normal in that they would not be unduly phased. Conversely, four adoptive parents commented that their child found the prospect of new situations challenging and could be nervous but, despite this anxiety, they still participated in new challenges. This group did not include Abbie's (low security of parental attachment) adoptive parents.

Foster carers

The majority of foster carers who commented (n = 7) described their foster child's behaviour as typical or normal, in that they might be a little apprehensive but not overly so and would be able to adjust and willingly participate in new situations and activities or, alternatively, relished the opportunities provided. In contrast, although Trevor's foster mother acknowledged that he could cope with change, she was aware that this was something he disliked. Three foster carers described their foster child as finding the prospect of new situations more challenging or anxiety-provoking. Both Dylan and Pol's carers talked about how their foster child's Asperger's Syndrome and ADHD (respectively) meant they required a daily routine and anything that deviated from this caused considerable anxiety.

Kinship carers

Four kinship carers who spoke about this issue considered their child to be able to take things in their stride in the context of new situations, whereas three carers identified difficulties of varying degrees and nature. Tierna's carers talked about her finding new situations "difficult", and although she had improved as she had become older, she remained essentially uncomfortable. Orlaith's aunt described her as somewhat nervous about new situations until becoming familiar; for example, she was nervous about starting secondary school and found the first week hard to settle, but thrived thereafter. Jessica's aunt described her as having little or no fear of new situations and requiring vigilance when out, which she attributed to her learning difficulties.

Residence order carers

The majority of residence order carers who addressed this issue (n = 6) considered that their child responded as would be expected in new situations, perhaps being slightly anxious or hesitant but quickly adapting. Greg and Kirsten's carers went slightly further, describing their children as being relaxed and taking new situations very much in their stride, and being confident in unfamiliar situations. Jo's carer described his response to new situations as more problematic. She talked about his dislike of large group gatherings, including family parties, as well as shopping centres, and typically avoiding such events or places. Although the carer associated this response with typical teenage attitude or behaviour, she also mentioned the fact that although Jo would happily attend a friend's birthday party, he refused to go to those of family members. Interestingly, this is the only occasion where the carer expressed concerns about the sense of security of a child who subsequently received a low security of attachment to carer rating on the IPPA–R.

Children's affection towards their parents/carers

Birth parents

There was no clear pattern amongst birth parents concerning descriptions of their child's affection. For three children there were no explicit displays of affection; with four children (including Alexandra who received a low security rating) there was some affection; whilst for Emma and Joseph there were high levels of affection. Three parents accounted for the lack or decline in explicit displays of affection on the basis of their child becoming a teenager and/or the fact that, as a male, the child was disinclined to give hugs and kisses. Furthermore, some of these parents discerned more nuanced displays of affection, such as humour, or close physical contact. Nina's mother talked about deliberately seeking to counter her physical withholding of affection by ensuring that they gave her regular hugs and kisses. Similarly, Jim's mother explained that, as Jim appeared clearly uncomfortable with displays of affection, she ensured physical contact in other ways, such as "play-fighting". Ashley's mother contrasted her (often extreme) rudeness towards her with her private tenderness and open affirmation of love and concern.

Foster and stranger adoptive parents

All foster adoptive parents and almost all stranger adoptive parents described their child as age-appropriately affectionate or very affectionate, mentioning open displays of affection, such as frequent hugs, cuddles and kisses. Justin's foster adoptive mother and Paul and Rory's stranger adoptive parents commented on the decrease in their children's overt displays of affection, as they had become older. Hugs and kisses were still given, but with less spontaneity. However, Claire's stranger adoptive mother described her as emotionally distant, never willingly offering any physical gestures of affection and being uncomfortable being given hugs and kisses by others.

Kinship carers

All kinship carers stated that their child displayed at least some physical affection, typically in the form of hugs and kisses. However, the degree of this affection ranged from regular and enthusiastic displays to the much more reticent. Most kinship carers (n = 6) talked about (sometimes very) affectionate behaviour shown towards both them and other members of the family. For others (n = 4), although affection was displayed, it was more curtailed and given only in specific circumstances. In Tierna's case, she had never been openly affectionate, giving only the occasional hug. For Jessica's aunt, her niece's affection was sporadic; Jessica could be affectionate, in that she gave hugs and kisses for a time, but then stopped. Although Nathan had been living with his grandmother for ten years (now aged around 13), it had only been in the past year that he had begun to give her a hug at night before going to bed; the grandmother considered this to be a significant "breakthrough". Rebecca's uncle described her as shy and therefore not spontaneously affectionate, except in relation to his (birth) toddler daughter, who Rebecca hugged and kissed all the time; she was less demonstrative towards her aunt and uncle. Orlaith and Eoghan's carers commented on a decline in explicit displays of affection, linking this to the children growing older/becoming teenagers.

Foster and residence order carers

All foster and residence order carers described their child as age-appropriately affectionate or very affectionate. For Patrick's foster mother, this affection was particularly important, given his otherwise aggressive and impulsive behaviour. In Sally's case, where the placement had recently broken down, her overt affection towards her foster mother was made all the more poignant given her otherwise offensive behaviour. Although recently removed from her care by Social Services and living in an assessment unit, Tony's foster mother talked about him as being openly affectionate during contact visits. Greg's grandfather (residence order) described him as very affection-ate, but considered this behaviour to be relatively "babyish"; he reflected on this as part and parcel of his grandson's continuing "clinginess", being the youngest of three children at home and, as such, possibly more indulged than his older siblings.

Although they still considered their child to be (openly) affection-ate, three foster carers, together with two residence order carers, commented that overt displays had reduced in the recent past as their child had become older and entered the teenage years. None considered this change to be anything other than age-appropriate behaviour.

Relationships with other family members

Birth parents

The majority of birth parents described their child as getting on (very) well (n = 4) or "normally" (n = 3) with (extended) family, including the typical ups-and-downs of family life (e.g. bickering/fights between children/siblings). For example, Joseph's mother described the close relationship between her son and his older brother, who now lived independently, as well as with her own sister and brother-in-law, with the latter being like a surrogate father to both her sons.

A number of birth parents rationalised their child's ongoing relationships with family members, both positive and negative, with reference to the specific circumstances of his/her previous foster care and current home life. Sometimes, these circumstances, particularly the physical separation and presumed consequent emotional distance this engendered, were considered to have prompted some degree of dysfunction within intra-familial relationships. For example, Jim's mother drew attention to resentment amongst her other sons, based on the fact that they had had to make (as they saw it) "sacrifices" to accommodate Jim's return:

When Jim came back . . . he [other son] was annoyed because then he had to start sharing with Jim and he didn't like that. And still he would say, 'This is my room'.

Conversely, others referred to their circumstances as having under-pinned their children's extremely loving and supportive relationships. For example, Emma's father accounted for her closeness to her grandmother (his mother), as well as her aunts and uncles, on the grounds that, as he was a single parent, all of his family had been very closely involved in her care.

In contrast, Ashley and Ronan's birth mothers described more problematic relationships. Ashley's mother explained her own parents' disinterest in and lack of affection for Ashley, on the basis that they resented her for "ruining" her life, as she had become pregnant as a teenager. Ronan's mother also highlighted feelings of resentment when she accounted for her son's perpetual fighting with his siblings:

When it was just me and [other son], and I think his nose was a bit out of joint . . . everything was his you see, he had his own room, and now he has to share a room with Ronan, he sort of pushed that line a bit because it was always him on his own in the house.

Foster adoptive parents

The vast majority of foster adoptive parents (n = 7) described their child as getting on well or very well with (extended) family. For instance, Bridget's adoptive mother talked about how well she got on with her adoptive male and female cousins (there were no other children in the family home), particularly those who lived very close by and were, essentially, like brothers and sisters. Steve's adoptive mother described him as being particularly close to his adoptive father and getting on very well with his two older (adoptive) brothers, both of whom had left home, but with whom he remained in close contact. His relationships with other (foster) children in the house were typical of siblings, sometimes getting on well, sometimes not. However, Joey and Laura's adoptive parents described more problematic relationships. Due to his autism, Joey's relationships with other children in the house were based on them giving him space, and being explicitly positive and accepting in their responses to him. With older family members, who understood and accepted his autism and consequent needs, relationships were very good. Although Laura had previously enjoyed very good relationships with her adoptive mother's birth children, this situation had deteriorated, as one older sister had recently returned home to look after her mother, who had a significant decline in her health, and Laura was unremittingly rude and aggressive towards her.

Stranger adoptive parents

All stranger adoptive parents described their child as getting on well or very well with (extended) family. For example, Abbie's (low security of attachment to parents rating) adoptive mother talked about her as getting on very well with the extended family network, helped by the fact that she was the youngest granddaughter/niece/cousin, and therefore tended to be favoured and indulged. Ciara's adoptive parents described her as getting on very well with everybody from within their very small family circle, helped by the fact that she was the only grandchild/niece and tended to be indulged. Similarly, when commenting on how well their son had been accepted by the family network, Rory's adoptive parents highlighted the fact that as he had been the first grandchild, he had been showered with attention.

Foster carers

The majority of foster carers (n = 12) described their foster child as getting on well or very well with (extended) family, despite the normal ups-and-downs of family life. For example, Dylan's foster carers talked about his "brilliant" relationship with their two birth daughters, both of whom (older than Dylan) were very protective of him. Tony's foster mother described her "estranged" foster son as being considered by all her (older) birth children as their brother. They still went to see him in the assessment unit where he now was and took him out for dinner. Jack's foster mother described him as enjoying close and loving bonds with her birth grown-up children and grandchildren. As well as describing him as regularly fighting with his birth brother (also fostered), Connor's foster mother talked at length about his close relationships with all of her extended birth family. Her five birth grown-up children treated him (and his birth brother) as part of the family, involving them in everything they did with their own children (her birth grandchildren), including overnight stays and holidays. Similarly, Martin's foster mother talked at length about his close and loving bonds with all of his foster family. She also had five grown-up children and numerous grandchildren; and all of these family members were counted by Martin as his family and they, in return, loved and cared for him:

> You know . . . our children, my own natural children, we did say that our love is like a piece of elastic and they just joined the pieces of elastic and we stretched it out a bit further . . . That is how it was and that is how my children see them.

For four foster carers, the situation was more complicated. Sally's foster mother described at length the volatile relationships Sally had had with all family members; all part of her very troubled behaviour that eventually led to the breakdown of the placement. Anna's foster mother described a problematic relationship between Anna and her birth brother whom she also fostered; they fought constantly. Although she reflected that this was most probably a case of sibling rivalry, she worried that they did not have a good relationship. Conversely, when talking about her foster son, Daniel's foster mother described him as very jealous of his sister to the point where if she was being shown any attention by herself specifically, he would become angry. Similarly, she described him as very close to her own father, having called him "granddad" at their first meeting, as well as with other family members, particularly her sister and brother whom he thought of as an aunt and uncle (and their children his cousins), and who were, in turn, very close to and fond of him. Sue's foster father described her as enjoying excellent relationships with her extended foster family, except for his birth granddaughter, of whom she was jealous. He lamented Sue's attitude, especially given that he, his wife, and members of the extended foster family all indulged her:

> The only thing she seems to have a problem with is a little bit of clashing . . . between her and my daughter's young girl . . . She sees that my granddaughter gets a lot of attention and . . . she kind of wants in on it all the time . . . She gets on great with the rest of the family.

Kinship carers

The majority of kinship carers (n = 8) considered that their child got on well or very well with (extended) family. For example, Annie's grandmother talked about her as getting on with all the family members. She liked to mother her younger cousins and was especially close to one uncle and partner, with whom she frequently stayed, helping to look after their young children. Orlaith's aunt talked about her getting on with everybody in the house. Her love and devotion were returned by the aunt's four older birth children, who had always considered her their "wee sister". However, for three children, relationships were more problematic. Accordingly, Tierna's carer described her as always having been extremely jealous of her own birth daughter (two years older), although she related better to her younger birth children:

I have a daughter . . . [Tiera] has always destroyed any presents [my daughter] got . . . she was very very jealous, you know, she would never have anything nice to say about her.

Jessica's aunt described her niece's relationship with family members as complicated, because of her learning difficulties. Nathan's grandmother described him as fighting with his older sister all the time, deliberately annoying her. Although frustrated by this behaviour, the grandmother attributed it to normal teenage rivalry.

Residence order carers

The vast majority of residence order carers (n = 13) described their child as getting on well or very well with (extended) family. For instance, Caoimghin's grandfather talked about how he got on very well with his own brother's and sister's grandchildren, all being of the same age, while Ryan's carer commented on his mutually loving relationships with all of her grown-up birth children. Jemma's aunt described her as getting on "great" with her four birth daughters, particularly one to whom she was close in age. Similarly, Gary was especially close to one of his carers' grown-up birth daughter's children, as the two were of a similar age, and saw themselves as brother and sister. Jonny was described as having a "great relationship" with the carers' birth grandchildren, several of whom were of a similar age.

Nicole's aunt and uncle reported more problematic relationships with their youngest birth son having resented their niece when she first came to live with them, feeling marginalised and resentful of her attention-seeking and possessiveness. In turn, Nicole had resented the presence of the two birth sons, compounded by the fact that they had largely ignored her initially. Although they now got on much better, Nicole did not have a close relationship with either of them. In relation to the extended family, the aunt and uncle described Nicole as enjoying very strong relationships on both sides of the family, being particularly close to one cousin of a similar age.

Developments in attachment security, and factors inhibiting/facilitating attachment security

Birth parents

All birth parents, including Alexandra's (low security rating) mother, considered their child's attachment security to have developed positively over time. However, the perceived nature of (developments in) attachment security differed depending on how parents understood the circumstances of their child's (placement in) previous care experience. Although Jim and Joseph's mothers acknowledged improvements in their sense of security, lingering fears of being taken away yet again meant that some degree of insecurity remained. Furthermore, Jim and Ronan's mothers drew a direct association between the frequency of movement between placements and ongoing problems in their ability to form attachments to them and other family members. In Ronan's case, this included siblings who had either never been in care or had been in care for less time. Jim's mother explained the reasons for his difficulty forming attachments:

> *Really basically, all the comings and goings. One minute he was with me, the next minute they took him, then they brought him back, and then they took him again. He didn't know where he was.*

Nina's mother linked Nina's ongoing deficit in attachment security to Nina's father's frequent imprisonment and associated lack of reliability in maintaining contact. Of those birth parents who considered their child's attachment security to have developed without any difficulty, Niall's mother and Bronagh's parents offered an explanation. Niall's mother drew a direct connection between the intensity of her son's attachment to herself and his siblings and the regularity with which she saw him when he was in care (four times per week), and his subsequent uninterrupted full-time return to the family home.

Bronagh's birth parents highlighted the significant emotional security and associated benefits (in terms of her cognitive and physical development) that their physically disabled daughter had gained from being re-united with her siblings.

Foster adoptive parents

All foster adoptive parents who spoke about this issue (n = 5) considered their child's attachment security to have developed positively over time. Three reasons for this were identified. First, Bridget's mother highlighted that she had been raised alongside a similarly aged child and had thus developed a close bond that remained very strong:

In all honesty, I think having [birth daughter] the same age actually helped her settle in ... much better than had she been here and no other children nearby ... and then with just copying [birth daughter], she came on leaps and bounds and took a lot less time than we thought it would have taken.

Second, Joey and Justin's adoptive parents suggested that their child's cognitive/developmental issues meant their dependence on and associated attachment to them had increased over the years, something that had been facilitated by their placement with them at a young age. Third, Bridget's adoptive mother also commented that adoption had promoted the development of attachment between adoptive parent and child over time.

Stranger adoptive parents

All stranger adoptive parents considered their child's attachment security to have positively developed over time, including Abbie's (low security of attachment rating) mother. Some provided behavioural indicators of growing security/confidence over the years. For example, Charlie was content to go off on his own for extended periods away from his parents and Tracy wanted to spend more "mother-daughter" time, which she had avoided in the past. Although they considered their child to be secure overall, some stranger adoptive parents acknowledged at least the potential for some

119

occasional insecurity. For instance, Morgan's adoptive mother highlighted her recent increased questioning about her birth parents and her past. She considered this to be the result of her growing older, and consequently developing an increased awareness of the reasons her birth mother gave her up for adoption. On the other hand, Rory and Ciaron's adoptive parents provided an explanation for their assessment of their child's attachment security as having been instantaneous, with both highlighting the importance of their placement at a young age.

Foster carers

All foster carers who spoke about this issue (n = 7) considered their child's attachment security to have developed positively over time. Two explanations were offered. Four carers highlighted how the children's felt security had grown over the years because of the stability each had been given. All of them had been moved from different placements, and needed to know that they now had permanency in their lives, as Trevor's carer stated:

I think basically it's probably me saying to him, you know, you're here and . . . I made sure to tell Trevor that this was his home and he wasn't going anywhere, he was here to stay.

Sue's foster father considered the primary factor to be the very young age she had come to live with them:

That was a big help because if a child comes late in life, you know, they don't know where they stand.

Kinship carers

A majority of kinship carers who commented (n = 5) considered their child's attachment security to have developed positively over time. Three explanations were offered. First, Joanne and Jessica's carers highlighted the importance of being fostered specifically by relatives, as they were able to provide strong reassurances about the permanency of the child's placement. Second, Nathan's carer stressed the presence of a birth sibling already known by the child who could thereby help him settle more readily. Finally, Orlaith and Maggie's carers emphasised that being placed with them at a young age facilitated their attachment, as it meant the child had limited experience of other relationships that could potentially interfere with the attachment process, as Orlaith's kinship carer stated:

Orlaith knows nothing . . . only here and we are her family.

Notwithstanding their assessment of their child as overall emotionally secure, Nathan and Maggie's carers explained that a problematic relationship with the birth mother adversely impacted on their felt security. In essence, the problems were ascribed to the birth mother's emotionally damaging attitude and behaviour towards the child, prompting feelings of reduced worth, resentment, vulnerability and anxiety, as Nathan's carer claimed:

She's (birth mother) got another two children now, you see, so maybe it's hard for him to understand . . . and he would be angry, if he was angry he would say it to her . . . she gave me and my sister up . . . awful, awful angry.

Only Marie's carers considered the child's attachment security to have been compromised over time, rooted in Marie's regular contact with her birth parents, which caused her considerable distress, being torn between her love for them and her knowledge of their alcoholism and associated behavioural issues and them frequently not turning up for contact visits, as described by Marie's carers:

When Marie went to see her mummy I think it mixed her up a bit . . . it's hard for a child to go to see their mother and father and then come away . . . all I said to her was, 'Marie, the ball's in your court if you don't want to see them' . . . but she couldn't do that.

Residence order carers
All residence order carers (n = 6) considered their child's attachment security to have developed positively over time. A number of reasons

were proffered. Four carers highlighted the importance of the granting of the residence order itself. Both Conall and Kirsten's carers stressed the explicit guarantee this gave the children concerning the permanency of their placement. Conall's carer commented that the residence order reassured him that he would be living with her on a permanent basis. She believed that, prior to this, he had worried that he could be removed and returned to his birth parents, as she described:

> *Before the residence order...he didn't want to go (to contact)... and he'd leave here screaming and crying and actually one time he put his fist through the window... since the residence order he knows now he's staying and that's it.*

In a slightly different context, Ryan's carer also underscored the importance of the residence order for his sense of security/attachment. She explained that, prior to the granting of the order, the family had tried not to bond with him too much, so that he would not become overly attached to them in the event of the placement coming to an end and the child experiencing trauma as a result:

> *You knew then that... there was no fear of him becoming too attached to you and then having to go through the trauma of moving, he was staying and that was it, so the bond developed.*

Caoimghin's grandfather highlighted the importance of the residence order for his own sense of security with his grandson (and his two siblings whom he also cared for under a residence order), as it meant he had been able to remain their primary carer during an unsettled period in his, and their lives.

Megan's carers highlighted a very different factor which helped the development of her attachment security, the absence of her birth father from her life in comparison to their own constancy, and the consequent lack of interference with the attachment process:

> *He had made his point. He wasn't there for them, whereas I was.*

Summary of main findings

- The IPPA–R indicated that the vast majority of children were securely attached to their parents/carers, irrespective of placement group and more children had insecure attachments with their peers than with their parents/carers.
- There was no significant difference in parent or peer mean attachment scores, or across the different dimensions of the IPPA–R, between the children in each of the five placement groups.
- The distribution of scores on the different dimensions of the IPPA–R, for both parents/carers and peers, were very similar for each of the five placement groups.
- Although mean differences between the groups were not significant, the profile of children in the kinship care group in terms of the proportion that had low, medium or high scores on the different dimensions of the IPPA–R, was more positive on peer attachment, than for the children in the other placement groups. Furthermore, the profile of children in the residence order group in terms of the proportion that had either low, medium or high scores on the different dimensions of the IPPA–R, was less positive on parent/carer attachment than for the children in the other placement groups.
- Most children in the foster adoption group considered birth family members to be part of their family. However, for those in the stranger adoption group, family membership tended to be restricted to members of the immediate and wider adoptive family. The inclusion of birth family members in the foster adoption group was consistent with how the family had been configured by children in the birth family, kinship care, foster care and residence order groups.
- For children in both foster and kinship care, the inclusion of birth family members in their family tended to be restricted to birth siblings, with birth parents being explicitly excluded.
- Only a small minority of children in both the stranger and foster adoptive groups wanted to be living with their adoptive parents at

age 16; whilst most of the children in all the other placement groups hoped still to be living with their current carers at 16 years old.

- In both the adopted groups, members of the immediate and wider adoptive family were almost exclusively cited in terms of who was most important and closest to them. However, only a small minority specified the adoptive parents alone in this capacity, and often this was extended to include other adoptive family members.

- Where both birth and foster/kinship/residence order members were specified as being part of the family, the current carers were more commonly specified as being most important and closest to the children.

- Children who were subject to a residence order with former foster carers were more likely to refer to them as "mum and dad", than those with former kinship carers, where difficulties tended to be experienced negotiating a form of terminology to represent "parenthood" that suited both the birth parents and residence order carers.

- Being placed at a young age was considered across all groups of parents/carers (n = 18) the most important factor in promoting ease of transition. This was followed by: presence of other birth siblings/kinships in the home; existing familial relationships and associated understanding /knowledge; presence of other children in the home; prior contact in the lead-up to the placement; placement heralding the end of contact with birth parent(s); and child placed in same geographical area, thus enabling established relationships to be maintained.

- Continuing contact with birth parents or previous foster carers (n = 5), and the child having experienced an excessive number of changes in placements (n = 5) were identified across all groups of parents/carers as the most important potential contributors to problematic settling in processes.

- Being placed at a young age was the most mentioned factor in promoting feelings of security across all groups of parent/carers (n = 15). Other reasons that parents/carers felt contributed to children feeling secure in their placements were: being cared for alongside birth siblings (n = 6); being cared for by relatives (n = 6); being adopted and thus provided with reassurance concerning stability of placement (n = 5); and repeated reassurances concerning stability of placement (n = 5).

- The vast majority of children across all groups of parents/carers were described as being comfortable being left on their own for (brief) periods of time. However, the children of foster adoptive parents were marginally more likely to demonstrate difficulty with being on their own.

- Although the vast majority of children across all groups of parents/carers were described as behaving normally/as to be expected on the parents'/carers' departure and return, the children of birth parents marginally displayed more overt signs of anxiety/concern. Ultimately, there were no significant distinctions to be drawn.

- More children in the foster adoptive parent group demonstrated problems in their behaviour with strangers and in relation to their attitude/response to new situations, compared to children from the other groups. Amongst all groups of parents/carers whose children displayed problematic behaviour in these contexts, the explanation most offered was cognitive/developmental limitations. However, birth parents offered this explanation less often than the other groups.

- According to their parents/carers, a higher proportion of children living with birth parents (7 out of 9) displayed a lack of, or were limited in, the expression of affection, compared to children in the other groups. In addition, four out of the ten kinship carers commented on limitations in the affection displayed by the children. Parents/carers in the remaining groups did not identify any problems, with all behaviour being described positively or considered entirely appropriate.

- Across placement types, a decrease in displays of affection was most frequently highlighted, occurring across all parent/carer groups, and was always associated with a child being less prepared to be overtly affectionate as they entered their teenage years.

- Although stranger adoptive parents were the only group to report exclusively positive or co-operative relationships between their child and all household/extended family, the majority of children across all groups of parents/carers enjoyed essentially good/positive relationships.

- Three core features/processes in the relationships between children and (extended) family emerged across the placement groups. First, it appeared that if a young child had come to live with older children, the age difference facilitated close/loving relationships. Furthermore, such relationships appeared to transfer generationally, so that loving relationships developed between a child and older children were then replicated when these older children had children of their own. Second, it was suggested that children coming to live in households or extended family as a young child where children of the same or very similar age lived, were likely to form close/loving relationships. Third, it appeared that problematic relationships were more likely to be described in situations where at least one (but more often both) of the children were related by birth to the carer.

- There was an essential uniformity of experience across all parent/carer groups concerning the development of attachment security over time, with only one child (in kinship care) being identified as facing issues impacting adversely on this process. The most frequently cited reason to promoting positive development of attachment over time was that of being placed with parent/carer at a young age. The most frequently cited reason militating against the positive development of attachment over time was problematic contact with birth parent(s).

5   Children's self-concept

Introduction

Children who have been abused or neglected are more likely to have an overall poor self-esteem and self-concept because of feelings of incompetence and lack of support and encouragement from parents (Fischer and Ayoub, 1994; Harter, 1998; Kim and Cicchetti, 2009). Conversely, those who receive affection, acceptance, safety and assistance from their parents are more likely to show higher levels of self-esteem (Peterson *et al*, 1983; Barnes and Farrell, 1992; Roberts and Bengtson, 1993; Kim and Cicchetti, 2003; DeHart *et al*, 2006).

Many children who enter the care system experience early abuse and neglect and negative relationships with their birth parents. However, some researchers would argue that being placed in care has the capacity to mitigate these early adverse experiences, particularly in the context of providing these children with alternative families. For instance, a new or additional version of "mum", "dad", or "mum and dad" can provide the type of long-term consistent support and encouragement that children with low self-esteem and self-concept appear to lack (Schofield, 2002; McSherry *et al*, 2008; Biehal *et al*, 2010). Contemporary theory would suggest that this is what happens when a child is adopted. Juffer and van IJzendoorn (2007) found no difference in self-esteem between adoptees (N = 10,977) and non-adopted comparisons (N = 33,862) across 88 studies. This was equally true for international, domestic and transracial adoptees. What is not so clear is the extent to which long-term care can provide the context for these children having similar self-esteem or self-concept to those who are adopted from care, or their non-care experienced peers.

Children's self-concept

This chapter provides an exploration and comparison of children's self-concept, level of happiness, and life satisfaction within and between the five placement groups. It is based on the findings that emerged from the quantitative analysis of the Piers-Harris Children's Self-Concept Scale 2 (Piers and Hertzberg, 2002) completed by the children, and the qualitative analysis of the interviews with the children themselves. The children were asked specifically about their level of life satisfaction, as well as their feelings and wishes when completing the "me-book".

Figure 5.1
Care pathway mean scores on Piers-Harris – Total self-concept

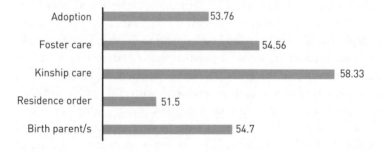

On the total self-concept dimension, higher scores are indicative of a more positive self-concept by the children. One-way ANOVA indicated that there was no significant variation in mean scores between the five pathway groups on Piers-Harris Total self-concept. Additionally, post-hoc Tukey HSD tests indicated that there were also no significant mean differences between any of the five care pathway groups. Although not statistically significant, there were differences between the mean scores (Figure 5.1). Children in the residence order group had the lowest mean score for overall self-concept, and those in kinship care had the highest. For children in the adoption, foster care, and birth parent/s groups, mean scores were similar, falling in between the largest and smallest means.

Figure 5.2

Care pathways by Piers-Harris Total score on the low/average/high range (n)

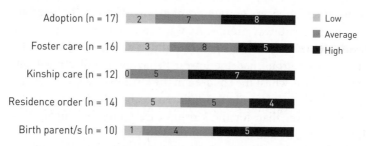

There was a degree of variability in the distribution of low, average and high scores between the five pathway groups in relation to total self-concept, as illustrated in Figure 5.2. The largest proportion of children with scores indicating high self-concept was in the kinship care group, whilst the residence order group had the highest proportion of children with scores indicating low self-concept. It can also be seen that the distribution of scores for total self-concept was very similar for the adoption and birth parent groups. In contrast with the other groups, none of the children in the kinship care group had scores that indicated low self-concept.

Behavioural adjustment: On this dimension, higher scores are indicative of more positive adjustment by the children. One-way

Figure 5.3

Care pathway mean scores on Piers-Harris – Behavioural adjustment

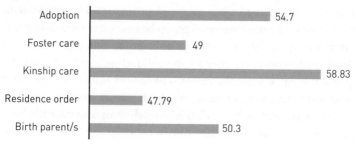

ANOVA indicated that there was a near significant variation in mean scores between the five pathway groups on Piers-Harris Behavioural Adjustment ($F = 2.31$, $p = .07$). Post-hoc Tukey HSD tests, however, indicated that there were no significant mean differences between any of the five care pathway groups. As was the case in relation to Total self-concept, although not a significant difference, the children in the residence order group had the lowest Behavioural Adjustment sub-scale mean score, whilst the children in the kinship care group had the highest. The mean score for the children in the adoption group was just slightly lower than for the kinship care group, but higher than both the foster care and birth parent/s groups.

Figure 5.4

Care pathways by the Piers-Harris – Behavioural adjustment subscale score on the low/average/high range (n)

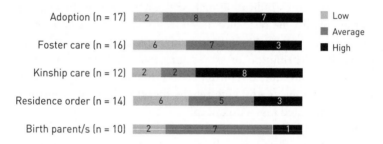

There was some variation in the distribution of low, average and high scores on the Behavioural Adjustment dimension between the different pathway groups, as shown in Figure 5.4. There was a marked difference between the kinship care and birth parent/s groups, with only one child in the birth parent/s group having a high score, whereas two- thirds of the children in the kinship group had high scores on this dimension. However, most of the children in the birth parent/s group had average scores. The patterns were very similar for the foster care and residence order groups, with both having high proportions of children scoring low and relatively small proportions with high scores. The adoption group had the second largest proportion of

Figure 5.5

Care pathway mean scores on Piers-Harris – Intellectual and school status

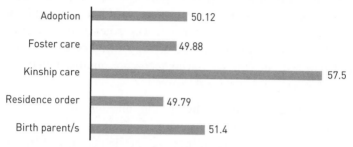

children who scored high on this dimension, but still only proportionally about half as many as in the kinship care group.

Intellectual and School Status: On this dimension, higher scores are indicative of more positive perspectives by the children. One-way ANOVA indicated that there was no significant variation in mean scores between the five pathway groups on Piers-Harris "intellectual and school status". Additionally, post-hoc Tukey HSD tests indicated that there were also no significant mean differences between any of the five care pathway groups. The mean score on this dimension was higher for the kinship care group than for the adoption, foster care, and residence order groups, with the birth parent/s group being slightly higher than these three (see Figure 5.5).

Figure 5.6

Care pathways by the Piers-Harris – Intellectual and school status subscale score on the low/average/high range (n)

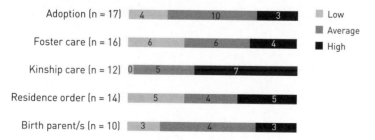

As shown in Figure 5.6, the pattern of distribution of low, average and high scores on "Intellectual and school status" was similar for the adoption, residence order, foster care, and birth parent/s groups, with a relatively even distribution of low, average and high score (with the adopted group having a larger proportion of average scores). However, the pattern of distribution of scores for the kinship care group was very different, with no children having low scores on this dimension, and almost two-thirds having high scores.

Physical appearance and attributes: On this dimension, higher scores are indicative of more positive perspectives by the children. One-way ANOVA indicated that there was no significant variation in

Figure 5.7
Care pathway mean scores on Piers-Harris – Physical appearance and attributes

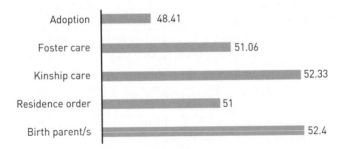

Figure 5.8
Care pathways by the Piers-Harris – Physical appearance and attributes subscale score on the low/average/high range (n)

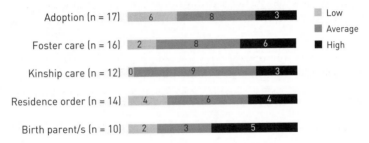

mean scores between the five pathway groups on Piers-Harris Physical Appearance and Attributes. Furthermore, post-hoc Tukey HSD tests indicated that there were also no significant mean differences between any of the five care pathway groups. The lowest mean score was for the adoption pathway group, with the other four groups having higher and relatively similar mean scores (Figure 5.7).

There is some variation among the groups in terms of the distribution of low, average, and high scores on Physical Appearance and Attributes (Figure 5.8). For the kinship care group, no child had scores that indicated a low score on this dimension, but only a small proportion had high scores. In contrast, the birth parent/s group had a small proportion of children scoring low, but also half the group scoring high. The adoption, foster care, and residence order groups had a reasonably similar pattern of distribution of low, average, and high scores, with a higher proportion of high scores in the foster care group, and a higher proportion of low scores in the adoption group.

Freedom from anxiety: On this dimension, higher scores are indicative of less anxiety in the children. One-way ANOVA indicated that there was no significant variation in mean score between the five pathway groups on Piers-Harris "Freedom from Anxiety". Additionally, post-hoc Tukey HSD tests indicated that there were also no significant mean differences between any of the five care pathway groups. However, Figure 5.9 does indicate that, although not significant, some differences were found between mean scores for the

Figure 5.9
Care pathway mean scores on Piers-Harris – Freedom from anxiety

Figure 5.10
Care pathways by the Piers-Harris – Freedom from anxiety subscale score on the low/average/high range (n)

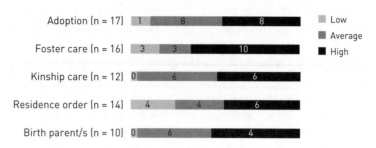

Figure 5.11
Care pathway mean scores on Piers-Harris – Popularity

groups, with the residence order group having the lowest mean score, and the foster care group the highest. The other three groups had relatively similar mean scores and were placed around the centre point between the lowest and highest mean scores.

The pattern of distribution of low, average and high scores on the "freedom from anxiety" dimension were very similar for the adoption, kinship care and birth parent/s groups, with a relatively even split between average and high scores (but with adoption having one child with a low score) (Figure 5.10). The residence order group had a fairly even distribution of low, average and high scores, whilst the foster care group had the highest proportion of children scoring high on this dimension, but almost a quarter scoring low.

Popularity: On this dimension, higher scores are indicative of more positive perspectives by the children. One-way ANOVA indicated that there was no significant variation in mean scores between the five pathway groups on Piers-Harris Popularity. Furthermore, post-hoc Tukey HSD tests also indicated that there were no significant mean differences between any of the five care pathway groups. Figure 5.11 indicates that the residence order group had the lowest mean score on popularity, whilst the birth parent and foster care groups had the highest. The adoption group mean score was lower than both the foster care groups, in addition to the birth parent/s group.

The pattern of distribution of low, average and high scores on the popularity dimension were quite similar for the adoption, foster care, kinship care, and birth parent/s groups, with relatively even splits between average and high scores (with the adopted and foster groups showing a small proportion of children scoring low on this dimension) (Figure 5.12). However, the pattern of distribution was quite different for the residence order group, with only a small proportion of children having high, a large proportion having average, and a small proportion having low scores on this dimension.

Happiness and contentment: On this dimension, higher scores are indicative of more positive perspectives on their level of happiness and contentment by the children. One-way ANOVA indicated that there was no significant variation in mean scores between the five

Figure 5.12
Care pathways by the Piers-Harris – Popularity subscale score on the low/average/high range (n)

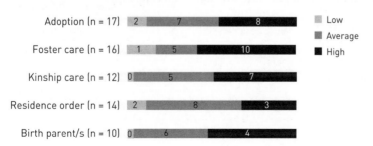

Adoption (n = 17) 2 7 8
Foster care (n = 16) 1 5 10
Kinship care (n = 12) 0 5 7
Residence order (n = 14) 2 8 3
Birth parent/s (n = 10) 0 6 4

Low
Average
High

Figure 5.13

Care pathway mean scores on Piers-Harris – Happiness and contentment

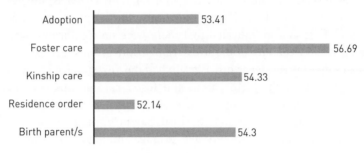

pathway groups on Piers-Harris "happiness and contentment". Additionally, post-hoc Tukey HSD tests indicated that there were also no significant mean differences between any of the five care pathway groups. The residence order group had the lowest mean score on this dimension, whilst the foster care group had the highest score (Figure 5.13). The other three pathway groups had very similar mean scores, and were positioned approximately midway between the highest and lowest mean scores.

The patterns of distribution of low, average and high scores on the "happiness and contentment" dimension was very similar for the adoption, foster care, kinship care, and birth parent/s groups, with a

Figure 5.14

Care pathways by the Piers-Harris – Happiness and contentment subscale score on the low/average/high range (n)

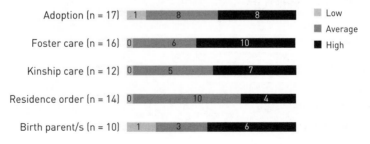

reasonably even distribution of average and high scores (but with the birth parent/s group having a small proportion of low scores) (Figure 5.14). In contrast, only a small proportion of the children in the residence order pathway group had high scores on this dimension, with the vast proportion having an average score.

Children's feelings about their lives

When completing the "me-book", the children were asked how they felt about the past, present and future, as well as being asked to depict on a "life ladder" how they were feeling currently – scores ranged from "0", depicting the worst feeling possible, to "10" depicting the best feeling possible.

The birth parent group

Nina was the only child in this group to receive a low Piers-Harris self-concept score. In terms of her responses when completing the "me-book", she stated she was "happy" about the present and future, and "alright" about the past. She gave herself a score of 8 on the life-ladder, which is quite high. Nina was 10 years old when she was returned to the care of her birth mother from foster care, and appeared to have a stronger relationship with her non-resident birth father.

Four children received average Piers-Harris scores, whilst another four received high scores. Alexandra did not register a Piers-Harris score (due to concerns about random responding). Every child in the birth parent group stated that they were "happy" about the present and life-ladder scores ranged from 7 to 10, with four children registering a score of 10. Two children stated that they were "happy" about their past, four were "OK", whilst Aidan was "scared", Bronagh "sad", and Jim "didn't know". Five children were "happy" about the future, whilst Joseph was "nervous", Niall had a "funny feeling", and three children "didn't know".

In this group only Ronan was "happy" about the past, present and future. He received an average Piers-Harris score and a "life-ladder" score of 10. He was four-and-a-half years old when returned to his birth mother's care from foster care, along with his two brothers.

The foster adoption group

Two children in the foster adoption group received low Piers-Harris self-concept scores, two received average scores, whilst the remainder received high scores. For the two who received low scores, both stated that they were "happy" at present, but in terms of the past, Danny "didn't know" and Justin was "OK", and for the future, Danny was "happy" but Justin was "scared". Justin also had the lowest "life-ladder" score of 5, with the others ranging from 8 to 10', and three having a score of 10.

With the exception of John, who stated he was "alright" about the present, all children in this group stated that they were "happy" about the present. Two children stated that they were "happy" about the past, with two being "OK", three "didn't know", whilst one child felt "a bit sad", and another was "kind of sad but happy". Six children were "happy" about the future, and two "didn't know".

Karl was the only child who was "happy" about the past, present and future. He was placed with his adoptive parents from hospital, shortly after being born. He also had a high Piers-Harris score, and a "life-ladder" score of 10.

The stranger adoption group

No children in the stranger adoption group received a low Piers-Harris self-concept score, five received average scores and three high scores. With the exception of Ciara, who said she was "grumpy", all children in this group were "happy" about the present and also "happy" about the future, except for Morgan who was "OK". However, only Ciara was "happy" about the past, with three being "OK" (Ciaron, Rory and Charlie), three "sad" (Tracy, Claire and Morgan), and Abbie "didn't know". "Life-ladder" scores ranged from 7 to 10, with three children having scores of 10. No children in this group viewed their lives in terms of their past present and future as altogether happy.

The foster care group

Three children in this group received low Piers-Harris self-concept scores, six average scores, and four received high scores. All three who received a low Piers-Harris score were "happy" at present, but "sad" about the past, although Mary was also "sad and nervous" about the future, while the other two were "happy".

The vast majority of the children in this group stated they were "happy" at present, with only Angela stating she was "OK", while Dylan refused to answer. Dylan also refused to answer regarding the past and the future. Two children stated they were happy about the past, with three being "OK", seven being "sad", and three children refusing to answer. Nine children were "happy" about the future, two were "OK", but Pol was "sad", and two refused to answer.

With the exception of Connor, who recorded a "life-ladder" score of 5, all other scores in the foster care group ranged from 7 to 10, with seven children registering a score of 10. Liam and Anna stated that they were happy about the past, present and future. Both were placed with their current carers in middle childhood (seven and five years old respectively), with Anna being placed alongside a birth sister. Both received average self-concept scores, with Liam having a "life-ladder" score of 8, and Anna one of 10.

The kinship care group

No children in the kinship care group received a low Piers-Harris self-concept score, four received average scores and six high scores. The majority of "life-ladder" scores ranged from 7 to 10, with the exception of Marie, who rated her current life satisfaction at 5. She also stated that she was "angry" about the past, although she was "happy" about the present and "excited" about the future. She was also the second oldest in the group when placed with her current carers at age seven.

With the exception of Rebecca, who stated she was "alright", all the children in this group commented that they were "happy" at present. Four children were also "happy" about the past, three were "sad", whilst Orlaith was "OK", Tierna was "weird" and Marie was "angry". The four children who were "happy" about the past were also "happy" about the future, as were Orlaith and Rebecca. Three children were "excited" about the future and Annie thought the future was "mysterious".

Four children were "happy" about the past, present and future. All four received high Piers-Harris scores and had "life-ladder" ratings of 10, 9.5, 7, and 10, and were six months, three-and-a-half years, two years, and four-and-a half-years old respectively when placed.

The residence order group

Five children in this group received low Piers-Harris self-concept scores, four of these were "happy" about the present, but "sad" about the past, with only Jo being "happy" about the past. Two of these children were "happy" about the future, whilst three were "not sure", and Jemma was "OK". All five of these children were less than a year old when they arrived at their current placement.

Five children received average Piers-Harris scores and four high scores. Every child in this group, with the exception of Gary who felt "normal", was "happy" about the present. Seven were also "happy" about the past, four were "sad", two "didn't know" and one was "OK". The vast majority of children were "happy" about the future, with three being "not sure", and Jemma being "OK".

Four children were "happy" about their past, present and future, with three of these being birth siblings placed together with their paternal grandfather. Two received high Piers-Harris scores, and the other two, average scores. For the whole group, "life-ladder" scores ranged from 8 to 10, with the exception of Kirsten and Roisin, who rated their current life satisfaction at 5 and 4 respectively.

Summary of key findings

- Most of the children, irrespective of placement type, scored within the average or high range across all dimensions of the Piers-Harris self-concept scale.
- There was no significant difference in mean scores across the different dimensions of the Piers-Harris scale between the children in each of the five placement groups.
- The distribution of scores on the different dimensions of the Piers-Harris scale was very similar for each of the five placement groups.

- Although mean differences between the groups were not significant, the profile of children in the kinship care group in terms of the proportion that had either low, medium or high scores on the different dimensions of the Piers-Harris scale, was consistently more positive than for the children in the other placement groups. The profile for the children in the residence order group was consistently less positive.
- Almost all the children, irrespective of placement group, stated that they were happy about the present, but many expressed negative emotions about the past, and a small proportion of children also expressed some nervousness about the future, again similarly across all five placement groups.

6   Children's health

Introduction

In Great Britain, recent research indicates that, compared with children of the same age and social status who live with birth parents, children in care are more likely to have incomplete immunisations; lower health surveillance; worse dental health; poorer nutrition and to make unhealthier lifestyle choices (Mather, 2010). Similarly, large-scale surveys in the USA (National Survey of Adoptive Parents – NSAP; and National Survey of Children's Health – NSCH) indicate that 54 per cent of children adopted from care have special health care needs, compared with 19 per cent of the general population (USDHSS, 2011). However, despite the fact that children in the UK have been adopted from care for over 30 years, there is a dearth of research examining how these children and their families fare post-adoption, particularly in terms of how the children's health needs are being met.

This chapter reports on the interviews with the children and their parents/carers. The interviews with parents/carers sought to ascertain their understanding of their child's health needs, their worries in relation to their child's health, the services received to meet those needs, and their satisfaction with these services. The "me-book" focused on the extent to which the children themselves felt healthy, as indicated on a "health thermometer".

Parent/carer perspectives

Birth parents

Overall, the majority of birth parents described their child as in good or excellent health (n = 7) and expressed no major concerns. Any issues tended to be discussed as relatively normal or trivial. For example, Jim's mother talked about her son's weight problem, describing him as "chubby", acknowledging that she should do more to control his weight and rationalising her failure to do so on the grounds of her time being taken up with looking after a large family. Aidan's mother talked about her son's recent stomach problems, which had been put down to "nerves" by her GP and by her to "attention-seeking", while Joseph's mother mentioned her son's asthma, stressing that he knew how to manage the condition himself and his fortnightly renewal of inhalers was kept in his schoolbag.

Five birth parents described more significant health issues. Nina's mother described ongoing problems with co-ordination/movement for which Nina was currently being investigated. Significantly, she highlighted that these problems were immediately obvious to her when her daughter was returned to her care, but had been left un-resolved, in her view, throughout the entirety of Nina's time in care. The lack of definitive treatment when in care was also highlighted by Joseph's mother, who described her son's bowel problems as being left untreated until he returned home; once referred to a paediatrician the problem was resolved. Bronagh's parents described their daughter's ongoing problems due to spina bifida, particularly those associated with a limited ability to walk.

Those birth parents of children with a designated behavioural condition/learning difficulty (Ronan and Niall) talked about regular review assessments, describing them as "routine". They also men-tioned receiving specific support, such as speech and language therapy. There was an underlying sense that these parents considered their child's health to be otherwise "normal", and that their behavioural issues were seen as independent of their "day-to-day" health.

Foster adoptive parents

A minority of foster adoptive parents (n = 3) described their child as in good/excellent health, with no major concerns. For example, Amy's adoptive mother mentioned her daughter's asthma, something that she appeared to have grown out of. However, the majority of foster adoptive parents (n = 6) highlighted more serious health worries/problems. Thus, Joey's adoptive mother talked about her son's autism and other health problems such as poor eyesight, gluten intolerance, and poor muscle strength – all associated with his diagnosis of FAS. Laura, another adopted child, had had both leukaemia and T-cell lymphoma in the past few years, which she had found had greatly impacted on her wellbeing.

Danny had FAS as well as ADHD; both had been confirmed as a result of Danny's adoptive mother's suspicions, based on her know-ledge of her son's birth mother's use of crack cocaine during pregnancy, as well as his facial characteristics. He also suffered from severe migraines, which consequently led to him missing most of the academic year, thus impacting on his educational needs. Karl had learning difficulties, poor eyesight in one eye, and a slight heart murmur. Justin's adoptive mother talked at length about her son's health issues, all associated with his FAS/mental health problems. Steve had also been diagnosed with FAS at birth and, when he came to his adoptive parents as a baby, was very weak and underweight; he was subsequently also diagnosed with ADHD.

Stranger adoptive parents
There was an even split amongst stranger adoptive parents, with four describing their child as in good or excellent health, and five high-lighting more serious health worries/problems. Morgan's adoptive mother talked about a relatively recent health issue concerning her daughter that was currently under investigation; preliminary tests were inconclusive but a thyroid problem was thought most likely. In relation to her other daughter, Claire (Morgan's sibling), she talked at length about serious concerns over her cognitive ability/development. She described persistent worries since first adopting her daughter that 'something wasn't right', quoting diverse examples of behavioural idiosyncrasies/developmental limitations such as emotional detach-ment ('there is this wee wall around her'), love of routine, slowness in speech development (she saw a speech therapist for several years) and lack of social skills. A number of years previously, a child psychologist had assessed Morgan as falling within the normal range (although problems with understanding/comprehension were identified). The

advice given was to allow her time to recover from her poor start in life. Morgan and Claire's adoptive mother was dissatisfied with this assessment and continued to be extremely worried for Claire and how she would be able to cope with life ('I worry about her all the time'). In addition to these cognitive/developmental issues, she talked about her daughter's heart murmur, ENT problems with glue ear and sticky eyes, as well as a one-off and unexplained seizure several years earlier.

Abbie's adoptive mother discussed a range of health problems concerning her daughter, some of them more serious than others. Firstly, hearing problems, for which she was required to wear a hearing aid, and which had significantly adversely impacted on her speech development until the age of five when she was fitted with a hearing aid. In addition, Abbie had been diagnosed with Cyclical Vomiting Syndrome (CVS), something from which she had suffered badly in the past and which was now under control; the CVS was thought to be the result of stress suffered throughout her early childhood.

Charlie had ADHD for which he took Ritalin and as a result his condition was well controlled. Ciara's adoptive parents shared their worries that their daughter had FAS, as her birth mother was an alcoholic. At the time of adoption, they had been advised by Social Services about this possible development, and over the years had observed numerous indicators in her behaviour and aptitudes (e.g. defiance, stubbornness, educationally "slow", poor concentration, etc.). Their daughter's academic limitations had been highlighted also by her school. They had approached their GP but his referral had not helped them resolve the issue, and they were considering going back to the GP in order to get a definitive diagnosis.

Foster carers

The majority of foster carers (n = 10) described their foster child as having no significant health concerns and any issues tended to be discussed as relatively non-serious. For example, Trevor's foster mother mentioned his headaches and stomach aches, Connor's foster mother talked about the problem of his bedwetting, which had recently been resolved, and Daniel's foster mother mentioned his eye condition for which he would need to use eye drops for the rest of his life. Interestingly, when asked about Martin's health, his foster mother described him as 'healthy as a trout'; however, she later described the brain damage that significantly adversely impacted on his behaviour.

Five foster carers highlighted more serious health worries/problems. For instance, Dylan's foster carers highlighted his ADHD and Asperger's Syndrome as well as a deformity in his penis caused by previous inept surgery. The cognitive/behavioural problems were described as increasing as Dylan became older, manifesting as impulsivity/aggression and impacting on all aspects of his life, including problematic relationships with other children at school. At the time of interview, and although Mary enjoyed otherwise good physical health, Mary's foster mother had initiated a series of consultations with different health professionals concerning her suspicions that Mary had FAS/ADHD, based on the behaviour/physical limitations she had witnessed in the two years Mary had been placed with her (e.g. hyperactivity and lack of physical co-ordination). Sally had also been diagnosed with ADHD shortly before coming to live with her foster carers. During her time with them, she had been prescribed Ritalin, something Sally's foster carers had disapproved of, because of its "zombifying" effect on children.

Similar to Mary's foster mother, James' foster mother had suspected that he had significant cognitive/behavioural issues, based on her observations of him in the first year or so of his placement with her. Not only had he still been in nappies when first placed with her (at six years of age) but he had no reading/writing skills whatsoever. On the basis of her requests for an educational psychologist's assessment, he was diagnosed with ADHD, although it is not clear what diagnosis was given for his delay in toilet training. James' brother Pol (in the same placement) had also been diagnosed with ADHD and had problems with co-ordination. Like his brother, he had previously been in receipt of speech therapy and educational psychology and was currently attending occupational therapy as well as child psychiatry (for monitoring his ADHD).

Kinship carers

The majority of kinship carers (n = 10) described their child as in good or excellent health, and had no major concerns. Any issues discussed were deemed to be "normal" or minor. For example, Tierna's kinship carer spoke about Tierna's hay fever; Marie's carers mentioned their niece's asthma; Rebecca's carer described her niece's relatively limited diet as she tended to eat the same things repeatedly; and Orlaith's carer listed her niece's psoriasis. Occasionally, previous health problems, which were now resolved, were mentioned. For instance, Joanne's carer described her niece's heart problems as a baby, before she was placed with her, which had required surgery. She was now completely free of any problems.

Tierna and Marie's carers contrasted current positive circumstances with past health problems, typically using this contrast as a means of highlighting the degree of improvement in the child's health since their placement with them. Tierna's carer talked about her persistent throat infections when she first came to live with the family, which she put down to neglect. Marie's aunt and uncle described their niece's very poor sleeping patterns when she first came to live with them. She saw a psychologist for three years, which revealed that she had been profoundly affected by the separation from her birth parents and insecurities from constant moves between foster carers. The treatment had helped her greatly. Jessica's aunt identified more significant health issues, talking about her niece's learning difficulties and the effect these had in all aspects of her life. Maggie's carers talked at length about the fact that, as grandparents, they were not allowed to take responsibility for consenting to medical treatment that Maggie may require. They had recently attended a number of "kinship courses", during which time they had been told that they could not legally sign/assume responsibility in a number of situations (e.g. school trips/medical treatment/sleepovers). They found this restriction wholly unacceptable, in that it diminished their role as grandparents and prevented Maggie from participating in activities with other children of her age, something which she could not understand and found upsetting.

147

Residence order carers

The majority of residence order carers (n = 9) described their child as being essentially healthy. At times, what were considered to be relatively minor ailments were mentioned. For example, Greg's grandfather described his perpetual head cold, something that had been investigated in the past and which he put down to likely sinus problems. He also talked about his other grandson Caoimghin's development of shingles and consequent taking of antibiotics, which had led to a weakening of enamel on his teeth, as a result of which he needed to be very careful about maintaining oral hygiene to prevent tooth decay. Conall's carer talked about his eczema, as well as unexplained spikes in temperature (controlled by Calpol); Kirsten's carer also mentioned her eczema, soothed by creams, etc. Luke's grandmother described his previous problems with crowding of teeth, such that he had to have ten teeth removed. She also described her concerted efforts to ensure all of her four grandchildren living with her retained good health, including giving them cod liver oil tablets every day and making them eat one or two oranges per day.

Six residence order carers highlighted more serious health issues. For instance, Ryan's carers expressed concerns about a heart murmur that he had been expected to grow out of but which still remained. It was not considered a serious threat to his health and he was an otherwise very healthy child. Gary was diagnosed with FAS, causing him to have problems with concentration that impacted adversely on numerous aspects of his life, from schoolwork to poor eating. Jo had been diagnosed with ADHD at around four years of age and had been attending a child psychologist since then. He was on medication to control the ADHD, as well as sleeping tablets. Sarah had also been diagnosed with FAS, which impacted on her academic ability. Apart from sinus-related headaches, she was an otherwise healthy child. Julie suffered from cerebral palsy and phenylketonuria (PKU), as a result of which she was severely brain damaged; in addition, she had developed epilepsy. Although Jonny's carers did not make explicit the root cause of his stated problems, they talked about him having "big problems", including hyperactivity and inability to concentrate, and he also had diabetes.

Children/young people's perspectives

In order to gain the children's own perspectives on their health, the "me-book" was designed to include a "health thermometer", which allowed them to rate their own health in the following range: very bad; bad; OK; good; and brilliant.

The birth parent group – None of the children within this group described their health as being very bad or bad. Three rated their health as OK, three as good, two as very good, Ronan rated his health as brilliant, and Alexandra didn't answer.

The foster adoption group – None of the children described their health as being very bad or bad. Four children rated their health as OK, three as good, none as very good, and two as brilliant.

The stranger adoption group – None of the children defined their health as very bad, bad or okay. Three children described their health as good, with the remaining five young people describing their health as brilliant.

The foster care group – None of the children described their health as very bad or bad. Two described their health as OK, four as good, with the remaining nine describing their health as brilliant.

The kinship care group – None of the children described their health as very bad. Marie described her health as bad, Annie as OK, Tierna as good, Rebecca as very good, whilst the rest described their health as brilliant.

The residence order Group – None of the children depicted their health as very bad or bad. Two described their health as OK, three as good, Roisin described her health as very good, and the remainder thought their health was brilliant.

Summary of main findings

- Across all groups, the data from the parent/carer interviews suggest that it is the children of foster adoptive parents who experienced comparatively poorer health, with seven out of nine children described as having significant health issues (the only group in which a majority of children were so described). This is compared with descriptions of significant health issues specified by five out of 12 birth parents; four out of nine stranger adoptive parents; one out of 11 kinship carers; five out of 15 foster carers; and six out of 15 residence order carers experienced the second worst health profile. Consequently, the children of adoptive parents experienced the poorest health.

- When the causes of poor health are examined, a distinct pattern emerges, in that five out of the six foster adoptive parent children and three out of the five stranger adoptive parent children were either suspected or confirmed with having cognitive/behavioural problems. Of these eight children, five had been diagnosed with FAS and the cause of a further two children's cognitive/behavioural problems remained undiagnosed.

- The issue of cognitive/behavioural problems underpinned a significant proportion of all health problems described: two out of five birth parent children; five out of the six foster adoptive parent children; three out of the five stranger adoptive parent children; one out of one kinship carer child; five out of five foster carer children; and, four out of six residence order carer children. Across all of these 20 cases, where a cause of the cognitive/behavioural problems had been confirmed (9 cases), eight were attributed to FAS, which is 10 per cent of the children interviewed.

- The children themselves, irrespective of placement group, tended to view their health positively, with only one child describing her health as bad. However, only one of the children in the birth parent group, and two from the foster adoption group, described their health as brilliant, compared with five in stranger adoption, nine in foster care, six in kinship care, and eight on residence order. These lower ratings of health by the children in the birth parent and foster adoption groups would appear to be consistent with the relatively complex array of health problems referred to by their parents/carers.

7 Children's behaviour

Introduction

The behaviour of children in care has often been portrayed as problematic or challenging, mostly due to the range of difficult experiences they have endured from an early age. Previous research has drawn attention to the prevalence of emotional and behavioural difficulties and mental health problems among children in public care (McCarthy *et al*, 2003; Meltzer *et al*, 2003; Richards *et al*, 2006; Sempik *et al*, 2008). Large scale surveys conducted in England, Scotland and Wales indicate that, across Great Britain, around 39 per cent of looked after children and young people have a conduct disorder, although percentages vary across the three countries (Meltzer *et al*, 2003, 2004a, 2004b). It has been found that the incidence of these difficulties is higher among older than younger children (Sempik *et al*, 2008), children who have experienced a greater number of placements (Pithouse *et al*, 2004), and those who enter the care system later in life compared to those placed as infants (Richards *et al*, 2006).

In this chapter, children's behaviour within and between the five pathway groups is comprehensively examined, through the quantitative analysis of the Strengths and Difficulties questionnaire (SDQ) (Goodman, 1997) completed by the children's parents/carers, and qualitative analysis of interviews with the parents/carers, together with observational notes taken by the research team during the interviews with the children.

Strengths and difficulties

This section presents the findings that emerged from the SDQ, which was completed by the parents/carers of the children in the different placements. In order to compare mean (total and scale) scores between the five placement groups, a one-way ANOVA was used. In identifying

Figure 7.1
Care placement mean scores for SDQ – Total difficulties

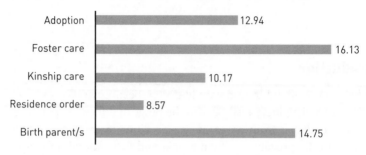

significant mean differences between any of the five groups, post-hoc Tukey HSD tests were used. All tests were conducted at five per cent significance level. P-values <0.05 were considered statistically significant.

Total difficulties: On this dimension, higher scores indicate that the parents/carers believe their children to have more overall difficulties. A near significant variation was found in mean scores between the five placement groups for "total difficulties" (F = 2.16, p = 0.08). In addition, there was a near significant difference between the foster care and residence order groups (p = .08). As shown in Figure 7.1, children in foster care displayed the highest mean score, while those in the residence order had the lowest.

Table 7.1
Percentages of children in the different placements within the abnormal range on the SDQ – Total difficulties

	% abnormal range
Adoption (n = 18)	28
Foster care (n = 16)	44
Kinship care (n = 12)	25
Residence order (n = 14)	14
Birth parents (n = 12)	50

The proportion of children in some of the groups in this study that scored above the clinical threshold for total difficulties was considerably high, particularly those living with birth parents (50%) and in foster care (44%). In contrast, fewer children in the adoption (28%), kinship care (25%) and residence order (14%) groups scored above the threshold (Table 7.1).

Figure 7.2
Care placement mean scores for SDQ – Emotional symptoms

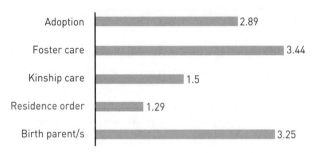

Table 7.2
Percentage of children in the different placements within the abnormal range on the SDQ – Emotional symptoms

	% abnormal range
Adoption (n = 18)	28
Foster care (n = 16)	44
Kinship care (n = 12)	17
Residence order (n = 14)	14
Birth parents (n = 12)	42

Emotional symptoms: On this dimension, higher scores indicate a greater degree of emotional symptoms. A near significant variation was found in mean scores between the five placement groups for "emotional symptoms" (F = 2.16, p = 0.08). In addition, there was a near significant difference between the foster care and residence order groups (p = .08). As shown in Figure 7.2, the foster care and birth

Figure 7.3
Care placement mean scores for SDQ – Conduct problems

parent groups had the highest mean scores, followed closely by the adoption group, while the residence order group had the lowest mean score.

Similar to the results for the SDQ total difficulties, nearly half the children in the foster care and birth parents groups scored within the abnormal range for emotional symptoms (Table 7.2).

Conduct problems: On this dimension, higher scores indicate that the parents/carers believe their children to have more conduct problems. One-way ANOVA indicated that there was no significant variation in mean scores between the five pathway groups on SDQ conduct problems. Additionally, post-hoc Tukey HSD tests indicated that there were no significant mean differences between any of the five care pathway groups. Although not statistically significant, there were differences between the mean scores (Figure 7.3). Children in the residence order group had the lowest mean score, while those living with birth parents had the highest.

As shown in Table 7.3, in terms of conduct problems, the contrast between the groups was less stark than before, with the proportion of children scoring above the threshold ranging between 21 and 50 per cent. In relation to mean scores, the birth parent and kinship care groups had the highest proportion of children in the abnormal range, while the residence order group had the lowest proportion.

Peer problems: On this dimension, higher scores indicate that the parents/carers believe their children to have more problems with their

Table 7.3
Percentages of children in the different placements within the abnormal range on the SDQ – Conduct problems

	% abnormal range
Adoption (n = 18)	28
Foster care (n = 16)	44
Kinship care (n = 12)	50
Residence order (n = 14)	21
Birth parents (n = 12)	50

Figure 7.4
Care placement mean scores for SDQ – Peer problems

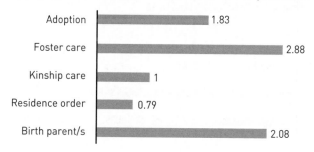

peers. One-way ANOVA indicated that there was no significant variation in mean scores between the five pathway groups on SDQ peer problems. Furthermore, post-hoc Tukey HSD tests indicated that there were no significant mean differences between any of the five care pathway groups. Although not statistically significant, there were some differences between mean scores (Figure 7.4). Children in foster care had the highest mean score, while those on residence order and in kinship care had the lowest.

In terms of peer relationship problems, the proportion of children scoring above the threshold was relatively low in the kinship care and residence order groups, with the adoption and foster care groups showing the highest proportions (Table 7.4).

Table 7.4
Percentages of children in the different placements within the abnormal range on the SDQ – Peer relationship problems

	% abnormal range
Adoption (n = 18)	28
Foster care (n = 16)	25
Kinship care (n = 12)	8
Residence order (n = 14)	7
Birth parents (n = 12)	17

Figure 7.5
Care placement mean scores for SDQ – Prosocial behaviour

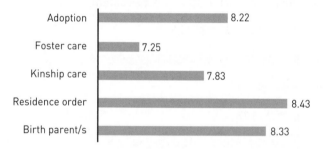

Prosocial behaviours: On this dimension, higher scores indicate that the parents/carers believe their children to be more prosocial (helpful) in their behaviour. One-way ANOVA indicated that there was no significant variation in mean scores between the five pathway groups on SDQ pro-social behaviour. Additionally, post-hoc Tukey HSD tests indicated that there were no significant mean differences between any of the five care pathway groups. Although not statistically significant, there were differences between the mean scores (Figure 7.5). Children in foster care had the lowest mean score, while those on residence order and living with birth parents had the highest.

Most children across all the groups scored in the normal range regarding prosocial behaviour, with only two children in foster care and two in kinship care having abnormal scores (Table 7.5).

Table 7.5
Percentage of children in the different placements within the abnormal range on prosocial behaviour

	% abnormal range
Adoption (n = 18)	0
Foster care (n = 16)	12
Kinship care (n = 12)	17
Residence order (n = 14)	0
Birth parents (n = 12)	0

Figure 7.6
Care placement mean scores for SDQ – Hyperactivity

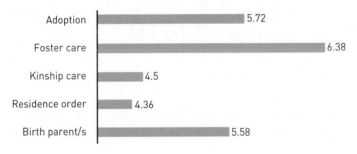

Hyperactivity: On this dimension, higher scores are indicative of a greater degree of hyperactivity in the children's behaviour. One-way ANOVA indicated that there was no significant variation in mean scores between the five pathway groups on SDQ hyperactivity. Furthermore, post-hoc Tukey HSD tests indicated that there were no significant mean differences between any of the five care pathway groups. Although not statistically significant, there were some differences between mean scores (Figure 7.6). Children in residence order and kinship care placements had the lowest mean score, while those in foster care had the highest.

Regarding hyperactivity, a third of children within most of the groups (adoption, kinship care and birth parents) had scores in the abnormal range, with a smaller proportion of children on residence

Table 7.6
Percentage of children in the different placements within the abnormal range on SDQ – Hyperactivity

	% abnormal range
Adoption (n = 18)	33
Foster care (n = 16)	56
Kinship care (n = 12)	33
Residence order (n = 14)	21
Birth parents (n = 12)	33

Table 7.7
Comparing SDQ total difficulties scores between 2004 and 2009

	No change	1–6 higher	>10 higher	1–6 lower	>10 lower
Adopted (n = 17)	2	7	1	6	1
Foster care (n = 13)	0	2	3	6	2

order having similar scores. However, the largest proportion of children in the abnormal range on hyperactivity was in the foster care group (Table 7.6).

In total, the parents/carers of 40 of the children interviewed in 2009 (Phase 3) had also been interviewed in 2003/4 (Phase 2). Two of these were kinship carers, two were carers of children on residence order, and six were birth parents, and these 10 cases were subsequently excluded from this analysis due to low numbers for comparison. As shown in Table 7.7, eight out of 17 adopted children scored higher (47%) in 2009 and seven scored lower (41%), while five out of 13 in foster care scored higher (38%), with eight scoring lower (62%). This suggests that, when measuring a shift in the children's scores between 2004 and 2009, there appears to have been a greater percentage of behavioural improvements and a lower percentage of behavioural deteriorations in the foster care group compared to the adoption group.

Specific difficulties

The children whose parents/carers were interviewed had a range of behavioural difficulties and conditions. Some had been given a formal diagnosis, but not all. Twenty-two were reported to have behavioural problems and 20 were said to have discipline problems (Table 7.8). Nine had been specifically diagnosed with ADHD and were taking medication for the condition. Most of these were in the foster adoption (n = 4) or foster care (n = 2) groups, with the remaining three being in kinship care, living with birth parents, and in stranger adoption. Two children with ADHD in the foster adoption group also had FAS, with one also having mild Asperger's. Another two children had autism (one in kinship care and one in foster care). Two of the children in foster care were also self-harming. Julie, who was subject to a residence order, had cerebral palsy and a profound learning disability that had become progressively worse since she had also developed epilepsy, and the combination of these conditions adversely impacted her ability to interact with others.

Parents/carers mentioned other specific difficulties and concerns they had with their children's behaviour, such as being "hyper" and hard to control or needing constant supervision, being easily led by peers, limited or poor concentration, being extremely insecure or anxious and not trusting anybody, staying out late and being interested in boys/girls, stealing and lying, being immature, attention-seeking

Table 7.8
Care placements by specific problems

	Behavioural problems	*Discipline problems*
Foster adoption (n = 9)	5	3
Stranger adoption (n = 9)	1	2
Foster care (n = 17)	8	6
Kinship care (n = 13)	1	3
Residence order (n = 14)	4	3
Birth parents (n = 11)	3	3

behaviours, being a loner (not mixing with other children), having no fear and being unaware of danger, disobedience, being prone to temper outbursts/tantrums, severe anger, impulsivity, treating their parent/carer badly (e.g. fighting, name calling, etc.), being bossy, obsessive, jealous of other children, having a lack of social skills, and being distant. The majority of these comments were made by birth parents (n = 7), foster carers (n = 6) (when excluding those whose placement broke down), and foster adoptive parents (n = 5), although a few carers of children in other placement types were also concerned about these types of difficulties.

Some parents/carers also mentioned that their children had been bullied (e.g. name calling), which seemed to make their behaviour more difficult, and one child appeared to regularly get into trouble with local children. In a couple of foster placements, the placement had actually broken down due to difficulties with the child's behaviour.

In some cases, the child scored highly in the SDQ and was believed to have behavioural or/and discipline problems, but during the interview, the parent/carer underrated these difficulties and explained that they did not have any major concerns about the child. In many such instances, the parent/carer knew how to deal with the child's behaviour, which meant that it was easy for them to manage it, and made the behaviour appear less problematic. They were also able to highlight many of the strengths of the children. For instance, Jonny's foster carers described him as a "charmer", a "good boy" and "quite popular", despite his high SDQ scores, his constant hyperactivity, limited concentration and being "easily led".

Jonny was working in a garage over the summer holidays, which he seemed to enjoy. His foster carers explained that he was good when kept occupied, as he loved working. Similarly, Nathan was described by his grandmother (kinship carer) as being a very angry child, especially after his previous placement broke down, and having very challenging behaviours, but she also explained how he was very good towards her, and worried about her health. Joseph and Aidan, both in the care of their birth mothers, scored very high in the SDQ, but during interview, the mothers did not express any concerns about their behaviour, and only mentioned relatively minor issues like "cheekiness".

Sleeping, eating and social behaviours

Despite generally high SDQ scores, most birth parents talked about their child's behaviour as essentially unproblematic and/or typical for their age (close to or entering their teenage years). Parents talked about having to compel their child to go to bed at a reasonable hour; cajole them into getting out of bed on a school morning; accommodate increased cheekiness, disobedience, occasional temper tantrums and general recalcitrance; and otherwise "reign in" a teenager's pursuit of independence. However, some highlighted problematic behaviour. For instance, Ronan and Niall's birth parents talked about their children as having some form of cognitive/developmental limitations, linking this to problematic behaviour, particularly displayed when out in public. At such times, they experienced difficulties with their child refusing to sit in one place for any length of time (Niall) or loud and otherwise unruly behaviour (Ronan).

Most foster adoptive parents described their child's behaviour as problematic. Joey's (autistic) behaviour, although improved over the years as his parents had learnt what to expect and how to respond appropriately, particularly in terms of establishing routines, remained difficult to deal with:

> Joey needs a very strict routine at bedtime . . . and probably getting that routine established was a big turn . . . it's very structured and he doesn't very well sway from it . . . Mealtimes, again, first thing in the morning he has his routine . . . That's probably the best way that we got him to be . . . even yet he's an awful anxious wee boy and he would work himself up into a total frenzy in no time at all.

Although Danny, diagnosed with FAS and ADHD, was essentially well behaved in terms of usually going to bed when asked, eating his meals, and when going shopping, he had become increasingly disruptive and volatile with age. Similarly, Justin's mother linked problems in her son's behaviour to his FAS and although he was essentially well behaved, he found it hard to control his more impulsive behaviour. Steve also had FAS, and his mother listed a number of behavioural issues, including his diagnosed ADHD, inability to sleep, lack of interest in food, and need to constantly be on the move to such an extent that, for example, he found it hard to sit still in a restaurant. Although Steve's mother considered his behaviour to have improved over the recent past, it remained immature in essential respects, for example, prone to outbursts if he did not get his own way.

However, some foster adoptive parents considered their child's behaviour as essentially unproblematic and/or typical of their age. Accordingly, Bridget's mother described her as typically well behaved; a preoccupation with food was linked to her neglect during the first few years of her life. Amy's adoptive mother referred to it being a pleasure to take her daughter out for a meal as she was very well behaved, tried everything on offer, and was always appreciative. Karl's adoptive father described his son as well behaved both inside and outside the home; any manifestations of a slight temper were rare and did not cause any concern. Finally, John's mother talked about him being 'a good child . . . he has his moods and his moments but he is eleven'.

In contrast with the experiences of foster adoptive parents, all the stranger adoptive parents talked about their child's behaviour as essentially unproblematic and/or typical for their age. They described their child as: having the odd "bad day"; avoiding doing chores around the house but otherwise able and willing to take on responsibility; a "normal" child, typically finding any distraction from doing homework; "wonderful" aside from having a volatile temper; well behaved/willing to do as told; not wanting to get out of bed in the mornings but 'I couldn't have asked for a better son'.

Similarly, the majority of kinship carers talked about the child's behaviour as essentially unproblematic and/or typical for their age. Accordingly, they described good/excellent behaviour both within the house and in public, a willingness to do things that were asked of them, adhering to a bedtime/mealtime routine, and good manners. At times, a tendency to complain, answer back or display "attitude" about having to go to bed/get up or contribute to household chores was put down to the normal vagaries of teenage behaviour.

Although describing her niece's overall behaviour as good, Marie's aunt raised some concerns, highlighting her recent "drifting", in that she had become cheekier and more likely to answer back, behaviours she associated with her becoming a teenager. Furthermore, she worried about the company Marie had begun to keep, namely, teenagers from what she considered to be "problem" areas. Jessica's aunt discussed her niece's behaviour in the context of underlying cognitive/learning difficulties, which meant a need for routine as well as acquiescence in relation to day-to-day behaviour. The only problematic behaviour was her tendency to isolate herself from the rest of the family.

Only two kinship carers talked about more problematic behaviour. Tierna's carer described how she refused to do as she was asked (e.g. would not get up in mornings) and could behave very badly when out (e.g. had run away and had punched the carer when she didn't get what she wanted). Such behaviour had increased since she had become a teenager. Nathan's grandmother described his behaviour as good in relation to her (i.e. co-operative and well mannered) but poor in relation to other people/contexts (i.e. could be aggressive with others). She believed this to be rooted in his hurt and upset at his mother's attitude to him and some of his siblings.

Most foster carers talked about their child's behaviour as essentially unproblematic and/or typical for their age, despite this group displaying high SDQ scores and a range of behavioural and discipline problems. For instance, Libby's foster mother talked about her foster daughter as "completely normal", typically well behaved in and out of the home, and Connor's foster mother talked about him as an affectionate, open person who was typically well behaved; some relatively minor issues were identified but in the context of essentially good behaviour. Both Mary's and Ben's foster mothers highlighted their children's problematic eating habits as well as their reluctance to sleep. Although emphasising how James and Pol followed very good routines in most aspects of their behaviour, their foster mother identified their relative hyperactivity (both diagnosed with ADHD) when out and about (e.g. shopping) to be, at times, problematic. In respect of their hyperactivity, both boys' behaviour had improved significantly over the recent past due to medication. Both Anna and Sue's foster mothers identified their daughters' problematic eating habits, as both girls were fussy concerning when and what they ate.

However, a sizeable number of foster carers (n = 6) identified overtly problematic behaviour. Dylan's foster carers described his significant behavioural issues, rooted in his Asperger's Syndrome and ADHD. His behaviour had deteriorated as he had grown older, and had been particularly difficult in the previous year (e.g. physical aggression/self-harming), a situation that had only been become tolerable through medication. He continued to be hyperactive, confrontational and domineering in his attitude, but was an otherwise funny and endearing child. Patrick's foster mother talked about his compulsive stealing and lying, as well as aggressive temper, which frequently caused violent outbursts of behaviour including the smashing of panes of glass and extreme physical aggression towards his birth brother (also fostered by her). Although she knew that his stealing, especially of food, which he hoarded, as well as compulsive eating of sweet things, were rooted in his early life experiences of abuse and neglect, she found it increasingly hard to deal with, especially as they had had multiple discussions with professionals concerning this behaviour, all to no avail. She described her son's subsequent embarrassment and shame over such behaviour and his otherwise tender and loving attitude towards her and other family members, as well as times of good behaviour.

In two cases, the deterioration of the child's behaviour had led to the breakdown of the placement. Sally's foster mother described initially good behaviour that had very quickly become extremely aggressive, deceitful and disruptive and eventually culminated in Sally making a number of accusations of physical violence against the foster father, which prompted disruption of the placement. Sally's foster mother was very upset about the disruption, and tried to rationalise the emergence of such behaviour, highlighting that it had started only after she began life story work sessions with a social worker that included a focus on her birth father, who was extremely abusive, as she explained:

> But things seemed to go into turmoil . . . The house was totally disrupted . . . it was really hard to cope with . . . and I'm not quite sure if it was maybe things that was brought up to her in the course of that life book that perhaps upset her . . . that maybe she hadn't known about her father . . . that really upset her . . . she just went off the rails completely.

Similarly, Tony had recently been removed by Social Services, placed in an assessment unit, and was awaiting return to his birth family. Tony's foster mother had found it increasingly hard, eventually impossible, to deal with his behaviour, which had deteriorated badly over the previous two years to the point where he could not be controlled (e.g. was non-complaint and placing himself at risk). She put this deterioration partly down to the loss of his foster father and then his birth brother to cancer in the previous couple of years. His birth brother had been fostered by another family living nearby and Tony had been very close to both his brother and his foster father.

Jack's foster mother described him as hyperactive and his behaviour as very hard to control. A number of investigations as to the cause of his hyperactivity had been inconclusive. She continued to suspect FAS due to Jack's birth mother's known heavy drinking during pregnancy. Although his behaviour was not "bad" as such, and had improved over the years, as he responded to her rules/advice, he could be cheeky and answer back, would wander off/hide from her when out shopping and was constantly causing himself physical injuries and/or getting into trouble at school, resulting in his foster mother to describe him as 'hard to cope with'.

Martin's foster mother talked about his behavioural problems rooted in brain damage he sustained in utero. Although these problems had diminished greatly over time, he remained volatile, prone to disruptive behaviour in school and extreme/aggressive temper outbursts, in addition to odd behaviour (e.g. would chew batteries). Martin knew that he was different and was profoundly upset by his inability to be "normal". In this context, his foster mother was critical of Social Services refusing to allow her to tell him the cause of the problems. She believed that such knowledge would help him understand that his behaviour was not his fault:

> But he is unpredictable and you need . . . to be one step ahead of him . . . He just took one night and he just went up the walls [smashing them] with frustration and I got built-in furniture . . . and he just tore lumps out of it . . . he'll say to me, 'Why can't I not be normal like everybody else'?

The majority of residence order carers talked about their child's behaviour as essentially unproblematic and/or typical for their age. At times, relatively minor issues were highlighted. Greg's grandfather talked about his grandson's behaviour as being somewhat disruptive in that he 'gets up to all sorts of bother', such as starting fights with his siblings or misbehaving when out shopping. Conall's carer discussed his recent poor bedtime routine, as well as his extremely fussy eating habits, but he was considered an otherwise well behaved child. Similarly, Ryan's carer described him as willing to go to his room, and avoiding actual sleep, but in all other respects, his behaviour was very good:

> Disastrous. He goes up to his room to go to bed and an hour later you can hear him thumping about the room . . . he's a rascal but he's okay . . . It's changed in the sense that he's grown up and he knows his boundaries now where he wouldn't have done when he was younger . . . and he knows there are rules he's got to keep.

Both Roisin's grandfather and Sarah's carer mentioned their children's fussy eating habits and tendency to refuse to eat certain foods. Jonny's carer talked about him never causing any trouble, but because of his hyperactivity, he was vulnerable to peer pressure so that she tried, whenever possible, to keep him away from large group activity, such as discos. In addition, he found it difficult both to eat and to sleep once his medication had worn off in the evenings, and was prone to wandering off on his own when out and about.

Two carers identified more problematic behaviour. Gary's carer linked his difficulties in concentrating/being easily distracted and inability to appreciate dangers, to his FAS. Luke's grandmother talked about his temper tantrums and associated verbal abuse of her, as well as his general stubbornness and non-compliance with going to bed, or helping to tidy the house:

> *Well he could blow up . . . for the slightest thing . . . and give me a mouthful of abuse and call you names, swear at you and every-thing . . . It's sometimes I think because he copies [older brother] . . . He can be stubborn ... You see, it's my fault too. I grounded him and then let him out 10 minutes later.*

Changes in behaviour

The majority of parents/carers, regardless of pathway group, believed that their children's behaviour had either stayed the same or improved. In terms of improvements, some children were thought to have become more mature, thoughtful, confident, secure, independent and reliable over the years, or not as "cheeky" as he/she used to be.

However, in a minority of cases, the child's behaviour had got worse. That was the case for Laura and Danny, who were both adopted by their foster carers. Laura's adoptive mother linked the deterioration in her behaviour over the previous two years to her own deterioration in health, suspecting that her daughter had been left feeling anxious/vulnerable. Danny's behaviour also became more difficult when he turned seven and he was subsequently diagnosed with ADHD and prescribed medication. It was a similar scenario for Ashley and Nina, who were both living with their birth mothers. Ashley's mother explained how they used to have a very positive relationship but when she started secondary school, her behaviour changed in that she started fighting with her, "speaking down" to her, and being cruel to her. Nina's mother also described a significant deterioration in her daughter's behaviour over the previous years, as she had become generally unruly, resistant and rude:

Before she was sort of shy and withdrawn, whereas now she is just a lunatic. She is just, if I want to do it I will do it now and you will not stop me.

For some children with ADHD and other problematic behaviours, the medication they were taking had resulted in significant improvements in their behaviour, for example, James and Pol, two birth siblings living with their foster carers:

The tablets are controlling a lot of the behaviour now that James is on so it has helped an awful lot.

Observed children's behaviour

This section describes the children's behaviour observed by the researchers during visits to the families. The notes taken during the interviews were used to complement the information recorded in the questionnaires and the interview transcripts.

Most children appeared comfortable and relaxed while completing the questionnaires and during the interview. Some were more engaged and open while others were more reserved, shy and/or quiet, with this being a feature across the groups.

The interviews conducted with children who had a high level of need and difficult behaviours (according to their parents/carers) did feel more challenging for the researchers, especially with children who had autism or/and ADHD. For instance, Joey had hyperactivity and mild Asperger's, and at his parents' request the first author visited him before the first interview to get to know him, as the interview was anticipated to be quite difficult. Joey was living with his foster adoptive parents. During the interview, he found it difficult to stay on task and used the "stop" sign to take frequent breaks. He had some difficulty understanding the questions, and he got side-tracked and distracted throughout. There were a number of topics he was unwilling to talk about.

Similarly, Dylan also had Asperger's and various behavioural problems, was bullied at school, and had self-harmed. He was living with his foster carers. During the interview, he moved about constantly and complained about the length of time the interview was taking. He became agitated when dealing with the topic of family, and refused to talk about his feelings because – as he explained – he was being bullied and did 'not want to go into that'. The interview with Jim was also challenging as it was very difficult to get him to expand on his answers. He was living with his birth mother who explained that he was paranoid that the researchers were from Social Services and would take him away again. His mother stated that he was a very clingy and insecure boy who did not trust anybody.

However, in a few cases, the views parents/carers had of their children, and which were reflected in the semi-structured interview with the researchers, seemed to be very different from what the researchers observed during the interviews. For instance, Steve (foster adoption) had FAS and ADHD, and was described as "hyper" and "immature". However, while completing the activities, he appeared to be able to concentrate well, was interested to know more about the study, and asked questions. Similarly, Martin was described by his foster carer as having hyperactivity, night terrors and losing his temper easily, but he appeared comfortable and calm while completing the activities and the "me-book", and took time to answer each of the questions. In the case of Claire, her adoptive mother had concerns about her behaviour, that she was "territorial", "distant", "cold", and lacked social and communication skills:

Claire is just different from other kids . . . there is this wee wall around her. You know what Morgan [birth sister, also adopted by them] is like, Morgan is the complete opposite, she is very outgoing and very friendly, and I know everybody can't be like that, but Claire is very distant. She is very cold.

However, during the interview, Claire seemed to be comfortable while being interviewed, appeared to understand all the questions, chatted freely, and was able to effectively express her views and feelings. In contrast to these cases, Trevor's foster mother and Abbie's adoptive mother had no concerns regarding their children's behaviour, but both Trevor and Abbie appeared anxious and uncomfortable during the interview.

Summary of key findings

- No statistically significant SDQ mean score differences were found between the children in the different placement types. However, some differences were found in terms of the percentages of children within each placement type that scored within the abnormal range. While lower proportions of children in the kinship care and residence order groups scored above the clinical threshold for total difficulties (although still higher than the 10% anticipated with a community sample), much higher proportions of children (i.e. around half) in the birth parent and foster care groups scored within the abnormal range.
- Conduct problems and hyperactivity seemed to affect a considerable proportion of children in each placement, especially those living with birth parents and in foster care, whereas peer relationship problems appeared to be especially prevalent among children in the adoption group. However, the majority of children in the study, regardless of placement type, were deemed by their carers to be considerate of others, helpful and kind (prosocial behaviour).
- Some of the children with high SDQ scores appeared to have a range of behavioural difficulties and conditions such as ADHD or autism.
- A considerable number of parents/carers considered their children to have behavioural and/or discipline problems. Most of these were foster carers and foster adoptive parents.
- Across placement types, children had a range of difficulties and conditions, including ADHD (and taking medication for the

condition), FAS and mild Asperger's, although these were more prevalent across both adoption groups. Parents/carers also described a range of other specific difficulties and concerns with their children's behaviour, including hyperactivity; poor concentration; insecurity; anxiety; impulsivity; lack of social skills; and risk-taking behaviours.

- Although some children scored high on the SDQ – Total difficulties scale and were believed to have behavioural and/or discipline problems, their parents/carers explained they did not have any major behavioural concerns about the child during the interview. These parents/carers considered that they knew how to manage and deal with the child's behaviour, which meant that the behaviour appeared less problematic, and as a "normal" part of their everyday lives. Many were also able to highlight the strengths of their children and their "positive" behaviours, over and above the problems they faced.

- Despite high SDQ scores, and occasional diagnosis of FAS, ADHD, and ASD, most birth parents, all the stranger adoptive parents, some foster adoptive parents, the majority of kinship carers, most foster carers and the majority of residence order carers described the child's behaviour as essentially manageable and/or typical of their age, with only minor concerns mentioned.

- Relatively more foster adoptive parents, birth parents and foster carers highlighted their children's problematic behaviours, while no stranger adoptive parents and only a few carers from the kinship and residence order group perceived their child to have any difficult behaviours.

- Reasons underpinning problematic behaviour, included cognitive/developmental limitations; teenage "attitude"; early life experiences of abuse and neglect and associated anger; low self-esteem; and anger as result of significant deterioration in carer's health. Interestingly, four out of the five children whose behaviour was described as problematic within the foster adoptive parent group had diagnosed cognitive/developmental limitations. Moreover, the single most prominent factor associated with problematic behaviour was cognitive/developmental limitations (mentioned by a total of 10 carers across four groups). The importance of these limitations for problematic behaviour is made all the more evident by the fact that it was mentioned by a further three carers when talking about specific behavioural issues. Although talked about much less often, the second most frequently identified factor was that of teenage-related "attitude" (mentioned by five carers/parents).

- Some children behaved contrary to their parents'/carers' expectations of how they would engage during interview, whilst other children with behaviour difficulties appeared to find the interviews difficult to manage.

8 Children's education

Introduction

Education is generally seen as a crucial issue in terms of facilitating social integration, with poor educational achievement often leading to long-term unemployment and social exclusion (Jackson, 2010).

Many children and young people in care experience a range of educational difficulties, such as poor school attendance, school exclusion and suspension, slow academic performance, and low scores on standardised tests of academic achievement in reading, writing and mathematics (Fernandez, 2008; Denecheau, 2011; Flynn *et al*, 2013). These difficulties may be caused by frequent placement moves and placement disruption, often leading to frequent school changes, behavioural and emotional problems, and low expectations. Furthermore, they may also have been present as difficulties in the children and young people's lives before they entered care, perhaps even to some degree precipitating their entry to care, particularly during the teenage years, or could be a consequence of early childhood trauma, occurring in utero, which may have impacted upon brain development.

In this chapter, children's education is examined across all the placement types, using the quantitative data emerging from the British Picture Vocabulary Scale (BPVS-II) and the parents' questionnaire, and the qualitative data from the interviews with the parents/carers and the children. A range of issues are explored, including the children's educational learning needs, the parents/carers' views on how the child was progressing at school, and the children's feelings about school and its different aspects, and their relationships with peers and teachers, as well as their own and their parents'/carers' expectations.

Educational learning needs

Children completed the BPVS-II which was used as a measure of scholastic aptitude (see Chapter 2). Scores are standardised on age reference groups which enables an individual's score to be compared with a large cross-section of individuals of the same chronological age. Standardised scores range from 40 to 160, with 100 being the average score. Scores below 90 are deemed low.

Figure 8.1
BPVS-II mean scores by placement type

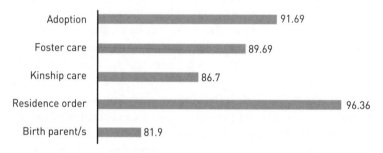

On this dimension, higher scores indicate that the children have greater scholastic aptitude. One-way ANOVA indicated that there was no significant variation in mean scores between the five pathway groups on BPVS-II mean score. Additionally, post-hoc Tukey HSD tests indicated that there were no significant mean differences between any of the five care pathway groups. Figure 8.1 shows the mean standardised scores for the different placement types, ranging between moderately low to low average scores. The lowest mean score was for the birth parent group, followed by the kinship care group and the highest mean score was for the residence order group, followed by the adoption group.

The children in the study showed a range of learning abilities and needs. Table 8.1 shows the percentage of children who scored below 90 in the BPVS, and who, according to their parents/carers, had learning difficulties, went to a special school, and were provided with

Table 8.1
Educational learning needs by placement type

	BPVS scores below 90	Learning difficulties	Special school	Additional supports
Foster adoption	25%	56%	22%	67%
Stranger adoption	50%	22%	0	22%
Foster care	50%	27%	7%	40%
Kinship care	50%	25%	0	42%
Residence order	36%	27%	20%	46%
Birth parents	78%	45%	27%	36%

additional supports (i.e. having a classroom assistant or a tutor, one-to-one teaching, going to a special school, or attending a special classroom with fewer pupils and more teaching staff). Three children were also receiving counselling at school. Some children had a classroom assistant because of their behavioural problems, rather than their learning disabilities.

As shown in Table 8.1, the group of children that received more additional educational supports, and were more likely to be deemed as having learning difficulties, was the foster adoption group, despite the fact that this was the group less likely to score below the average range in the BPVS. In contrast, even though seven out of the nine children living with birth parents who completed the BPVS had low scores, only four of them received any learning support. In total, nine children were attending a special school: three with birth parents, three on residence orders, two adopted by strangers, and one in foster care.

The majority of the parents/carers of children who were attending a special needs school or a support unit, or who had classroom assistants, believed that their child had benefited from the consistency and stability of these supports. For instance, Steve's foster adoptive mother commented that her son's classroom assistant had really helped him to be confident and independent, and she felt fortunate that the same classroom assistant had worked with him for five years, since he was in nursery school. Similarly, Jessica's kinship carer explained that she had had the same "resource teacher" for seven years, which the carer believed made a great difference, as 'that teacher had a really good understanding of the child' and 'had a great patience with her'. James' foster mother believed that going to the special school had been 'the best thing that had happened to him', as it had increased his confidence 'because he can see there's people worse than he is'.

However, some parents/carers, such as Jonny's residence order carers, were worried that these extra supports were making their child feel different. Jonny was attending a special support centre, which consisted of a small group of six pupils, and his carer believed it had 'worked wonders'. However, she also believed it made him feel different and had discussed enrolling him in the nearest school, but she was advised that it would be better for him to remain in a smaller group as he could end up 'with the wrong company'.

Some children had had extra help in the past but not at the time of the interview, while others were due to receive supports in the future. For example, Niall had a one-to-one special needs teacher the previous year, which his birth mother believed had helped him. However, the school felt he no longer needed additional support, which was a concern given his low BPVS score. Similarly, Gary also had a low BPVS score, and his residence order carer believed he was a 'bit behind'. He had received extra help in the past, but then the carer was told that he could 'cope alright on his own'. She believed he needed extra help, as he used to perform better at school, when this was available to him. According to his birth mother, Aidan was going to receive extra support that year, because he needed more help with English, as he was having difficulties with his reading comprehension. Aidan's BPVS score was also low. In contrast, Ciara had an average BPVS score, but her adoptive parents (stranger adoption) wanted to 'push' for extra help at school (one-on-one help) for her, because they believed that she needed it. They were advised that she was meant to obtain additional support, but this had not materialised.

A few parents/carers were dissatisfied with the previous school their child had attended, while others criticised previous teachers. For instance, Eoghan's kinship carer recalled having seen 'a vast improvement in his work', especially since he had moved to secondary school. In his primary school, she was told that he was very poor at English and 'was going to struggle', but in his secondary school, they told her that 'there is nothing slow about him'. She believed that in the primary school, 'they didn't put the effort in'. She only became aware that his classroom assistant was not spending enough time with him after Eoghan left the school, and regretted not having fought harder for his interests.

The Eleven Plus test was mentioned in some of the interviews with parents/carers (n = 10) and children (n = 2). This examination used to be taken by the majority of 10–11-year-old children in Northern Ireland, in their last year of primary school, as part of a selective secondary education system. Thus, it governed admission to various types of secondary school. This test is no longer in use in Northern Ireland, and has been replaced by a transfer test for selection to grammar school, but at the time of the interviews, it was still being undertaken. Some of the children in the study had sat the exam (n = 9), with seven passing with As, B1s and B2s and two failing (one with birth mother and the other in foster care). Of the seven who passed the test, three were on residence order (two of them siblings living with their grandfather), one in foster adoption, one adopted by strangers, one in foster care, and one in kinship care. Martin's foster mother reported injustice within the system, as she had to insist that Martin be permitted to sit the test, which he was being prevented from due to his behavioural problems. Subsequently, Martin did achieve well in this test, which he may not have had an opportunity to sit had it not been for his foster mother advocating on his behalf:

I had to fight with Social Services to get him to do the Eleven Plus . . . They weren't going to let him do it . . . and I felt that he should do it. I says because he has problems, why should he be punished, because of that? That he is quite capable of doing it . . . the Education Board wasn't going to let him do it . . . At the end, they allowed him to do it but he had to sit in a room on his own . . . in case he would disrupt the class . . . He had to sit in a room by his own and he had to have somebody there especially for him. So they made him, from when he went to school, he's been made different. I'm trying to make him normal, the same as everybody else, but he is made to feel different, which I felt ... it wasn't fair and manys a time I had words with the teacher over it ... he got a B1. I was all delighted.

Ashley's birth mother also felt compelled to fight against the teacher's low expectations about Ashley passing the test. However, Ashley did not want to sit the examination, and failed. The mother expressed her regret at her insistence on Ashley sitting the examination:

When I went to speak to her P6 teacher, he said Ashley is refusing to learn therefore I am refusing to teach her. 'She will never pass the Eleven Plus, she is not capable of it, and do not put her to [name of school] either because of Ashley's attitude, she will go downhill'. See, the more he said that to me, the more I wanted to prove him wrong, so what did I do? I put her in for the Eleven Plus. Ashley didn't want to do it, but I said, 'Ashley, as long as you try your best, regardless of the outcome, you try your best, that will be fine.' ... No, I did not get her tutored, how could I afford to get her a tutor? ... I helped her and she got work home and that ... we done that at home. She got a D, and see, as a parent, that is the worst feeling I have ever felt ... because I pushed that child knowing that he had said to me that she wasn't capable of it. I pushed that child, and pushed her, and she got a D, so I made her feel like a failure ... that's the way I felt, but she accepted it ... when the results came through, and I opened it Ashley says, 'I knew that would happen,' as casual as that.

Parental views and expectations about the child's educational achievement

The majority of parents/carers in all the groups claimed that their child was doing well or alright at school, and that was often the case even if the child had a low BPVS score, was in a special school, had learning difficulties, and/or was receiving extra help. In these latter cases, the parent/carer often specified that they were doing well in the class/school they were in, or at the level they were achieving. However, in four instances (i.e. two foster care, one kinship care and one adopted), while the child scored considerably below the average in the BPVS, the parent/carer claimed their child was achieving the same or above the average for the children in their age group. For example, although Ben scored extremely low in the vocabulary measure, his foster mother asserted that he 'came top in the class in English'. In addition, in four other cases (child in kinship care, foster care, on residence order and foster adoption), while the child presented a low average score (although considered within the normal range), their parents/carers claimed that they were doing extremely well, and considerably above average. It is impossible to ascertain the reasons behind these discrepancies. However, it may have been the case that the child might not have performed as well as he/she usually did in the classroom when completing the scale; the BPVS might not have been able to show the "real" capabilities of these children; or the parent/carer might not have been aware of their child's academic limitations.

Despite stating that their child was doing very well or OK at school, some parents/carers mentioned minor concerns such as their child being able to do better in all his/her subjects, not doing homework, being adversely influenced by another child in the class, or being slightly behind the other children academically.

Some parents/carers (n = 12) highlighted the problems that their child was having at school, such as behavioural problems (n = 7), being bullied (or/and bullying) (n = 6), or poor school attendance (n = 1). In addition, most of these children had learning difficulties and were underachieving. These were spread across the five placement groups: three in foster care (one of them had recently broken down); three in kinship care; two living with birth parents; two foster adopted; one stranger adopted; and one on residence order. Bullying appeared to be a relatively common problem for some of these children. For instance, Ryan's residence order carer identified older children playing tricks on him as one of the reasons why he was finding it difficult to settle into his secondary school:

> *Well, now in secondary school, he's finding it pretty hard to settle in, you know, from being the oldest in primary to being the youngest in secondary. You know the way in primary you go into your class you're there the whole day. Now he's moving from class to class, and he's finding it a wee bit hard, and some of the bigger boys would play tricks on the first years, you know, that sort of thing, and he's finding it a wee bit hard to cope with now.*

In Laura's (foster adoption) and Patrick's (foster care) case, the parents/carers mentioned that their child was not only being bullied, but were also bullying other children, as Patrick's foster mum explained:

> *He can get still into a lot of bother. He can still be bullied at school. His report is not good at school . . . I hear reports that he is bullying some young one that started.*

In terms of behavioural problems, parents/carers stressed their child's general poor or bad behaviour at school, as well as more specific issues, such as having a short concentration span or being aggressive. For instance, Sally's previous foster carers (the placement had recently broken down) recalled that her behaviour in school was particularly bad, and she had many detentions. According to Niall's birth mother, he hated school, was starting P7 although he should have been starting first year in secondary school given his age, and had behavioural problems at school:

> *Niall sitting there kicking the teacher and all, under the chair, and he wouldn't leave him, because he's doing this and mostly off the chair doing it as well.*

According to Danny's adoptive mother (foster adoption), he had many difficulties in school, particularly since he was seven years old, when many things changed (i.e. moving from junior school to senior school, moving out of the main school into temporary accommodation, and having a new teacher). According to her, these changes affected his behaviour, going 'from being a model pupil in school to being a nightmare', and this challenging behaviour continued, although she had not heard of any incidents since he last went back to school:

From the end of September until January, he was out of school. Then he went back January to Easter, two days a week and from Easter to June three days a week. School really was a big stress and I mean, because he travels 20 miles to school out there and 20 miles home again.

Danny's adoptive mother believed that school was very stressful for him because of his lack of social skills and difficulties in his peer relationships (e.g. didn't like criticism and could react by getting verbally aggressive).

In other cases (n = 5) across placements, parents/carers claimed that there had been issues regarding school in the past, but these had improved, and the child was now coping well. For instance, Jim's birth mother claimed that he had recently had a good report from school, although the previous year had been difficult, with 'ups and downs', as he was fighting with other children and failing to attend. She believed that his teachers' encouragement had a role in his change of attitude:

They [the teachers] keep encouraging him by saying, 'Oh, your attendance is now 76', you know, he likes to get encouragement, so you know, that boosts his confidence, and that makes him want to go.

According to Abbie's adoptive mother (stranger adoption), Abbie's achievement and attitude at school had greatly improved since she changed schools. She used to attend a special needs primary school, but was going to a mainstream secondary school at the time of the interview. Abbie's mother believed that at the special school teachers were not sufficiently 'under pressure for to be getting all those kids at a certain standard in the key stage'. Thus, she was convinced that the school change was the main reason for the improvement in Abbie's educational outcomes:

> *Looking back, I think possibly that we should have just moved her over into a primary school, because since she has got into the high school and been one of the normal people, she has really come on in leaps and bounds, and her attitude has changed.*

Abbie's view appears to echo that of her adoptive mother, as she told the researchers that she did not like her primary school, as it was 'not a nice school', and she did not have many friends then.

Children's perspectives on their school lives

Children listed the subjects and aspects that they most liked about school. In this section, these have been grouped into the following categories:

- Active and practical subjects: physical education (PE), sports (e.g. netball, football, etc.), technology, woodwork, using the computers, and home economics (HE);
- Academic subjects/formal aspects: science, maths, English, history, geography, biology, foreign languages, doing work, having exams;
- Creative subjects: art, drama and music;
- Social aspects of school: meeting friends, "mucking about", break/ lunch time, school trips, after school clubs, youth club; and
- Being off school: school holidays and home time.

Table 8.2 presents the number of children within each placement group that claimed they liked these subjects and aspects of school.

Active and practical subjects appeared to be very popular among the children in the study as they were listed by nearly all of them, regardless of placement types. Children appeared to enjoy playing a range of sports and PE, as well as practical subjects, such as home economics, which appeared to mostly involve cooking and baking; and technology, which children tended to describe as "making things"

Table 8.2
Children's likes about school by placement type

	Academic subjects	Act./pract. subjects	Creative subjects	Social aspects	Being off
Foster adoption (n = 8)	5	8	8	8	7
Stranger adoption (n = 9)	3	8	7	8	3
Foster care (n = 15)	4	15	11	13	7
Kinship care (n = 10)	7	10	10	10	7
Residence order (n = 14)	10	13	11	12	10
Birth parents (n = 10)	3	9	8	8	6
Total (n = 66)	**32**	**63**	**55**	**59**	**40**

or "building stuff". For instance, Kirsten's (residence order) favourite subject was woodwork:

I like the different types of wood, and it's fun to hammer and stuff and you get to make different things.

The social aspects of school were also mentioned by most of the children and creative subjects were almost as popular. Some children talked about meeting friends and talking with their peers during their breaks, as well as going to after-school clubs. For instance, Áine (kinship care) was a very bubbly girl, who enjoyed the breaks because of the fact that she could then talk:

Yeah, we can't talk [in school]. I absolutely hate it but . . . in break time, you can talk with your friends for fifteen minutes, and in lunch time for half an hour or something like that.

Charlie (stranger adoption) also enjoyed the social aspects of school, his favourite being school trips, because 'they are fun, you get to meet new people that you haven't met in school'.

Some children enjoyed subjects such as art, music and drama. Both Sue (foster care) and Danny (foster adoption) felt it boosted their self-esteem, as Danny explained:

My favourite, this is quite a difficult one, can it be two? . . . music and drama . . . let's see, it gives me more confidence . . . it gives you confidence to speak out loud and all.

Annie (kinship care) also detailed her reasons for liking art and drama:

[I like drama because] you can go mental and express yourself . . . [I like art because] it's fun and you get to listen to music too, while you're doing it . . . when we're doing art, you get to paint anything you want.

Academic subjects were less frequently selected as things that children liked about school, and fewer than half of the children mentioned one or more academic subjects as something they liked. The residence order and kinship care groups had the highest proportion of children that liked academic subjects (71% and 70%), whereas the foster care, birth parents and foster adoption groups had the lowest (26%, 30% and 33% respectively).

A few children (n = 6) claimed that they hated or did not like school. These included two adopted children, three with birth parents, and one in foster care. Caomhan (with birth mother) claimed he did not like school, and in terms of subjects, only liked art, but also liked sports and using the computers three days a week. He said he did not enjoy doing any work because he was "tired"; and felt happy at the time of interview as it was during the summer months, and he was "off school":

[Circles "school holidays" in the school page of the "me book"] School holidays, because it gives you a rest from it. You deserve a school holiday.

Particular subjects/aspects of school that were often mentioned as being disliked were maths (n = 18); exams (n = 9); R.E (n = 9); science (n = 8); and English (n = 5). The reasons most often mentioned for not liking a particularly subject was the teacher, the subject being boring or difficult/hard, and the feeling of not being good at it. For instance, Tracy (stranger adoption) explained why she did not like to have exams:

'Cos you get into a different class . . . and they are hard, and you have to revise for them, which I don't really revise, and I end up falling asleep, and they are not that great . . . they stress me.

Megan (residence order) did not like maths:

It's very boring. And there's computing. Especially algebra. It's very confusing.

Most parents/carers either did not comment on what the children enjoyed or their views mostly coincided with what the children told us. However, the comments of a few parents/carers (n = 12) did not correspond with the views expressed by the children in terms of their likes and dislikes. For example, Jim stated he liked music, PE, sports and technology, although his birth mother appeared to have a completely different view of the subjects he enjoyed and did not enjoy:

He loves art. I don't think he's that keen on the rest of them. PE he definitely hates. Will do anything to get out of PE . . . It's because of his weight, you know he's self-conscious about it, but apart from that, he has no interest in the other subjects like, but he does them, but he would rather do art.

The majority of children across placement types appeared to have developed good relationships with their peers at school. As already mentioned, many identified meeting friends and other social aspects of school as one of the things they liked about school. However, a few children seemed to have difficulties in this area, as they said they had no or very few friends who were important to them (n = 6), or they were being bullied by other children (n = 2). For instance, although Jonny's residence order carer believed he had friends at school, Jonny said in his interview that he did not like school, and did not have any friends there (although he had some outside school). Similarly, although Abbie (stranger adoption) admitted not having many friends at school at present (she had moved from primary to secondary school), she explained that it was worse in the past:

> Abbie (A): *I didn't have much friends and I didn't go to a nice school.*
>
> Researcher: *You didn't go to a nice school in the past?*
>
> A: *No. I didn't like my primary school.*

Despite her carer not referring to this during her interview, Sarah (residence order) was not happy at school, since she was being bullied:

> Sarah (S): *That wee boy, uhm . . . he's the teacher's pet, and he really annoyed me today, so he did. Normally, he used to be calling me fat, and ugly and all, and a lesbian . . . and then we got that sorted out. And he agreed with the fat and ugly, but he didn't agree with the lesbian.*
>
> Researcher (R): *Right, and how does that make you feel, whenever you go into school?*
>
> S: *I don't really worry when I get on my bus, and then we get near to the school, I get really, really scared, because I don't know if he's going to do something to me.*
>
> R: *And had your mum talked to the teachers and stuff about it?*
>
> S: *Yeah, but I don't think they have listened.*

Although Rebecca (kinship care) seemed to enjoy school in general, when she moved to live with her uncle, she had to change schools and make new friends, which she did not find that easy.

In terms of other school relationships, some children across all the groups (n = 15) identified their teachers as people important to them. Sometimes, they were identified as a generic group, but often it was also a particular teacher or teachers whom they found especially supportive. Anna (in foster care) specified their teachers (any teacher) as important to her, but also identified her assistant teacher as her favourite:

Researcher (R): *And why would your teacher be important to you?*

Anna (A): *Because they give you a good education, so when you grow older, like, you can get yourself a job and all.*

R: *Well, do you have a favourite teacher?*

A: *Yeah, my assistant teacher.*

R: *Right, and why is your assistant teacher important?*

A: *Because she helps me with my maths. She helps me because I have trouble with my maths and like she's really kind and generous . . .*

While others did not identify them as important people in their lives, some children liked a particular subject because of the teacher (n = 7) or explained that the teacher helped them with a particular subject (n = 3). But the converse was also the case. For example, Ben (foster care) explained the reasons why he did not like his maths teacher:

> *[I don't like] maths. He is useless, the teacher . . . I hate him . . . no one likes him in our class . . . he never gives a free period, like. Like, the other teachers would give one maybe every two weeks. Not one a year, not even near the summer holidays would he give one. He never lets you take a break at all . . . he's wild annoying. He doesn't even give you time to do your work. What you don't get done in class, extra homework.*

Bronagh (living with birth parents) explained why she felt put off geography by her teacher:

> *She kind of just didn't understand, didn't make us understand it more, and she didn't really explain it better very much and that, so she didn't, and then if you done something wrong in her class, then she would shout at you, so she would actually shout at you.*

Children's ambitions and parent/carer expectations

Most children interviewed had an idea of the employment they wanted when they grew up. This ranged from being a doctor or a chef to being a plasterer. Many mentioned earning lots of money. As expected, there were gender differences regarding the children's ambitions, but no differences between placements were found. The professions most cited by boys in terms of what they would most like to do or be were professional sports player (football, ice-hockey, rugby, etc) (n = 10); join the army (n = 6); mechanic (n = 4); run their own business (n = 4); builder (n = 3); chef (n = 3); policeman (n = 2); vet (n = 2); and performing (e.g. singer, actor) (n = 2). The professions favoured by girls were performing (i.e. singer or actress) (n = 5); hairdresser/beautician (n = 4); show jumper/hockey (n = 4); help people in need (n = 3); fashion designer (n = 3); teacher (n = 2); vet (n = 2); and doctor (n = 2).

While most children believed they would end up doing what they wanted to do (n = 31), others expressed doubt about what they would turn out to be (n = 8), and/or listed other professions that they would most likely have in the future (n = 14), such as a hairdresser, or a clothes shop assistant in the case of girls, or for boys, a farmer, a builder or an electrician. These latter children, who were spread across all placement types, were not completely confident that they would be able to achieve their dreams, or identified these other options as more "realistic". For instance, Patrick (in foster care) wanted to be a chef, but had reservations about whether he would be good enough to be one, and thought he might turn out to be a farmer instead. Similarly, Emma (living with birth father) dreamt about being a fashion designer, but was not confident she would become one, as she believed you needed to be "brilliant" to be one and did not think she was brilliant enough. She thought she would work as a hairdresser instead, because she always did her friends' hair and they thought it was good.

Ben (in foster care) acknowledged that whatever he did when he grew up would depend on his school qualifications:

If I don't get good enough results, I would have to think about it what would be the best for me.

His wish for the future was to have a good job, and he was looking forward to his future, and appeared excited about the possibility of travelling and of having a job. Similarly, Kirsten claimed she felt happy about her future, because she hoped to get a good job, despite the fact that she had doubts about whether she would end up being a solicitor for which she thought 'you'd need a lot of talent'. Annie (in kinship care) was less optimistic about her future. She explained that she wanted to be a scientist:

Because it's fun. You get to find out loads of new things and discover new things and prove things.

However, she did not think she could be a scientist in the future because 'you need to know loads of maths', and she did not like maths. She joked that she would 'probably end up working in a MacDonald's'. Despite her low expectations, she scored in the 78th percentile in the BPVS measure (high average score).

In contrast, some children, like Roisin (residence order), were particularly focused and confident that they would achieve their goals. Roisin wanted to be a doctor in a US city, and claimed that she would 'work to get her aspiration'. She explained the reasons why she wanted to become a doctor:

You just get to help people and I suppose you'd be very happy with yourself, you know, like saying that you've saved someone's life and that.

Roisin scored in the 94th percentile in the BPVS (the highest score for the whole sample), and according to her grandfather, was performing extremely well at school, as her report was 'all As and A+'. She maintained that she felt happy and confident about her future:

I think I will have a really good job, and I'm gonna live in, like, a really nice place, and my life will be better than here.

Most parents/carers appeared aware of their children's ambitions (n = 28), although many talked about their children changing their minds very often (n = 11) and not really knowing what they would like to do in the future. Others appeared completely unaware, or their views did not match those of their children (n = 21). According to her residence order carer, Sarah changed her mind all the time about what she wanted to be, but this was not a concern of her carer:

> *Because she's young yet and she has all the time in the world to think, I don't push her into a corner. I don't . . . I mean I'd love her to get a good education but if she never gets it, as long as she can cope and survive and get enough to get a job and keep herself, I'll be happy with that. I mean there's not an awful lot of brain surgeons about and she'll never be one and again, I never put any on the other two, [older birth children] was the same. Do your best at school, it's all you can do and if you do that and you try, well, that'll be it.*

Other parents/carers, like Ryan's residence order carer (see quote below), seemed to concur with Sarah's carer that they only wanted their children to be happy in the future, regardless of their occupation. They wanted their child "to do well", and would encourage them in their studies, but their priority was their child's happiness:

> *I tell Ryan the same as I told my own son when he was growing up, I used to say . . . 'I don't care what you do as long as you're happy doing it.' I said, even the bin men are needed. But I'll encourage him to do well in school and all the rest of it, but I won't pressurise him. Whatever he wants to do with his life provided it's, you know, on the right road. We'll support him, we'll support him whatever he decides to be.*

Most parents/carers wanted their child to do well at school, and a few specified that they would like their child to attend third level education. For instance, despite Ben's low score in the BPVS, his foster mother stated that she wanted him to go to university:

That would be my dream for him to graduate in something that he, you know, really likes. That would be my dream and if we get that, well, I'll be happy enough then.

Similarly, Kirsten's residence order carer wished for her to go to the university that her older birth daughter went to, even though it was further from their home:

There is no doubt now, I will be in tears if that happens, you know, because she will be away for a week and not coming back at the weekends, maybe even stay up in [local city], you know, but I would love it if she would keep on with her education, have a good life, a good job.

Some parents/carers were convinced that their children were going "to do well" in the future, and had a strong belief that their child would attain their aspirations, which for some were very high but for others less so. For instance, Joanne's kinship carer believed she was going to 'do great! She has great people skills and she also will do very well academically'; and Abbie's adoptive mother (stranger adoption) thought that Abbie would be a chef in the future, as she wanted. She argued that, although Abbie knew her limitations (i.e. learning disabilities), these did not worry or bother her, because she was extremely focused, hence her mother's belief that she could accomplish her dreams. Similarly, Bronagh, who has a physical disability, expressed her dream of becoming a teacher. However, her birth parents thought she was not being realistic about what she could actually achieve:

Bronagh's birth father (BF): *She loves kids ... she wanted to be a teacher and then she wanted to do child ... she wanted to do child care ... and then she wanted to be a cook and then she went back to being a teacher and then she's back.*

Bronagh's birth mother (BM): *There's none of it is actually practical like ... not for her.*

191

BF: *Not with her disability.*

BM: *Well, I'll tell you what, she'll not sit back and she'll not let anything beat her.*

Nicole's residence order carers were aware of her wish to be a doctor, and described her as having 'set certain goals'. They believed she was doing well at school, and could 'see her going to university'. However, they were not convinced that she should aim as high as aspiring to be a doctor, but found it more plausible that she would become a nurse or a paramedic:

> *So I always would say to her, well, maybe, if it's medical you like, you know you can always be a nurse or a paramedic.*

A few parents/carers expressed worry about their children's futures, and had low expectations. These were parents/carers with children who had a range of difficulties, such as behavioural problems. Danny was diagnosed with ADHD when he was seven years old, and he had a range of behavioural issues. Danny's adoptive mother (foster adoption) worried about his future, not just in terms of his future educational achievements, but his capacity to become an independent adult:

> *I just wonder how he'll fit in, you know, as he's only 13 and he really is sort of . . . he would act more like a nine- or a 10-year-old, and I've been accused today of being overprotective by my daughter. And I suppose I am overprotective but he's not at the stage where he's asking to go but I worry about the future when he does go out into that big world, because he's very much cosseted in our sort of world now, so that would be my fear.*

Other parents/carers appeared to have low expectations for their children's futures; Mary's foster carers and Conall's residence order carer were not expecting 'great academically' from them.

Summary of main findings

- There was no significant variation in mean scores on the BPVS-II, and no significant difference between mean scores for any of the groups. Mean scores for all the groups were relatively low (ranging between moderately low to low average scores). The lowest mean score was for the birth parent group, followed by the kinship care group and the highest mean score was for the residence order group, followed by the adoption group.
- The foster adoption and residence order group had the lowest proportion of children with low BPVS scores, whereas over three-quarters of children living with birth parents and half of the children in the other groups scored very low on this measure.
- In terms of additional learning supports, the majority of children in the foster adoption group and nearly half of those in foster care were in receipt of some support. However, the birth parent group had the lowest percentage of children receiving supports, despite displaying the highest level of need.
- A few children appeared to do very well at school and had passed the Eleven Plus test. Low expectations for these children from teachers and Social Services were apparent in some cases.
- Although the majority of parents/carers in all of the groups believed their children were coping very well or "alright" at school (considering their limitations), a few identified problems, such as bullying and behavioural problems.
- The subjects/aspects children most liked about school across placements were: active and practical subjects, the social aspects, and creative subjects. Academic subjects were the least liked, especially by children in the foster care, birth parent and foster adoption groups.
- Teachers emerged as crucial for children liking or disliking particular subjects, and even as people important in the children's lives, in terms of support.
- The majority of children across placement types appeared to have formed friendships at school, despite a few children claiming to have none or only a few friends, and being bullied by others.

9   Parent/carer stress

Introduction

Parental psychological wellbeing has been demonstrated to have an impact on parenting style, and in turn, the child's behaviour (Morgan *et al*, 2002; Kuhn and Carter, 2006). Although all parents experience parenting stress to some extent, research evidence identifies children's challenging or externalising behaviour, characterised by problems such as non-compliance, inattention, impulsivity and aggression, as a strong predictor of parenting stress (Hastings and Brown, 2002; Morgan *et al*, 2002; Spratt *et al*, 2007). Abidin (1995) explained that the effect of life events that occur outside the parent–child relationship depletes parents' emotional resources and their ability to cope with their parenting role. In contrast, some studies have found that a strong sense of self-efficacy (i.e. an individual's belief in their own ability to successfully perform a task) in parenting acts as a buffer against adversity, helps parents promote children's wellbeing, and can reduce levels of parenting stress (Coleman and Karraker, 1997; Oyserman *et al*, 2004; Raikes and Thompson, 2005). In research literature, it is not yet clear which comes first, the child's challenging behaviour causing the parental stress, or the parental stress causing the child's challenging behaviour (Palacios and Sanchez-Sandoval, 2006).

Several studies have explored stress experienced by foster carers (Lipscombe *et al*, 2004; Schofield and Beek, 2005; Sinclair *et al*, 2005; Wilson, 2006; Morgan and Baron, 2011) and have found evidence of strain, anxiety and depression related to the stressors of the caregiving role. It is widely recognised that the strength of the carer and child relationship contributes to the success of a placement and to carer wellbeing and satisfaction (Hodges and Tizard, 1989; Morgan and Baron, 2011). Placements where carers have shown greater consistency, sensitivity and warmth, despite the child's challenging behaviour, are rated as successful in terms of the child's wellbeing, and in reducing the likelihood of placement breakdown (Quinton *et al*, 1998; Wilson, 2006). Lipscombe *et al* (2004) identified a number of factors which influence the critical point of stress for carers, such as the carer's own expectations of the child's behaviour, their ability to manage it, how they express their feelings about it, and whether the behaviour is harming other children in the household.

Kinship carers can have additional stressors (Whelan, 2003). Often, a child is placed in their care at a time of crisis and they have little or no time to prepare or to make the necessary lifestyle adjustments (Coakley *et al*, 2007). Other stressors include lack of financial resources; the ongoing, often fractious, relationship with the birth family; and its impact on the child, family members and family dynamics (ibid). Such stressors have been found to negatively impact on child and carer wellbeing, and have implications for placement disruptions (Whelan, 2009).

Adoption research has largely focused on psychological investigations of children, their behaviour needs and outcomes. However, despite adoptive parents and stress being an under-researched area, several studies have explored parental stress with adoptive parents who experience additional difficulties, such as parenting children with special needs, or who have had institutional experiences, or parents seeking advice (Bird *et al*, 2002; McGlone *et al*, 2002; Judge, 2004). In these studies, adopted children's behaviour is closely associated with their parents' stress levels, with parents of more troubled children experiencing higher levels of stress (McGlone *et al*, 2002; Judge, 2003). Additionally, the adoption of more than one child has been correlated with stress (Bird *et al*, 2002). Some studies have suggested that adopted children may be more troubled than their non-adoptive peers (Quinton *et al*, 1998), and consequently, it might be expected that adoptive parents would experience higher levels of stress than their non-adoptive counterparts (McGlone *et al*, 2002). Yet, in other studies, adoptive parents have reported low levels of stress (Bird *et al*, 2002; Judge, 2003, 2004; Ceballo *et al*, 2004; Palacious and Sanchez-Sandoval, 2006).

In this chapter, parenting stress within and between the five different care placements is examined, through the quantitative analysis of the Parenting Stress Index questionnaire (PSI/SF – Abidin, 1995), which was completed by the children's parents/carers.

Parenting stress index

The Parenting Stress Index (PSI/SF) (Abidin, 1995) measures for stress in the parent–child relationship system, and contains 36 items divided into four subscales: Defensive Responding, Parental Distress, Parent-Child Dysfunctional Interaction and Difficult Child (see Chapter 2 for more details). It provides a total stress score in addition to a score for each of the four sub-scales. The normal range of scores is within the 15th to the 80th percentiles. High scores are considered to be scores at or above the 85th percentile, and to be indicative of clinical need.

In this study, the measure was administered by a researcher. Each item was read out to the parent or carer who then indicated their preferred response, which could be any one of the following four responses: strongly agree, not sure, disagree or strongly disagree.

Parent/carers level of stress

In order to compare mean (total and scale) scores between the five placement groups, a one-way ANOVA was used. In order to identify significant mean differences between any of the five groups, post-hoc Tukey HSD tests were used. All tests were conducted at five per cent significance level. P-values <0.05 were considered statistically significant.

Total stress: On this dimension, higher scores are indicative of greater levels of parent/carer stress. One-way ANOVA indicated that there was no significant variation in mean scores between the five pathway groups on PSI Total Stress. Additionally, post-hoc Tukey HSD tests indicated that there were no significant mean differences between any of the five care pathway groups. However, it was found that there was a near significant variation in mean scores between the five placement groups (F = 2.11, p = .09), and there was a near significant difference between the adoption and birth parent groups (p = .08) (Figure 9.1).

Figure 9.1
PSI Total stress mean score by placement type

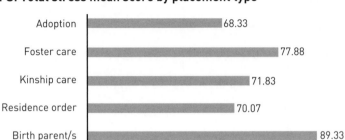

As shown in Table 9.1, high proportions of parents/carers across the five placement groups in the current study were experiencing clinical levels of parental stress. This is particularly evident for birth parents (50%), foster carers (44%) and kinship carers (33%). There were lower levels of parental stress experienced by parents/carers from the residence order (21%) and adoption (22%) groups.

Difficult child: On this dimension, higher scores indicate greater child-related problems for parents/carers. One-way ANOVA indicated that there was no significant variation in mean scores between the five pathway groups on PSI "difficult child". Post-hoc Tukey HSD tests indicated that there were no significant mean differences between any of the five care pathway groups. As shown in

Table 9.1
Percentage of parents/carers across the five different placement groups within the high/clinical range on PSI – Total stress

Placement group	% high range
Adoption (n = 18)	22
Foster care (n = 16)	44
Kinship care (n = 12)	33
Residence order (n = 14)	21
Birth parents (n = 12)	50

Figure 9.2
PSI – Difficult child mean scores by placement type

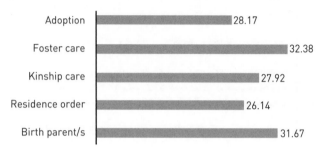

Adoption	28.17
Foster care	32.38
Kinship care	27.92
Residence order	26.14
Birth parent/s	31.67

Figure 9.2, differences in mean scores were minimal and were not found to be significant between any group. However, the highest mean scores were displayed by the foster care and birth parent groups.

As illustrated in Table 9.2, large proportions of parents/carers in this study perceived their child's difficulties to fall within the clinical high range. Both the birth parent and kinship carer groups had the same proportion of high scores (42%); as had the adoption and foster carer groups, although lower (33% and 31% respectively). In contrast, the proportion of residence order carers scoring above the clinical range (21%) was less than half that in the kinship carer and birth parent groups.

Parent–child dysfunctional interaction: On this dimension, higher scores are indicative of greater problems between parents/

Table 9.2
Percentage of parents/carers across the five different placement groups within the high/clinical range on PSI – Difficult child

Placement group	% high range
Adoption (n = 18)	33
Foster care (n = 16)	31
Kinship care (n = 12)	42
Residence order (n = 14)	21
Birth parents (n = 12)	42

Figure 9.3
PSI – Parent–child dysfunctional interaction mean scores by placement type

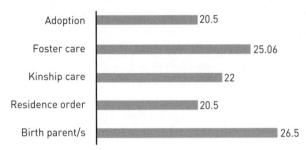

Adoption — 20.5
Foster care — 25.06
Kinship care — 22
Residence order — 20.5
Birth parent/s — 26.5

carers and their children. One-way ANOVA indicated that there was no significant variation in mean scores between the five pathway groups on PSI "parent–child dysfunctional interaction". Additionally, post-hoc Tukey HSD tests indicated that there were no significant mean differences between any of the five groups. Figure 9.3 indicates that the foster care and birth parent groups had the highest mean scores on this dimension.

Table 9.3 shows that the proportions of parents/carers scoring in the high/clinical range were not as large on this sub-scale of the PSI measure, in comparison to the previous subscales discussed, with three groups within the 10 per cent threshold level for a community

Table 9.3
Percentage of parents/carers across the five different placement groups within the high/clinical range on PSI – Parent–child dysfunctional interaction

Placement group	% high range
Adoption (n = 18)	6
Foster care (n = 16)	19
Kinship care (n = 12)	8
Residence order (n = 14)	7
Birth parents (n = 12)	33

sample. However, as might be expected, both the foster care group (19%), and the birth parent group (33%) in particular, had large percentages of children within the high/clinical range.

Parental distress: On this dimension, higher scores indicate that the parents/carers experience greater distress when caring for their children. One-way ANOVA indicated that there was significant variation in parental distress mean scores across the five placement groups (F = 5.11, p = .00). Furthermore, post-hoc Tukey HSD tests indicated that there were significant differences between the birth parent group and the adoption (p = .00), kinship care (p = .02) and

Figure 9.4
PSI – Parental distress mean scores by placement type

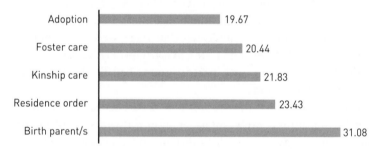

Table 9.4
Percentage of parents/carers across the five different placement groups within the high/clinical range on PSI – Parental distress

Placement group	% high range
Adoption (n = 18)	0
Foster care (n = 16)	6
Kinship care (n = 12)	8
Residence order (n = 14)	14
Birth parents (n = 12)	50

foster care (p = .00) groups. There was also a near significant difference between the birth parent and residence order groups (p = .07).

The scores across the care placements for parental distress were generally low apart from the birth parent group, with half the children in that group (50%) receiving scores in the high/clinical range (Table 9.4). In contrast, no adoptive parents had a clinically high parental distress score.

In terms of changes over time, of the 72 parents/carers interviewed for the current study in 2009/10 (Phase 3), 40 had been previously interviewed in 2004 (Phase 2). Therefore, it is worthwhile to compare parental stress scores over this period of time with this same group of parent/carers, to ascertain the extent of change (if any) in parental stress levels over time.

In Table 9.5, the total PSI scores are compared for this sub-sample of parents/carers between 2004 and 2009 for children in adoption and foster care. Interestingly, the majority of adoptive parents' parental stress scores increased (10 out of 17) in 2009, whilst the majority of foster carers' parental stress scores decreased (8 out of 13).

Table 9.5
Comparing PSI scores for children between 2004 and 2009

	No change	1–10 higher	>11 higher	1–10 lower	>11 lower
Adopted (n = 17)	1	2	8	4	2
Foster care (n = 13)	0	2	3	2	6

Summary of key findings

- Large proportions of parents/carers were experiencing clinical levels of parental stress across the five placement groups. Thus, half of the birth parent group (50%), followed closely by the foster care group (44%), a third of the kinship care group (33%) and just over a fifth of the residence order (22%) and adoption (21%) groups experienced clinical levels of parental stress. There was no statistically significant variation across these five placement groups, although there was a near significant difference between the birth parent and adoption groups.

- The birth parent group scored higher clinical levels than the other placement groups across all the PSI domains (although it shared joint highest place with the kinship care group in the child difficulty domain). On the parental distress domain, there were significant differences between the birth parent group and the adoption, kinship care and foster care groups, and a near significant difference with the residence order group. This raises particular concerns regarding the high level of parental distress being experienced by birth parents.

- The foster care group was the second highest to score clinical levels of parental stress. They had the second highest proportion of parents/carers scoring high in the parent–child dysfunctional interaction domain, but had the second lowest percentage in the parental distress and child difficulty domain.

- The kinship care group was the third highest among the placement groups to score clinical levels of parental stress. Although this group scored similarly with birth parents in the child difficulty domain, its percentages of high scores in the other domains of parent–child dysfunctional interaction and parental distress domains were low at eight per cent, and were the third lowest across the groups.

- The residence order group had the second lowest clinical levels of parental stress. Although this group had the second largest proportion of parents/carers scoring high in the parental distress domain, it had the lowest proportion of all groups in the child difficulty domain, and second lowest in the parent–child dysfunctional interaction domain.

- The adoption group scored the lowest clinical levels of parental stress across the five placement groups. Despite this group scoring second highest in the child difficulty domain, it scored lowest in the parent–child dysfunctional domain. The adoption group did not score clinically high on the parental distress domain, and therefore was the only group to experience normal levels of parental distress.

- There were changes in the levels of parental stress in the sub-sample of those parents/carers from the adoption and foster carer groups from the period of 2004 to 2009. Over this period, the majority of adoptive parents' parental stress increased, whilst the majority of foster carers' parental stress decreased.

10 Contact with birth families

Introduction

The issue of contact with the birth family for children in foster care and adoption has been a focus of debate within the research literature for the last 20 years, driven by a dramatic shift in policy and practice towards increased contact in the UK, and in other countries, such as the USA (Grotevant, 2000), Sweden (Andersson, 1999), Australia (Humphreys and Kiraly, 2011) and Spain (del Valle *et al*, 2009; Palacios and Jiménez, 2009). The current legal framework in the UK (Children Act 1989, Children (NI) Order 1995) actively promotes contact with birth families, especially for children in care. In the last couple of decades, that has led to an increase in contact and its frequency for children in care (Cleaver, 2000), and to the promotion of a more open approach to adoption.

However, it is a controversial and complex issue, in that research findings have highlighted both the benefits of contact for enhancing children's sense of identity and continuity (Masson, 1997; Cleaver, 2000), but also the difficulties, such as potentially placing children at risk of physical/sexual abuse; triggering "loyalty conflicts" for children; deterioration of children's emotional wellbeing and conduct (Leathers, 2003; Selwyn, 2004; Sinclair *et al*, 2004, 2005; Moyers *et al*, 2006); and negative consequences for the stability of placements (Wilson *et al*, 2000; Macaskill, 2002; Sinclair *et al*, 2005; Loxterkamp, 2009). In fact, recent research evidence indicates that contact with birth family members can have both positive and negative outcomes for children in the care system, depending on a range of interacting factors. In other words, contact cannot be governed by a simple rule of thumb, or a one size-fits-all approach (Wilson and Sinclair, 2004).

This chapter focuses on contact with birth family members and previous carers, through a detailed examination of the level and quality of contact arrangements; the attitudes of the parents/carers in relation to contact; and children's feelings towards their birth family and contact with them. This information was extracted from the interviews with both the children and the parents/carers in the study. Comparisons are made in relation to the quality and type of contact arrangements that the children have within and between the five different placement types.

Contact: a definition

Contact, because of its physical connotation, creates the idea of a mutual experience between parents and children, including the possibility of physical care and intimacy as well as emotional relatedness. (Lyndsey, 1995, p.36)

Since the implementation of the Children Act 1989, the concept of "access" has gradually been replaced by the term "contact" among professionals in the field, underlining a shift in attitude from the parental right to see the child to the acknowledged right and need of children to see their parents (Lyndsey, 1995). This is specified in the 1989 United Nations Convention on the Rights of the Child, with Article 9 stating that every child who is separated from one/both parent/s has the right to stay in contact with both parents, unless this could potentially harm them.

Contact has been broadly defined to include different types of direct and indirect communication between a child and a range of people important in the child's life, or those who have a relationship with him/her, i.e. birth parents, siblings, grandparents and other relatives, previous foster carers, etc. (Quinton *et al*, 1997). "Direct" contact mainly involves face-to-face meetings, which can be supervised (or not) by social workers, foster carers or other professionals, whereas "indirect" contact includes letters, phone calls, messages passed by third parties, e-mails, etc. While children in foster, kinship and residential care are more likely to experience both direct and indirect contact, indirect contact – especially letterbox contact – is still the main form of contact for adopted children (McSherry *et al*, 2008; Sen and Broadhurst, 2011).

The frequency of contact arrangements varies widely in the different types of placements. For the current study, a categorisation was adapted from Brown and Moloney's (2002) work. *No contact* (categorised as "no access" by Brown and Moloney) refers to those cases where children do not have contact visits. *Regular and frequent contact* means that visits take place on a regular basis, and quite frequently (between once or twice a week to once a month). In the third category, *regular but infrequent contact* visits also happen regularly, but not as frequently (between one to six times a year). In the final category, *irregular contact* (categorised as "infrequent" by Brown and Moloney), children are uncertain when to expect visits, and visits tend to occur about once a year or less.

Contact arrangements

The majority of the children interviewed in the current study (n = 46; 62%) had some form of face-to-face contact with at least one birth relative, mostly a sibling or parent. The percentage was higher in the foster (93%) and kinship care (75%) groups, than in the residence order (67%), birth parent (50%) and adoption (44%) groups. In terms of the adoption group itself, a much higher proportion of children in the foster adoption group had face-to-face contact with at least one relative than those in the stranger adoption group (66% vs. 22%).

In total, 31 children (47%) had face-to-face contact with at least one parent, with 22 having contact with just one (16 with the mother, and 6 with the father), and nine having contact with both parents. Most of the children who had no face-to-face contact with birth parents were in the residence order (n = 8), stranger adoption (n = 7), foster adoption (n = 7), and kinship care (n = 6) groups. In addition, the majority of children living with one birth parent (n = 6) did not maintain contact with the non-domicile parent, although in two cases, impromptu contact with this parent occurred when, for example, the child was visiting relatives. In two other cases, there had been contact in the past, but it had diminished and eventually stopped over time.

Reasons impeding or preventing contact with birth parents for

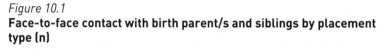

Figure 10.1
Face-to-face contact with birth parent/s and siblings by placement type (n)

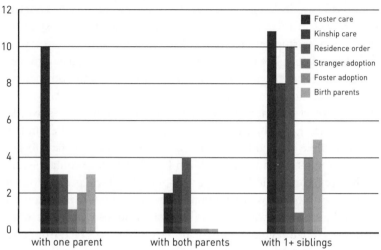

children in all placement groups were mentioned, and included stated disinterest on the part of the birth parent/s; birth parents' mental illness or alcoholism; birth parents' lack of attendance; and child's refusal to have contact.

Most children in foster care, kinship care and on residence order had face-to-face contact with at least one separated sibling (69%, n = 29), whereas this was only the case for five (out of 18) adopted children, as shown in Figure 10.1. It can also be seen that five children living with their birth parent/s also had contact with their separated siblings. Some of the children who had no contact with siblings either did not have any (n = 7), or they were already living with them (n = 6). Thirteen children had contact with their grandparents (six in foster care, three foster adoption, two kinship care, and two on residence order). Three children were not included in these descriptions of current contact arrangements, as their placements had recently broken down at the time of interview, and the carers were not aware of their current level of contact with the birth family.

The frequency of contact also varied within and between placement types (Figures 10.2 and 10.3). *Regular and frequent contact* with birth parents was particularly common in kinship care, where children saw their birth parents as often as every day, for a few minutes or hours, or even stayed in their house for the entire weekend. The rest of the children in kinship care had no contact; in three of these cases, visits had stopped, and in two of these, the children were refusing to have contact anymore. *Regular but infrequent contact*, on the other hand, was more common for children in foster care, often up to six times a year. The most common arrangement for children on residence order was *no contact*, and in six of these cases, regular visits had eventually stopped, while in the other two, there had never been any face-to-face contact. Only three adopted children had face-to-face contact with a birth parent: one child in stranger adoption had *regular and frequent contact*; and two in foster adoption had *regular but infrequent contact*. The children living with one birth parent who also saw their other birth parent had regular and frequent face-to-face contact, from once a month to four times a week.

A considerable number of children had regular and frequent contact with their birth siblings. Regular but infrequent contact with siblings was particularly common among children in foster care.

The type of contact differed between placement groups. Thus, supervised contact either by social workers and sometimes by parents/carers occurred mostly in foster care (n = 9), but it was barely the case for children in kinship care (n = 1) or on residence order (n = 1). However, sometimes, parents/carers were present when the birth family visited the child, often in the carer's home or out in public places. For many children in kinship care (n = 6) and on residence order (n = 7), contact was unsupervised, while that was the case for only four children in foster care. In adoptive placements, face-to-face contact was generally arranged informally between the adoptive and birth parents themselves, and usually the adoptive parents were present when the birth family visited, or the adoptive family together visited the birth family.

In total, 24 children had some form of indirect contact, with only 14 children having no form of contact at all (6 in stranger adoption,

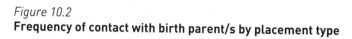

Figure 10.2
Frequency of contact with birth parent/s by placement type

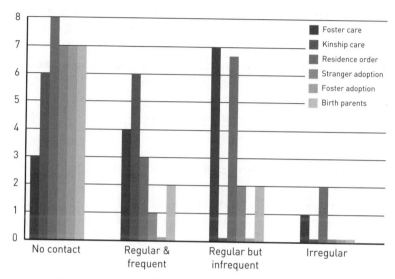

Figure 10.3
Frequency of contact with sibling/s by placement type

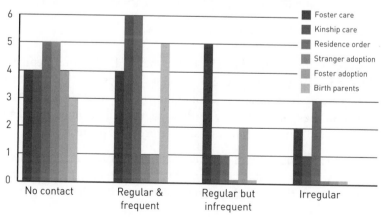

4 with birth parent/s, 2 in kinship care, 1 on residence order, and 1 in foster adoption).

- 13 children had telephone contact, i.e. texts and phone calls (5 in foster care, 1 in kinship care, 3 on residence order, 1 in stranger adoption, 2 in foster adoption, and 1 with birth parent/s);
- 14 children had post-box contact, i.e. letters, photographs, seasonal cards and presents (2 in foster care, 4 in kinship care, 3 on residence order, 3 in foster adoption, and 2 in stranger adoption); and/or
- Two children had digital contact, i.e. Skype, e-mails, social networking sites (1 in kinship care and 1 on residence order).

This contact was with birth mothers (n = 11), birth fathers (n = 7), siblings (n = 12), and other family members (n = 1). In the majority of cases, texting occurred with siblings, while telephone calls tended to happen with birth parents. Sometimes, that type of contact complemented face-to-face visits, as was the case for Daniel, living with foster carers:

> Researcher (R): *And do you think about your brothers much, are you in contact with them all?*
>
> Daniel (D): *Yeah, I get to see them in some contact as well.*
>
> R: *Okay, and would you text them or anything outside of it?*
>
> D: *Yeah, I would text my two big brothers.*

However, this was often the only contact they had with some members of the birth family. That was also the case for most post-box contact arrangements. For instance, Caoimghin, Roisin and Greg received post from their birth father, and that was the only contact they had with him, as their grandfather (residence order) explained:

> He [birth father] sends the kids birthday cards, he sends them money in the cards, he keeps that contact with them but he doesn't see them, so they don't have any contact that way.

In many adoptive placements, particularly foster adoption, face-to-face contact with birth parents had stopped some years previously, and had been replaced by post-box contact arrangements. In some of these placements and other adoptive placements, post-box contact arrangements had also stopped, and the child was not having any form of contact. That was the case for John (foster adoption) who had had monthly face-to-face contact with his birth parents before the adoption went through. His adoptive mother explained how post-box contact had also stopped:

> We would have sent maybe a letter and a photograph and they sent a letter back and they used to send presents at Christmas and birthdays ... but they stopped all that. They're back on the drink again so they stopped that.

In Trevor's case (foster care), one of his birth sisters, who had a different father, refused to have any more face-to-face contact with him because it affected her negatively, but agreed to have telephone contact instead, as his foster mother explained:

> But she did have one contact and then after that I think she tried to commit suicide because she'd seen the daddy in Trevor, Trevor was too much like his father ... So she only agreed that she could text and he could text her on the phone, but she didn't want to see him again.

Children's reactions to contact

Children's reactions to contact did not seem to differ depending on placement type. They responded differently to contact with birth family members, and these reactions also changed with time, as they grew older and contact arrangements were modified. Parents/carers often reported negative effects of contact, when the children were younger, including being really upset, frightened, even screaming and crying, when being "forced to go" (n = 20). This was mostly the case for children on residence order (n = 7), in foster care (n = 6), and in kinship care (n = 4). For instance, Conall's carer explained his upsetting experience of contact before the residence order came through:

> When he was young before the residence order . . . he didn't want to go, he didn't understand and then social workers would come here, particularly one, and she was just adamant he was going and there was no in between and she would make him go and he'd leave here screaming and crying and actually one time he put his fist through the window . . . Since the residence order, he knows now he's staying here and that's it.

In these cases, as expressed in the previous quote, the situation had improved, as a result of modifying the contact arrangements (e.g. from being in a family centre to being activity-based in the community) (n = 4: two in foster care and two on residence order); stopping contact altogether, thus children being listened to and not "forced" to go (n = 6); and/or the child being able to understand the purpose of contact and having fully settled into their placement (n = 4). As an example of improving children's experiences of contact by modifying the arrangements, Pol's foster mother gave the following account:

> But things seem to be going well this last year or so, better than it had been, so I mean the kids come back and I don't have any problems now. Whereas at the beginning there was a lot of problems with behaviour and different things, but that has all settled down and things have been going well this past year because they have been doing more family orientated things. Whereas before they were in a Family Centre and the kids would be bored, but now that they are doing things together, maybe going bowling or something, wee picnics and things like that to make it a wee bit more interesting for them.

On the other hand, Orlaith's kinship carer explained how she was not having any more contact as she was refusing to go:

> Well, she doesn't like going to see her mother, because in the past her mother has been aggressive at visits and Orlaith would

have got very frightened at that. She went along to the visits just to please her mum, but now it has got to the stage where she is refusing to go, you know, she totally does not want to go . . . and she refuses, she refuses and I wouldn't let anybody force her to go.

According to her carer, Kirsten (residence order) was feeling more secure in her placement, and contact had improved as a result of that:

I think she feels now that she can just say whatever and she is listened to and she knows when she comes back to us if there is a problem, we'll sort it the best we can or get advice on it.

In fact, a number of residence order carers, like Kirsten's carer, emphasised the importance of the order in enabling their child's and their own preferences/needs to take precedence. For example, both Ryan and Sarah's carers commented on the benefit of the residence order in enabling the children to end contact with their birth parents, as prior to its granting, contact was largely determined by the conditions imposed by Social Services and/or the wishes of the birth parents. Kirsten's carer commented that at times she did not want to see her birth mother; previously she would have been 'forced, very much', something that her carer considered to be fundamentally wrong. However, the granting of the residence order had enabled Kirsten to be able to choose whether or not she went, which was something that her carer welcomed.

It was not just the carers who explained how situations had improved, but sometimes children, like Sue (in foster care), were able to give us their own perspectives on what contact was like, and what had happened for things to get better for them:

Researcher (R): *What part of your past are you feeling sad about, do you think?*

Sue (S): *When I used to see my mummy and daddy and all, just.*

R: *And what is it about seeing your mum and dad that makes you feel sad?*

S: *They used to argue all the time. They used to say stuff about each other all the time.*

R: *Right, would that have been in front of you?*

S: *Aye.*

R: *Just during the visits?*

S: *Aye.*

R: *Right, and that was difficult. And what about now with visits?*

S: *It's alright. I only see my mummy.*

R: *You only see your mummy, so there's none of that going on?*

S: *No.*

R: *Ok. And do your visits go okay?*

S: *Aye.*

Sometimes, children were coping with sad memories, painful stories and feelings of abandonment, as well as with their parents' mental illnesses, their family history of domestic violence, offending, or alcohol abuse. For example, Jonny's carer (residence order) reflected on how he was dealing with his mother's alcohol abuse:

She (birth mother) phoned here last Friday night and Jonny handed the phone to me, 'Here ma, I don't want to speak to her, she's drunk' ... So he's beginning, you know, to realise that and he knows when she's on the phone and that she's drunk he won't talk to her. Now if she rings and she's sober ... he will talk to her and I suppose it's good, you know, we don't stop him.

As explained by her kinship carers, Marie was dealing with her family's domestic violence:

She said that to me, she says, 'I'm looking to see if my daddy's hitting my mummy or anything'... she'll always scan [birth mother] to see if there's any marks on her or bruises.

In fact, some children expressed their feelings, when coping with these types of scenarios, often wishing particularly for their parents to stop drinking, as exemplified by Anna and Patrick's (both in foster care) comments below:

Anna (A): *[I wish] For my mummy and daddy would stop drinking.*

Researcher (R): *Okay, and would they still be drinking a lot?*

A: *I don't know.*

R: *Would you think about them drinking?*

A: *No.*

R: *What about when you're going to contact, would you think about them much?*

A: *Yeah. I can smell drink off their breath and all and smoke.*

R: *What does that make you feel like?*

A: *Sad. Well it's not sad because I know they have a problem, so they can't help it.*

Patrick (P): *Sometimes she [birth mother] does stuff like I don't like her doing.*

Researcher (R): *Whenever you're visiting?*

P: *Aye, she always does it.*

R: *Does she? What type of thing?*

P: *Drinks and smokes and all.*

R: *Drinks and smokes, and would you prefer if she didn't do that?*

P: *Aye.*

Annie was living with her paternal grandmother, and both her parents were mentally ill. Her birth mother had tried to stab her during a contact visit, and after that, contact had stopped. However, she still visited her birth father in an institution, and was seeking to understand the issues around his mental illness, as stated by her grandmother:

> We go up to see [birth father] every fortnight, that's her daddy. And she will say to me, 'Why is my daddy sitting talking to himself?' you know and I'll say, 'That is part of the illness Annie, it's just part of the illness', but we don't spend long with him. We would spend . . . it works out that it suits her daddy, about 10 minutes, and it suits Annie. This 10 minutes every fortnight just absolutely suits him because I notice her understanding him more, not letting it go on like, say, 20 minutes would be too long or half an hour would be far too much, and too much for her to watch or see. See this is just at levelling things out; it is actually working out well, where she doesn't see her mummy. Her mummy doesn't want to see her, and she doesn't want to see her mummy after the episode with the knife.

According to some carers, contact with siblings could have a positive effect on children, since they were able to help them deal with these difficult memories and/or feelings of abandonment, as stated by David's kinship carer:

> But you know, he [birth brother] will just say, 'Well, David, she treats us the same, you're not the only one that she treats that way, she treats all of us the same,' making him realise it's not just him.

A few children (n = 4) were still experiencing mild negative reactions to contact, noticeable especially when they returned home, being clingy, withdrawn, or cheekier, as described by Jo's carer (residence order):

> The only time [after contact], when he's down with his natural mum, he'll not speak, you know, he'll be a wee bit cheekier.

Jo was one of the two children on residence order who received a low security of attachment to carers on the IPPA–R.

Similarly, Kirsten (residence order) was still feeling insecure around contact, as reflected by her carer:

> *Kirsten would go to visit her natural mum once every two months and she is just waiting at the window for us coming back. And at that stage she would be clingy and huggy more than usual. You know, I think it is a case of 'are you coming back for me?', even when you say to her, you know, I will be back at five o'clock or whatever, she is still waiting at that window for you coming back.*

Sometimes children were disappointed, angry or saddened by birth parents failing to turn up or leaving early, as Sue's foster mother claimed:

> *She sees the sisters quite often, and the mother just doesn't show up half the time for the visits and, I don't know . . . When she comes back, she's a little moody and you've got to give her her space for a while, you know, because if she goes to a visit and her mother just doesn't show up, she's devastated.*

According to his foster mother, Jack felt angry when his birth mother showed little interest in having contact with him and his siblings:

> *He went to see the rest of the siblings last Wednesday and he came back and mum only stayed something like half an hour, and she left, the excuse was that she had an appointment with the doctor. So he was a bit angry about that and he just came back and he said, 'Granny, you are my true Mum' . . . ach, he was really angry when he came back.*

On a few occasions, birth parents would interfere in the child's contact with other birth family members. For instance, in Trevor's case (foster care), his birth mother, who did not want to have contact with him but was living with his sister, was creating some trouble in relation to this contact.

He was telling me that [birth sister] said to him yesterday that the mum said that when they were younger that Trevor was very jealous of [sister] and he used to pull her hair and stuff . . . she's maybe just trying . . . now that there's contact going that she's only trying to put [sister] against Trevor.

A few children, like Patrick (foster care) and Paul (stranger adoption) (see quotes below), were described as not caring or worrying about contact, since they were not that close to their birth families, or because they were older and were not as disappointed as they used to be when it did not happen:

He doesn't care, he doesn't care, he just comes in and it's over. That's it for another time. He doesn't worry about it.

He can be sometimes upset if he goes for the contact and it doesn't happen . . . we keep reminding him that it's his mother that he is going to see and that she has problems and she can't help it. There are times when I think it doesn't really bother him one way or the other, sort of. Maybe it is just his age at the minute . . . I don't know.

However, many children (n = 14), especially in foster care and on residence order, enjoyed contact and had a very positive relationship with their birth family, as reflected by Connor's foster mother, and by Eoghan (kinship care) and Daniel (foster care) respectively:

R: *And how do you think contact affects him? Does it affect him in any way?*

Connor's foster mother: *Not really, they would get to see their mum, very affectionate towards her. As I said, hugs and that . . . so, they seem happy. They are happy to see her, yet during . . . the rest of the week or fortnight it's not mentioned. And I would say, you know, it is your mum's visit on Wednesday, okay . . . that's good.*

Eoghan: *Well, I like it up here but I don't really like it down there, but I like going down and seeing my mum.*

Researcher (R): *And what makes contact visits good?*

Daniel (D): *Just seeing them.*

R: *And is it different living in foster care and then going to see your mum and dad?*

D: *No.*

R: *Or is it just something you just get used to?*

D: *It is, yeah.*

R: *Is it, yeah? And do you look forward to those visits?*

D: *Yeah.*

R: *Yeah, and what do you think about them in general?*

D: *They are good.*

Despite enjoying the visits, Daniel was still dealing with complex feelings, and explained how sometimes he felt a bit sad after contact:

Daniel (D): [Draws a sad face L and writes 'sad'] *[I feel] Sad.*

Researcher (R): *Okay. Can you say why then?*

[Writes 'I don't like thinking of it']

R: *Okay, are there things you don't like thinking about?*

D: *Why I am in foster care and all.*

R: *Okay, and would you think about that much?*

D: *Sometimes, not all the time.*

R: *And is there anything that can make that feel a bit better?*

D: *Not thinking about it.*

R: *Is it hard sometimes not to think about it?*

D: *Yeah, like when you have just came from a visit with your mammy and daddy.*

R: *And what kind of things would that make you feel like?*

D: *Sad.*

R: *Do you feel that way before you go for the visit or is it just after?*

D: *No, it's just after.*

R: *What way does it affect you then when you come back from the visit and feel a bit sad?*

D: *Like grumpy and don't talk.*

Children's wishes and feelings, and the concept of ambiguous loss

The concept of ambiguous loss (Boss, 1980) has been found to be useful in making sense of the experiences of foster children (Lee and Whiting, 2007). It refers to three types of loss: family members being physically present but psychologically absent; physically absent but psychologically present; and in transition, in terms of these positions not being permanent (ibid). With regards to the experiences of contact with the birth families, these types of circumstances seemed to reflect the experiences of some of the children in the current study, across all five placement types.

In some instances (see Table 10.1), the birth parents were physically absent from the lives of the children, but psychologically present, in that they remained in their thoughts. In other words, although some of the children did not see their birth parents, they still considered them to be part of their family (n = 14). For example, Luke's mother had died, so she was physically absent, but she remained in his thoughts. Luke was living with his grandmother (residence order) and he still very much saw his deceased mother as

Table 10.1
Ambiguous loss of birth parents

	No contact		Contact	
	Part of family	*Not part of family*	*Part of family*	*Not part of family*
Foster care	4	3	6	2
Kinship care	2	3	5	0
Residence order	4	4	5	1
Foster adoption	2	5	1	1
Stranger adoption	2	6	1	0
Living with 1 birth parent	0	2	6	0
Total	**14**	**23**	**24**	**4**
	Physically absent but psychologically present		Physically present but psychologically absent	

part of his family, and wished her back. Similarly, Claire and Morgan, two sisters who were adopted (stranger adoption) together, did not have any contact with their birth parents, as it was a closed adoption, but both of them considered their birth parents as part of their family:

Claire (C): *I feel sad because I miss them.*

Researcher: *So when you think about your past, you feel sad because you miss them? And who would them be?*

C: Uhm . . . *[birth mother] and [birth father].*

At times, the parent/carer seemed totally unaware of the children's feelings towards their physically absent birth parents. Bridget's adoptive parents (foster adoption) seemed completely oblivious of the fact that she considered her birth parents to be part of her family, to be really close to her, and that she was curious about them:

Researcher (R): *So, if you had to pick somewhere you were going to live when you were 16 or 17, it wouldn't be anywhere but just with your friend, just living with your friend* [child had initially indicated she would like to live with friends]?

Bridget (B): *Well, I might go and live with my birth parents.*

R: *Your birth parents? You might like to live with them? Why do you think you would want to live with them?*

B: *Because I've never seen them before and I don't know anything about them.*

R: *So you'd like to find out a bit about them, would you?*

B: *Mmm* [assenting noise].

In fact, there was post-box contact with Bridget's birth father, but Bridget did not know this, as her adoptive parents did not tell her, because they believed she was "not interested":

Adoptive mother (AM): *Her father will send cards to Social Services and they send them on.*

Researcher (R): *Would that be regularly?*

AM: *Birthday and Christmas.*

R: *Right. And how does she respond to that?*

AM: *We haven't given them to her yet. Because she's not really ... she's not interested. We have them all for her, but he does send, to my mind, inappropriate cards. Like it'll be 'Happy birthday darling daughter'.*

R: *And would she know that you receive them, but that you haven't given them to her?*

AM: *No, I don't think she does, because he sent gifts and things through too in the early days. So they're all there for her when she wants to talk about him. I mean she can have them all but as I say, anytime we try to broach it, she just doesn't want to know.*

A few children, however, had contact with one or both birth parent/s but they were not mentioned as being part of their family. Thus, they were physically present at contact visits, but psychologically absent from their lives.

Most of the children interviewed either perceived the birth parent/s that they had contact with as part of their family, or had no contact with one or both of them, and did not regard them as family (Table 10.1). Some of the children who had no contact with birth parent/s expressed that it was their choice, and conveyed feelings of sadness, fear and anger towards them. They had to make sense of very painful personal stories that were either part of their own memories or told by somebody else, as Annie (kinship care), Sarah (residence order), and Martin (foster care) told the researchers:

Annie (A): *No, I haven't seen [birth mother] since I was two because she smashed a glass bottle and started hitting my nanny.*

Researcher (R): *Oh, did she? So you're not allowed to see her, okay.*

A: *But it's my choice if I wanted to see her.*

R: *Oh, was it your choice? And what did you decide?*

A: *No.*

Sarah (S): *Yeah, it's kind of bad, because uhm ... my dad and my mum got into the car and my dad got me in the car seat, and threw me in the back and didn't put the seat belt on me, and flew around the town speeding. And I went everywhere.*

Researcher: *And what do you think about it? Do you ever think about it? Do you ever think about him?*

S: *He gives me nightmares ... I think to [birth father], I'm his daughter, but I'm not actually. I think he thinks that ... but I'm not part of his life anymore.*

Martin (M): *[I feel] annoyed . . . well, because it's just I wish my mum, my real mum did care about me and I feel good and glad that I'm up here now and I'm getting looked after better than I was . . . it's better up here and I get into less trouble.*

Researcher: *Do you have memories of how it was, or do people tell you what it was like?*

M: *Yeah, my sister said that . . . she didn't even feed me, she was that drunk, and her and [other sibling] had to feed me biscuits in my cot because my mum was drunk, and she didn't care.*

However, those who had face-to-face contact, especially if it was regular and frequent, had much more positive views of their birth parent/s and, in a few cases, longed for more contact or even to move back to live with them. Although these children did not live with their birth parents, they were psychologically present in their lives, as part of their family. For instance, Pol (foster care), Jo (residence order), Marie (kinship care), and Justin (foster adoption) had contact with their birth parents, and expressed their feelings about them:

Researcher: *And why do you think [foster mum] and [birth mum] are the most important people to you?*

Pol: *Because they are nice.*

Jo (J): *My birth mum.* [Circles "Birth Mother" in the family section of the "me-book"

Researcher: *Is she part of your family?*

J: *Yeah, she's always there for me, so she is.*

Researcher (R): *What would you wish for your family if you had a wish for them?*

Marie (M): *Uhm, I don't know, it would either be that they didn't die or they all wised up.*

R: *What do you mean wise up?*

M: *Like my mummy and daddy stopped drinking and they got me back and all and they would have a better life.*

Researcher (R): *So, if you want to just write in who you would like to live with when you are older.*

Justin (J): *Birth parent* [Writes "birth parents"].

R: *So you would like to live with your birth dad? Because your birth mum, she's passed on, hasn't she?*

J: *Yeah, my birth parents.*

R: *So why would that be?*

J: *Uhm, I just want to get to know them a bit better.*

It is also interesting to note that Jo received a low security of attachment to his carers on the IPPA–R, which might suggest, on the basis of the quote above, that his primary attachment remained with his birth parents, rather than his current carers. For Rebecca, who was living with her uncle (kinship care), the reason why she wanted to go back to live with her birth mother was more about her wish to be the same as her friends in school, rather than because of her feelings towards her:

Researcher (R): *And what about where you live now, anything you would wish for?*

Rebecca (RE): [Writes "To live back with my mummy"]

R: *Okay, to be back with your mummy. Why would you wish that?*

RE: *Because it's hard in school.*

R: *Because it's hard in school because of girls not understanding or not knowing [about you being in care]?*

RE: *They ask why and all.*

Siblings were considered part of the family by the majority of children whose siblings were not living with them (see Table 10.2). For many, like Rebecca (kinship care), they were a big part of their lives:

Table 10.2
Ambiguous loss of siblings

	No contact		Contact	
	Part of family	*Not part of family*	*Part of family*	*Not part of family*
Foster care	2	3	10	2
Kinship care	2	–	7	1
Residence order	1	1	8	–
Foster adoption	2	–	2	1
Stranger adoption	–	–	1	–
Living with 1 birth parent	1	–	5	–
Total	**8**	**4**	**33**	**4**

Physically absent but psychologically present

Physically present but psychologically absent

Rebecca (RE): *I lived with my brother for ten years as well.*

Researcher (R): *You lived with your brother?*

RE: *Nine years, ten years, I don't know. Nine years anyway.*

R: *I'm sure he enjoys seeing you too.*

RE: *Aye, it's like a completely different person whenever I see him.*

R: *In what way?*

RE: *Because he would be, like, getting into mischief and stuff, but then whenever he would see us he would just be a completely different person.*

R: *What way would he be when he sees you?*

RE: *He is, like, all happy and all.*

However, differences between siblings were often pointed out, with some siblings being considered closer than others, as expressed by Marie (kinship care) and Anna (foster care):

Researcher: *So he [brother] would be the most important to you, okay, so just write it there, and why would he be the most important to you?*

Marie: [Writes "Brother"] *Because, I don't know, I can trust him and rely on him, and he is always there for me, whenever he is not in jail.*

Anna (A): *Put [brother 1] and [brother 2] in "1" [highest level of closeness represented in the "me-book"] and [brother 3] and [brother 4] in the other [lower level of closeness] because I haven't really seen [brother 3] or [brother 4].*

Researcher (R): *Okay, so [brother 3] would be in "2"?*

A: *Mmm* (assenting noise).

R: *Okay, and what about your two sisters?*

A: *Number 1.*

R: *Both of them? And why would they be in number 1 then?*

A: *Because we would fight and all but like have a laugh together and they would do everything, like, for me. If I ask them to do something for me, they would do it.*

Similarly, Amy (foster adoption) felt closer to her adoptive siblings (with whom she lived) than her birth siblings, who she only saw a few times a year:

Amy (A): [writes "sisters" and sticks it between circle 1 and circle 2]

Researcher: *Would they all be as important?*

A: *[Sister 1] and [Sister 2] would be, .'cos [Sister 3] I don't see her much.*

R: *So, [Sister 1] and [Sister 2] would be your real sisters?*

A: *No, they're adopted ones.*

Some children, like Ben (foster care) and Laura (foster adoption), did not see some birth siblings, but they still considered them to be part of their family. Thus, these siblings were physically absent, but psychologically present in the children's lives. These children were often disappointed, upset, and longing to see these siblings:

Researcher: *How often would you see them?*

Ben (B): *It used to be that I got to see them like once every two months, but that went off.*

R: *Has that stopped for a good while?*

B: *Over a year.*

R: *Right. Are you happy enough with that stopping?*

B: *No.*

R: *You're not. So you'd like to see them again, would you?*

B: *Aye (assenting).*

Researcher: *Can you think of anything that could make your life even better?*

Laura: *I have a wee sister and she's seven and I never see her . . . I seen her whenever she was four.*

Other children, like Mary (foster care) and Caomhan (living with birth mother), would have liked to see their siblings more often than they did, or wished to live with them:

Mary (M): [In the "me-book" writes "see my family more" as a wish for her family]

Researcher (R): *See your family more . . . would that be your family in [local city]?*

M: *In both. Because I used to get to see my family, my birth family, once a month, and now I only see them twice a year.*

R: *And you would like to see them more often?*

M: *Yeah.*

R: *Would that be your brothers and sisters?*

M: *Yeah.*

Researcher: *If you had a wish for your family, what would you wish for your family?*

Caomhan: *I wish that we could all live together with my wee sister* [Writes 'I wish my wee sister would be living with us'].

Thus, the children in this study were dealing with different kinds of losses, and their relationships with family members were diverse. Some children wished to see particular family members more; some were happy with the level of contact; some felt sad, frightened, or angry about their past and their birth families. These differences were evident across all the different placement groups.

Parent/carer perspectives on contact and its effects on them

Across the placement groups, the majority of carers/parents, whose children had face-to-face contact with the birth family, reported having no problems regarding contact (n = 22; 9 foster carers, 5 foster adopters, and 4 with residence order), and a few, like Connor's foster mother, even mentioned having a good relationship with one or both birth parents:

Researcher: *And how do you find contact yourself?*

Connor's foster mother: *[I find contact] Fine, fine. I would have a relationship with [birth mother]. You know, I would know her well . . . I would chat away to her just as I would chat to you and you know, she would talk and ask me how they were and if there were any problems.*

Similarly, Danny's adoptive mother (foster adoption) and Charlie's adoptive father (stranger adoption), considered contact to be a "family thing":

Researcher (R): *Okay, so how's that contact arranged?*

Danny's adoptive mother (DAM): *We just phone each other and say, you know, will we do something on Saturday or Sunday or whatever, and that's it . . . I'm sitting here doing nothing so I just think, I must give Danny's birth granny a wee ring and you know, she's very good, you know, Danny calls her granny as well as [own daughter], you know and she's very, very good to them as well. You know, they're a part of contact.*

R: *So you all go together?*

DAM: *We all go together, it's very much a family thing.*

R: *And so what sort of things do you do?*

DAM: *Well, our last one was up at the [entertainment centre], we did the golf up there and then went over to ten-pin bowling.*

Researcher: *What about the contact with the brothers, how do you find it?*

Charlie's adoptive father: *Very good, we're fond of the brothers too . . . they seem pretty much part of the family, you know.*

However, a few carers reported tensions in the relationship with birth parents (n = 7). These were mostly kinship carers (n = 5). For instance, Maggie's grandparents were hurt because Maggie's birth mother wanted Maggie back, despite the fact that it was the grandparent who suggested that Maggie should have more contact with her. They were worried because although the contact was supposed to be supervised, there were times when it was not, and Maggie would come back very quiet and not talk about what happened. They were concerned that the birth mother was 'filling her head with white lies'. Similarly, Jo's carer (residence order) had a difficult relationship with his birth mother:

> It was hard sometimes, it was, just listening to what's coming out of her mouth and that there you know ... but she had to be put in her place a couple of times but she's the sort of girl, you know, and she thinks if she just shouts at you and runs off with her mouth, you know, you'll be feared [afraid]. But she's seen another side of me. I'm not saying I'm a hard person or anything like that there, but I just had to put her in her place. Because if I didn't, she would have ruled the roost ... she would call me a c**t and a fat b*****d and all the rest of it, and then a day later she would be like 'will you do me a favour?'

It could be argued that this difficult relationship between Jo's carer and his birth mother, and the fact that Jo felt that his birth mother was always there for him, might explain to some extent the low security of attachment to the carer rating that Jo received on the IPPA.

A few parents/carers explained how things were better now that the children were not forced to have direct contact. They had found it very hard to watch their children screaming and crying while leaving the house to go to contact visits, as recalled by Kirsten's carer (residence order):

> [I find contact] Better now. Better. Definitely better, because she doesn't have to go if she doesn't want to go. She is not forced into it anymore. You know, when she was a baby, I felt very much she was forced into going. When the child was going out of the house squealing, holding on to me and crying, I don't think that was fair ... I found that very hard because the child was really upset and she just knew herself she didn't want to go.

Similarly, Ryan (residence order) no longer had contact with his birth parents, as he refused to go. His carers described contact as a "nightmare", and Ryan's parents as "weirdos":

> *And then he would have seen his siblings and his mum . . . It was a nightmare to be honest with you . . . a real nightmare but anyway and then . . . he never wanted to go, you had to sort of blackmail him . . . If it was Easter I'd say sure, there's Easter eggs there for your brothers and sisters . . . And there was one contact in particular, a good wee while after the residence order, when he just said he wasn't going and I couldn't make him go, and the social worker phoned and she said, 'Ryan, if I change it to a different place, if I make it different will you come?' and he said 'no'. Now his mother got on the phone then, and she was very nasty, she said, 'that wee b*****d,' she said, 'has to remember he has another family. I am going to come down to your house and I'm going to pull the head off that wee c**t,' was her words exactly . . . She came in here, him and her came in here, they sat down, I made a cup of tea, the children they laughed and they giggled, she opened her purse and she threw him £20, he opened his wallet and threw him £20 and they never said, 'you didn't appear at access', never mentioned it . . . they're weirdos, I tell you.*

While many parents/carers had a positive or indifferent attitude towards contact, a few adoptive parents were not keen on the idea of contact. John's adoptive mother (foster adoption) was not keen on having contact with his birth family. John used to have monthly face-to-face contact with his birth parents, but it stopped with the adoption. After the adoption, there was letterbox contact, which had also recently stopped because the birth parents were drinking again. John's adoptive mother appeared to be content with this:

> *I would prefer that they're not in touch but we had to go by the court . . . I just don't like them being in touch, you know. They're not their parents, we are. I did go along with it, but they are the ones that have broken the contact.*

John's adoptive mother did not appear to realise that John still considered his birth parents to be part of his family:

John (J): [On the page in the "me-book" that dealt with family – long pause] *Birth mother* [Circles "Birth mother"].

Researcher (R): *Do you see her much?*

J: *No . . . But still . . . and birth father* [Circles "Birth father"].

R: *Do you see him?*

J: *No . . . no, but still consider them in my family.*

Two other adopted children, Rory and Ciara (both stranger adoption), had also had previous letterbox contact with their birth parents over a period of several years, which had only recently ended. Rory's adoptive mother did not seem to consider post-box contact as an important aspect of Rory's life, and had stopped sending letters, as she did not think it worked for them for two reasons: 1) because they did not know whether the letter was forwarded straight away by the social worker or it was just sitting in their offices; and 2) because they were concerned that they were "giving too much away", and they did not want the birth family to know which school Rory was attending and so on. These adoptive parents appeared to have judged the situation well, as during his interview, Rory explained that he did not consider his birth parents to be in his family, that he had never seen them, and that he 'would rather be in the family he is in'.

Parents/carers worried about the potential harmful effects that contact could have on their children. Aidan's birth mother worried about him having unsupervised contact with his birth father who was an alcoholic and could have been drinking prior to the contact visit. A few parents/carers worried particularly about their children's contact with siblings, and the detrimental influence they could have on them. Nicole's foster carer decided to take action regarding this and confiscated Nicole's mobile phone, as she felt she had no control over her contact with her older siblings, which could potentially be damaging for her:

You see . . . they were giving her £10 top up every week. Where she would have got £10 maybe to do her the month or six weeks or something like that, or a birthday or something, you might get a top up but . . . I couldn't control it. And they were having, I mean the texts that were going on . . . and there was more rows . . . they were texting her and she was texting them and [birth sister] was telling her all about her boyfriend and all that was going on . . . Oh! I just was reading a text and there was far too much information for Nicole's age, you know.

Steve's adoptive mother (foster adoption) was also concerned that his younger birth sister (who was also adopted) had made contact with him and was possibly going to have face-to-face contact with him. The problem that this presented was that their birth mother had remained in contact with the sister but not with Steve. Thus, she was concerned that when the sister would see him, she would tell him this, and he would feel rejected again.

Satisfaction with the contact arrangements that their children had often depended on the amount of control and say that parents/carers felt they had about the decisions concerning the arrangements, and on how social workers and statutory providers dealt with their different situations. Eoghan's grandmother (kinship carer) had control over the contact that he had with his birth mother and siblings, which usually happened at her home every weekend, and she was pleased with that:

It is simple. You know, we went to court whenever he was a baby, and that's what the judge said, 'You are the luckiest boy here today because you have the best of both worlds'. You know, there is nothing . . . more than an agreement than anything, I don't have him adopted. I just have parental control over him. I didn't get that done. Because he is free to come between the two houses at my discretion. I make the decision. You know, where his mummy, she would ring me up, and say is it okay if Eoghan's comes, and that's fine.

In contrast, Amy's adoptive mother (foster adoption) was unhappy that a social worker had got involved in the contact arrangement with

Amy's birth siblings. Previously, the siblings' foster mother and herself had successfully arranged this between themselves:

Well, we managed it in the initial stages and it is only, I would say, within the last few years that Social Services actually wrote it down . . . an actual schedule, which personally I don't know that I am enamoured with, you know . . . [name] who is the foster mother, we did it and we managed it very well, and then, I don't know whether Social Services had to be seen to be doing their bit or whatever, I don't know, but they stepped in. I can't remember what this girl's title was, but basically she was in charge of this sort of thing. And . . . she agreed with us, and then wrote it down and then sent us each a copy of letter. But to me I don't think there was any need for that, you know.

Pol's foster mother was more positive in terms of the help that she had received from social workers in re-arranging contact:

Researcher (R): *And how do you arrange the visits?*

Pol's foster mother (FM): *Well, it usually comes from the social worker, but I would take the kids there and leave them and pick them up later on, after. I don't have any bother now, no.*

R: *And when you did, would you have had good support?*

FM: *Oh yes, from the social workers because they were able to sit and we could have said 'why not try something like this?' you know, maybe the kids are bored, sitting in a room with nothing really to do, so why not try something that the kids would enjoy more, so that's what they have been doing.*

Joey's adoptive parents (foster adoption) were also happy with the help they had received from the Trust adoption team in relation to contact. Joey had post-box contact with his mother, and this worked well, until there was an issue with Joey's birth mother signing off as "mum". Someone from the adoption team "had a word" with her, and she agreed to sign it with her name in future.

According to Claire and Morgan's (birth sisters) adoptive mother (stranger adoption), Social Services had pushed for a "closed" adoption with no contact, despite the fact that the adoptive parents were open to the girls having some form of contact with their birth family. The following extract highlights the fact that the adoptive parents had not been properly informed as to why Social Services felt that there should be no contact with the children's birth family:

Adoptive mother (AM): *No contact. It wasn't even our choice because we had . . . [adoptive father] and I had discussed this at the time, you know, are the children able to go and see their parents? Not for our sake, it would kill me, [adoptive father] is the same. But we have to think of the girls, it's their wee lives, we have to think of them, but we were told from day one, basically no contact. They will never know where they are or anything about yous, nothing.*

Researcher: *Did they ever explain to you why there would be no contact?*

AM: *Just because the kids were "freed". Social services had applied for a freeing order. This was before we even knew about the children.*

Summary of key findings

- Only a small number of children had no form of contact with their birth family, most of whom were adopted (stranger adoption). A range of contact arrangements existed within all placement types. Regular face-to-face contact with birth parents and/or siblings was particularly common for children in foster and kinship care, on a residence order, or living with birth parents, but was rare amongst stranger adopted children, who were more likely to have post-box or phone contact.
- Contact arrangements changed over time, often reducing or stopping altogether, across placement types. Sometimes, change occurred as a result of the child or/and parent/carer being listened

to, but other times, it occurred due to the circumstances of the placement or of the birth family.

- A few children appeared to feel powerless to effect any change around contact arrangements, and had little hope of getting their opinions heard and acted upon. However, in instances where children had been listened to, considerable improvements were made.

- Contact visits in family centres always appeared to be unsatisfactory for both children and their parents/carers.

- Children's reactions to contact were very diverse, ranging from being upset, angry or disappointed and not wanting to go to visits, to being happy with the arrangements and level of provision. Reactions did not appear to be determined by placement type, although most of those reporting negative effects of contact in the past (when the children were younger) were foster carers and carers of children on a residence order.

- The concept of "ambiguous loss" was found useful to describe the experience of the children in the study in relation to contact: 38 children considered their birth parents to be part of their family (psychologically present) but either had no contact with them (n = 14) or had contact but were not living with them (n = 24) (physically absent), and 41 children considered their sibling/s to be part of their family (psychologically present), but either had no contact with them (n = 8) or had contact but were not living with them (n = 33) (physically absent). Some children were happy with the level of contact, while others longed for more contact with their birth family members or even wished to live with them.

- The majority of parents/carers of children who had face-to-face contact with birth family members reported having no problems in relation to contact, although where tensions existed, they tended to occur within kinship care.

11 Family communication

Introduction

Family communication has been defined as 'a spontaneous and symbolic process in which the members of the family share information through words, gestures and expressions', and positive communication involves 'the exchange of clear and congruent messages that contain empathy, give support, and show an effective ability of problem resolution' (Tabak *et al*, 2012, p. 27). Good quality communication enables parents and children to share their wishes, feelings and perceptions, while forming close and intimate bonds, with the child feeling well cared for and supported. It has also been linked to enhancing self-esteem, mental wellbeing, and resilience in adolescents (Kernis *et al*, 2000; Levin and Currie, 2010 – cited in Tabak *et al*, 2012).

In foster and adoptive families, over and above normal family exchanges, there is the need for additional communication about being adopted or fostered, including the issue of birth families. Within adoption research, Brodzinsky (2005) developed the concept of "communicative openness", as involving the process of examining the meaning of adoption for members of the adoptive family. There has been some research exploring communicative openness within adoptive families (Freeark *et al*, 2008; Jones and Hackett, 2008) and its associations with children's wellbeing, self-esteem and adjustment or contact (Beckett *et al*, 2008; Brodzinsky, 2008; Von Korff and Grotevant, 2011). However, less is known about communication between foster carers and their foster children.

In this chapter, the issue of family communication is examined in detail, with a particular focus on the level and quality of communication between the children and their parents/carers, including the level of difficulty that children and parents/carers experience when talking about feelings and worries, or sensitive issues regarding the birth family. Communication was one of the topics discussed in the interviews with the parents, and was indirectly referred to in the interviews with the children, as well as being one of the dimensions in the IPPA–R. Quantitative and qualitative analyses address comparisons of children within and between the five different placement types.

Comparing children's communication with peers and parents/carers (IPPA-R)

This section presents the findings that emerged from two of the dimensions of the IPPA–R, which are communication with parents and communication with peers. The IPPA–R was completed by the children in the different placements. The IPPA–R was described in Chapter 4, and the full results of the measure are reported there. In Figure 11.1, comparisons are drawn between the level of communication the children had with their friends and their parents/carers across the different types of placements.

A considerable number of children, especially those in the foster adoption, kinship care, foster care and residence order groups, had high communication scores with both parents/carers and friends. A larger number of children had higher communication scores with their parents/carers than with their friends, and this was particularly

Figure 11.1
IPPA–R communication with peers and parents/carers by care placement types

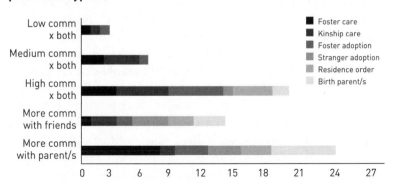

the case for children in foster care and living with birth parents. Gender was found to be a statistically significant variable regarding peer communication scores (F = 6.11, p<0.05), but not parent communication scores. As commonly found, girls had significantly higher communication scores with their peers than boys did.

However, these findings should be treated with some caution, as contradictions between IPPA–R communication scores and qualitative data were found in a large minority of cases, across the different placement types (n = 20). For ten children, while their IPPA–R communication scores for friends were low, these children had described, especially when completing the "me-book", talking with their friends and receiving support from them and that they were important to them. In contrast, three children had high IPPA–R communication scores for friends, but while completing the "me-book" had indicated that they did not consider their friends to be important or did not talk to them. For five children, while the IPPA–R communication scores for parents/carers were high or medium, the parent/carer described the child as reserved, and not sharing their feelings/worries with them. Finally, for two children, IPPA–R scores were low for both peers and parents, but according to the child and/or parent/carer, the child appeared to communicate with both friends and parents/carers.

Children's communication with their parents/carers

Independent of placement type, the majority of parents/carers found it easy to talk to their children and considered themselves able to communicate well/very well with their child, about a wide range of issues. They were confident that if their child was experiencing any problems or had significant worries, he/she would disclose these to them, either immediately or after a period of time and/or encouragement from themselves. Even if some of these children were a bit reserved about their feelings, their parents/carers believed that there were no communication difficulties, and eventually the children would tell them about their worries. A few parents/carers, like Joseph's birth mother, Maggie's grandmother (kinship) and Bridget's foster adoptive parents (see quotes below respectively), also thought that they would be able to tell if something was amiss, just by the look on the child's face or their behaviour:

He's (Joseph) easy to talk to, so he is. It's easy . . . if he comes in from school and I know there is something wrong with him, I'll say are you alright, he would sort of kind of grunt. I'll leave it and then he has his dinner and if he wants to he just comes out . . . it takes him a while to tell you.

I would know if there was something wrong with Maggie . . . I say . . . 'What's wrong with you today? Has somebody said something to you?' She wouldn't tell you right there and then but then she would maybe wait and say, 'Nanny, do you remember how you were asking me . . .' then she would tell me something. But it's nothing serious.

But you know when she's (Bridget) worrying about something because she'll come in and she'll stomp on down to her bedroom and not say a word, you know . . . Or she'll get in the car and say nothing. You know, because normally she would be... she'll get in the car and be 'how was your day, what did you do at work?'

A few parents/carers (n = 4) assumed that their children did not have "real" worries or serious problems. Thus, Rebecca's uncle (kinship carer), Maggie's grandfather (kinship carer) and Roisin's grandfather (residence order) did not believe their children to have 'any worries now', and hoped that they would talk to them if they ever did, while Bridget's adoptive mother (foster adoption) believed her daughter's problems tended to be trivial issues around friendships, as she explained below:

Her worries tend to be about . . . [name of friend] told me I was such and such today and blah, you know the usual, name calling, that type of thing, so she would, you know, she would talk about things like that, but if it worries her, it doesn't worry her for very long, to be honest.

Some of the topics that parents/carers expressed difficulty/uneasiness talking about were related to puberty. That was often more difficult for male parents/carers with female children. For instance, Roisin's grandfather (residence order) was reluctant to talk to her about puberty. In this instance, Roisin talked to his ex-partner who was still very involved in her life. Similarly, Emma's birth father found it hard to talk about "women's things", so his sisters were able to step in and have a chat with her:

> I wouldn't have known what to do. I would have probably had to go looking for help there, because we weren't brought up that way.

In six cases (one foster care, two kinship care, two birth parents, and one residence order), parents/carers acknowledged that the children felt more comfortable talking with others in the family, like siblings or aunts/uncles, than with themselves, particularly if the subject was sensitive. For instance, Annie's grandmother explained how Annie used to talk about her worries with her, but since her husband died, she talked with her uncle, about missing her grandfather and not her:

> She would have talked to me, now, but I think she would go more now to [son] and tell him, because she doesn't want to worry me, and I think it is mostly about her missing her granddad, and she would be upset.

The parents/carers of 15 children described communication as particularly problematic. These children were living in different types of placements:

- stranger adoption: 3
- foster adoption: 3
- foster care: 2
- kinship care: 2
- residence order: 1
- birth parents: 4

The problems identified on the part of the children included their being very reserved or/and not open about their feelings; being afraid of or finding it hard to identify/express feelings; never mentioning the past/birth family/care; finding it difficult/hard to talk with each other; being too open about worries/feelings; and talking to parent/carer as if they were their best friends. For instance, according to his birth mother, Jim never talked about his feelings with her:

> *Jim doesn't like really talking. Unless it's about something he wants to buy or is looking to buy and he'll talk to no end, apart from that, how he's feeling or what he's done, he doesn't really, unless something real funny happened in school that he can't wait to tell.*

Nathan's grandmother (kinship carer) found that he never disclosed much information about himself (i.e. worries, interests, feelings, etc) to her:

> *He doesn't tell you much. If he talks about anything it will be TV, you know, or what he done outside.*

According to Danny's foster adoptive mother, apart from not talking about his worries, he found it hard to talk about his feelings:

> *Sometimes if he has had a blowout, I'll say to him, 'What was that all about Danny?', and he'll say, 'I don't know', or I would say to him, 'Did we need to go there, did that need to happen?' . . . 'But I can't help it' . . . Yes, he can identify feelings that he's happy, he's sad, but I think he would find it hard, you know, to talk about it . . . Comes upon him and when something's happened, that's it, it's over, it's done, he wants it boxed and forgotten about.*

For Dylan, communication problems appeared a bit more severe, as he had very complex behavioural problems, and seemed to understand things differently to what happened in reality, as his foster carer explained:

Sometimes he bottles things up . . . he's very deep, but if something happens in school, you'll get his version of it . . . which often is very true in his mind. He doesn't generally make up stuff or lie . . . but how he sees things is not maybe exactly how it happened. But he still believes that's it, and the number of times that I have totally believed him and gone in guns blazing, to find out that that's not what happened at all.

Some parents/carers mentioned the possible reasons underpinning their children's perceived difficulties in communication. These reasons included:

- previous emotional abuse/trauma (Jim's birth mother);
- cognitive developmental limitations (three foster adopters, Jessica's kinship carers, and Ronan's birth mother);
- lack of emotional security/maturity (Laura's foster adopter);
- low self-esteem (Patrick's foster carer); and
- the child's sex (Martin's foster mother).

Jim's birth mother described her son's reluctance to talk about the emotional abuse he suffered at the hands of his birth father; consequently, he had withdrawn into himself as a means of self-preservation:

Because I don't think he has had that, you know, with his dad and all, he couldn't go asking anything or tell him anything, you know, without being hit or whatever, so he finds it better if he just keeps it all in, it will all go away, and everybody is happy.

Both Joey's and Danny's foster adoptive mothers believed that communication with their sons was heavily influenced by their learning/cognitive limitations and lack of emotional intelligence, which made it difficult for them to be aware of/able to express their feelings, and reluctant to disclose them. Nonetheless, both parents were confident that meaningful communication was possible so long as they actively enabled their sons to communicate in ways that made sense to them, as Joey's adoptive mother explained:

Talking with him is easy . . . if you do it at his level. [When talking about feelings] he gets agitated; he doesn't know why he's agitated. You have to sort of explore what's been going on and then make sense of it for him . . . He would be inclined to push something aside and, you know, when he's pushing that aside, that that's what the problem is. And he doesn't like to visit it and see what it is, can we sort it.

Jessica's kinship carer found communication with her difficult, as she was not sure if Jessica could understand her, and also believed that she found it 'difficult to get the words', as 'she needs a lot of time to digest, she needs a lot of time to think about something'. According to her carer, Jessica was not able to communicate her feelings, as she was afraid of feelings. Conversely, Justin's adoptive mother (foster adoption) talked about her son as being a 'very open' child; a relative lack of insight meant that he tended to disclose personal information inappropriately. Ronan's birth mother found it hard talking with Ronan, because whenever she tried to discuss a certain issue, he went on to talk about something else; she thought that this problem could be caused by his poor concentration:

I don't know if it's because he doesn't want to talk about it or it's just his concentration. If something comes into his head he just spits it all out. It's like maybe you're having a serious conversation with him but he's maybe been up at the cinema that day, and he'll really want to tell you about this film that he saw.

Laura's foster adoptive mother associated her daughter's communication issues with her lack of emotional intelligence and inability to express herself concerning personal feelings:

She can't get a handle on what's wrong with her, you see . . . she doesn't know, she can't talk about it.

According to his foster mother, Patrick was very reserved regarding personal issues and worries, and she believed that this was caused by his low self-esteem:

He's very, very reserved. Very, very reserved, very, as I said before, Patrick has very low self-esteem and tries to hide things that should be talking about, you know, always covering things up, you know, this way, not outspoken . . . [birth brother] would be the one that would come in the door bubbling and bubbling, but not Patrick, no, no, no.

Martin's foster mother attributed his reluctance to talk about his worries to his being a man:

He doesn't confide very well, but then that's a man thing.

In total, 31 children across the different placements mentioned talking with their parents/carers as one of the activities that they did with their family:

- stranger adoption: 5
- foster adoption: 4
- foster care: 4
- kinship care: 7
- residence order: 7
- birth parents: 4

Tracy explained that she would ask her adoptive mother (stranger adoption) when she was not sure about how to do something, and she added that she would tell her most of her secrets. Nicole (residence order) also claimed that she talked with her parents/carers:

Usually my daddy sometimes picks me up from school and asks how I was and what did I do today, just that stuff, just stuff anyone would ask you if they picked you up from school. Or if you're watching TV you'd make conversation.

James understood communication with his foster family as being compulsory, as he talked with them, because although he did not like talking, he had to. In contrast, Joseph (with birth mother) also talked with his family, but understood communication differently, as he expressed when describing his favourite family activity, 'family time':

> *Like sharing what we feel, like ... say if you, like you've done something, then you tell your family. [Writes down 'saying what's inside you'] I do that once, like, every three days.*

Sometimes, the information gleaned from the children's interviews did not correspond with their parents/carers' views. For instance, although Rebecca's uncle (kinship carer) thought she would talk to him or his wife if she had any worries, Rebecca never mentioned talking to them, but said that she talked to her birth siblings (despite not living with them); she talked to her birth brother on visits, and to her sister via the computer every night, as well as her birth father on Skype, as he lived abroad. In addition, she claimed that the person with whom she talked the most was her little cousin (aged three years old), with whom she lived, with the second most important person being her birth mother, with whom she talked on the phone 'every wee while'.

Talking about birth families and sensitive issues about their past

Parents/carers revealed how, and to what extent, they talked to their children about the birth family, going into care, or being adopted. There were different attitudes towards the disclosure and sharing of information with their children about the birth family and being adopted or fostered. For instance, some parents/carers (n = 12: two stranger adoption, three foster adoption, three foster care, two kinship care, one residence order, and one birth parent) stated that they had shared all the information they had with their child. One of those was Orlaith's kinship carer, who revealed that she did not find it difficult to talk to Orlaith about her birth family, and the difficulties they had with contact. She stated that she had told her "everything" and "the truth". Ben's foster mother explained that if he asked something about the birth family that she did not know, she would have actually told him to ask questions to the social worker, but everything else she would have shared with him. Libby's foster mother did not talk much about her birth family, but she did not hide any information either, even though the social worker suggested as much at one stage:

> *[One of Libby's siblings' father] thought for a long time he was Libby's daddy and then when him and the mother split up he asked for DNA to be taken and it turned out he wasn't Libby's father . . . Libby was about seven at that time, and they [Social Services] thought that she was too young to tell her. And I thought to myself that's nonsense because I knew my own child better than anybody else, and I told her. I said [siblings' father] is not your daddy. Not a bother . . . you know, why lie to her? What age is the appropriate age? Maybe 12 or 14? Maybe it's going to have a worse effect on her . . . [Libby] didn't even pass any remarks, because she had no relationship with him anyway.*

The views of Kirsten's carer (residence order) would appear to concur with those of Libby's foster mum, as she too believed she had to be honest with Kirsten:

> *If she would have asked us questions that we know the answer to, we would be honest with her and I think that's how you have to be.*

However, not all parents/carers shared this same belief, and although most revealed some information, some of them actively concealed some facts that they deemed to be too potentially upsetting for the child, or too difficult for the child to understand due to their age or ability. That was the case for seven adoptive parents (four stranger and three foster adopters), two birth parents and one residence order carer. Ciaron (stranger adoption) knew that his birth mother was dead, but his adoptive mother did not tell him that she had been murdered, as she felt he was too young to know that, and believed he did not need to know. John's and Bridget's adoptive parents (foster adoption) also concealed information from them regarding their birth parents' alcohol problem and Ashley's birth mother had never talked to Ashley about her experience of the care system, leaving Ashley apparently unaware that she had ever been removed from her mother's care:

> She has no memories. She actually said to me a few weeks back, 'Mummy, that woman who used to babysit me, did you have to pay her?' . . . She has memories of staying there, but she doesn't have memories of being separated from mummy . . . I don't want to tell her . . . She knows what fostering is. There was a wee girl in Year 4, P4, who was in Ashley's class and was actually living in a care home and Ashley, God love her, came home and said, 'Mummy, I feel so sorry for her living there with no mummy and no daddy', you know. Inside I'm feeling guilty as hell, because I am thinking you were once away from me due to my actions basically.

For Claire, the fact that her adoptive mother (stranger adoption) had concealed certain information about her and her sister's birth family meant that she had imagined a reality that did not exist. Claire and her sibling Morgan's adoptive mother explained that, as they grew older, she would give them more information, such as 'that their mum and dad as a couple weren't happy together', but Claire disclosed that she missed her birth parents, but thought that 'at least they are with each other', which was not the case.

Eight adoptive parents (five stranger and three foster adopters) explained the child's past in what they considered an "age-appropriate" way, which often involved masking the truth to make it sound "nicer" or less "ugly", and could sometimes lead to the child romanticising about his/her past and birth family. These parents were struggling to explain the harsh realities to their children, as Amy's adoptive mother (foster adoption) stated:

> It is trying to find the right way . . . without being too cruel and horrible, you know, which obviously you don't want to be, but at the same time it is a fine line, you don't want to have painted this

picture of this perfect mother that gave you up and was so good at giving you up, you know, because you know there is no point in doing that either. Obviously, eventually, we are going to reach the point that she will know the facts, but there is no point at this moment in time.

Others, like Tracy's adoptive mother (stranger adoption), explained how they actually emphasised the positive aspects of their child's story, while omitting the negative ones:

She knows everything. All the good things . . . In terms of the bad things . . . I suppose they hear things . . . so you sort of, maybe they come out with something, and you sort of lighten it a bit you know, you didn't want to lie but you didn't want to be looking like bad guys either . . . I do not really want to tell the children the exact nasty things that went on.

Laura's adoptive mother (foster adoption) gave an example of how she communicated her story to her daughter, in a positive way, in order to reduce her feelings of being abandoned/not wanted:

I worry about her because she has it, I suppose, in her head that she's adopted, she wasn't wanted . . . I tried to put it that she was wanted and her mummy just wasn't able to look after her and then how much I wanted somebody and I got her.

Danny's adoptive mother (foster adoption) explained how she had been able to share a lot of information with him about his birth family, as she had previously facilitated contact with his birth mother and got on well with her. In addition, Danny had a life story book and current regular contact with his birth brother and paternal grandmother. Laura's adoptive mother (foster adoption) tried 'not to be negative in any way or to put blame on them at all', whilst Tracy's adoptive mother (stranger adoption) told Tracy that her birth mother 'didn't know how to look after children, not to look after her, but to look after children', as she was very young.

Claire and Morgan's adoptive mother (stranger adoption) told a similar story to her daughters:

Mummy and Daddy loved them very much, they loved them more than anything . . . they just didn't know how to look after a wee baby and a wee toddler. And I just say some people are like that. They love children, they love to have children but they just don't really know how to look after them properly, that is all, you know. What other way can I put it?

Ciara's adoptive mother (stranger adoption) had also told her a simplified version of her story, as she believed her daughter was too young 'to really understand it':

Just she didn't grow in Mummy's tummy, she grew in somebody else's tummy and then we picked her specially. So that is really as far as she understands. So far. You say that to her and she will repeat it, you know, but that is it.

As previously noted, some of these adoptive parents and other parents/carers struggled to talk about these issues, as they found it hard having to communicate potentially emotionally damaging information, especially in relation to birth parents, such as their alcoholism, mental health problems, rejection and physical abuse/neglect of the child. For instance, Jessica and Joanne's kinship carer found it extremely difficult to be positive and open about their birth parents, since their birth mother had two other younger children living with her in a neighbouring country, but at the same time, had failed to keep contact with Jessica and Joanne. Paul's adoptive mother (stranger adoption) found it hard to talk to him about his birth mother's mental illness, as she felt she did not know enough about it herself:

Would be the major thing because I don't know an awful lot about the illness myself and for me to try and explain it to him without maybe making him concerned would be an issue.

According to their parents/carers, some children asked questions and

Table 11.1
Children talking about birth family/past, according to parents/carers, by placement type

	Asking questions /talking	Used to ask but not recently	Not talking no questions
Foster adoption	3	4	1
Stranger adoption	2	3	2
Foster care	4	3	3
Kinship care	1	1	2
Residence order	4	1	3
Birth parents	1	1	6
Total	**15**	**13**	**17**

talked about their birth family/past (n = 15), others did not talk about their birth family/past or ask any questions (n = 17), and several had already asked in the past but had not brought up the subject recently (n = 13) (Table 11.1).

In general, most children across the placements did not tend to bring up the subject of their birth family, or their past in care. However, some of them were asking questions about particular issues. For instance, according to his foster mother, Patrick talked only about his twin siblings, who had been adopted, and wanted to know where they were. Ben was hurt by the fact his birth mother kept one of his siblings, but abandoned him, and he had asked his foster mother if she would ever give one of her children away. Annie was curious about mental illness, which affected both her birth parents, and asked her grandmother (kinship carer) questions about it. Steve asked his adoptive mother (foster adoption) questions about his birth sister, who had been adopted, and about his birth mother not coming to see him:

> At times, I just say about his sister, and he will ask why did she go to somebody else, and I say that when people are adopted that is sometimes what happens, but that you are very lucky now . . . sometimes he would ask about his mum, why did she

not come and see him, and I say, 'Well dear, I really can't answer that.' Because I really don't know why she didn't do it.

Other children had asked more questions when they were younger, and more conversations had been had at earlier stages, whereas at the time of interview, it was felt that they had already discussed and knew most of the issues, and thus they were not a topic of conversation any more. For instance, Trevor's foster mother explained how he used to talk about his past in foster care, as he was already over 11 years old when he came to live with her, but he had not talked about this recently. On other occasions, the child simply refused to talk about the birth family, as in the case of Ryan (residence order), who had had regular contact with his birth mother in the past:

We would have done [talk about birth family] right up until after the court there last year, whenever his mother took us back to court over access and that . . . Now we wouldn't really talk about her because he just doesn't want to . . . he just doesn't want to know anything about her, you know, and he doesn't want contact or phone calls or anything . . . not now, as I say, because it's a closed door now as far as he's concerned . . . But yeah, he would have asked why did my mum not look after me, normal questions you know.

According to their parents/carers, some children never talked or asked questions about their birth family or their past in care, either because they already knew everything, had forgotten, or were not curious/interested in finding out. That was the case for most of the children living with their birth parents. For instance, Emma and her father never talked about Emma's birth mother, who was not living with them. According to Bronagh's birth parents, she did not bring up the past, 'she just has forgot about it because she sees that there's no drink or nothing'.

Jack's foster mother explained how he never talked about his birth mother, what happened to her, and why he was taken into care, as he knew all the information and did not need to ask the questions.

253

In some cases, the views of the children and their parents/carers differed. Thus, while some parents/carers believed their children were not interested in finding out why they went into care/were adopted, these children appeared curious and wanting to know more about their birth family/past. For instance, Justin's adoptive mother (foster adoption) stated that he had not been asking many questions recently, but he had done so when he was younger, and they had shared all the information with him then. However, Justin revealed that he wanted to know 'more about what actually happened' in his past, about his 'mum and things that were going on' in his life. Similarly, while Claire and Morgan's adoptive mother believed Claire was not interested in her birth family, as she never asked any questions about them (while her sister Morgan did), Claire disclosed that she sometimes felt sad about her past because she missed her birth parents.

In Rebecca's case, her uncle (kinship carer) believed she had asked no questions about why she was living with them because she knew that her mother was in a rehabilitation centre; but he seemed completely unaware that Rebecca felt sad, embarrassed and different from her peers, because of living with them and not with her birth mother and siblings.

Summary of key findings

- Many children had high communication scores for the two scales (parents/carers and peers), especially those in the foster adoption and kinship care groups; and a higher number of children had higher communication scores with their parents than with their peers, especially those in foster care and living with birth parents. However, significant differences between placement types were not evident.
- Across placement types, most parents/carers described communication with their child as easy, and believed that they would disclose their feelings and any problems/worries to them, either immediately or after some encouragement on their part; although some acknowledged that their children would sometimes rather talk with

somebody else in the family about certain issues.

- A minority (n = 15) described some communication problems with their children, e.g. being extremely reserved about feelings/worries and rarely talking. The majority of the children were either living with birth parents (n = 4) or adopted (n = 6, three stranger and three foster adoptions). A range of possible reasons for these difficulties were described, including cognitive developmental limitations, previous emotional abuse and low self-esteem.

- Some children across the different placement types (n = 31) mentioned talking with their parents/carers. Some of them talked about communicating everyday issues, but a few also revealed that they shared their secrets and feelings with their parents/carers.

- Some parents/carers across the different placements (n = 12) claimed that they had shared all the information they had about the birth families/the child's past in care with their children. However, others (n = 10) had actively concealed some facts that they deemed to be potentially distressing for the child or too hard to understand. These were mostly adoptive parents (n = 7; four stranger and three foster adopters). In addition, eight adoptive parents (five stranger and three foster adopters) had offered a simplified or romanticised version of the child's past.

- According to their parents/carers, not all children were curious, talked about or asked questions about their birth families, their past in care or being adopted/fostered, and in fact some never did (n = 17), while others had done so in the past but not recently (n = 13). Some did ask questions and talked about the birth family/past (n = 15), but not often. The majority of children living with birth parents did not talk about their past in care (n = 6), whereas most adopted children were asking questions or used to in the past (n = 12: five stranger and seven foster adoptions).

- A few contradictions between the parents' and the children's accounts were found regarding this issue, as a few children were curious about their birth family but their parents/carers appeared unaware of this.

- If children had worries, some parents/carers found it was best not to pressure them for information, but to let them talk about this in their own time.

12 Social Services' involvement and social support

Introduction

Children in care and their carers have a formalised relationship with Social Services, which is the conduit, in principle, to the provision of support services. However, the formal/statutory nature of this relationship ends when the child is adopted from care. Any future relationship, and consequently access to support, then depends on the attitude of the particular Social Services department to this form of support (in the context of increasing pressures on budgets for children in care), and the will and determination of the adoptive parents to lobby for post-adoption support. Likewise, parents whose children return home from care, unless under a care order, have no formal right to support services. In England and Wales, the adoption process has come under renewed focus, particularly the nature and function of post-adoption support, and arguments have been presented to improve current provision (Luckock and Hart, 2005; McSherry *et al*, 2008). This chapter explores the extent of Social Services' involvement that the families involved in this study received, and the type of social supports (if any) that were availed of.

Social Services' involvement

Birth parents

Ten out of the 11 birth parents interviewed addressed this issue, evidencing significant disparity in the nature of their involvement with Social Services and their assessment of its quality. Three parents were complimentary of the support received, two identified positive and negative aspects, such that involvement was characterised by both as fundamentally "okay", and five parents were critical, sometimes highly so.

For the two parents whose involvement with Social Services was portrayed as "okay", their accounts included descriptions of both supportive and undermining actions and were characterised by the use of language that emphasised the "ups-and-downs" of interaction over the years. Aidan's mother recalled Social Services' responsiveness to her requests for additional educational support for Aidan, alongside their marginalisation of her concerns about contact between him and his alcoholic father.

The more disparaging parents directed their criticism at actions that impacted on themselves as well as their child/children, reserving the most damning criticism in relation to the latter. In this regard, Social Services were condemned, inter alia, for failing to provide, as far as possible, continuity in the lives of children, including repeated moves between birth parents and foster carers such that the children were left deeply fearful of being moved again; failing to keep birth parents informed of relevant developments such that they themselves were compromised in their ability to ensure their child's best possible welfare; being heavy-handed in terms of supervision of contact; and failing to ensure that birth siblings remained together whilst in care. Joseph's mother remembered her frustrating contact experience when he was in care:

> It was at the ... family centre. She had the cameras on and listened to every word that was being said and it was horrible ... She [social worker] kept making excuses and she spent more time with my kids than I did ... I had to wait once a week to go and see the kids ... My solicitor had asked why we were being filmed and being listened to, so that was stopped ... Contact was horrid, it wasn't nice at all, and it wasn't nice for the kids.

Birth parents' criticisms of Social Services tended to focus on their lack of confidence, trust or interest in them, as individuals, particularly as this compromised their ability to care for their child. In general, lack of support was discussed in relation to a variety of issues, including lack of consultation/provision of information concerning their child's ongoing care; heavy-handed scrutiny of their ability to care properly for their child; preventing adequate contact between parent and child while the latter was in care; removing their child from their care without due consideration/investigation; lack of consultation/support in the period leading up to and immediately following their child's return to their care; conniving to keep birth parents apart so that they would not reunite as a prelude to getting their children back; and insensitivity concerning the parent's emotional well-being. Emma's parent explained:

> *Every month now, it used to be every two weeks, now they've started coming up less . . . 'We can call to your house when we want.' I says, 'I haven't a problem, but can you not lift the phone?' . . . There was no set time, so you'd be sitting from 8am to 5pm, you had no life.*

At times, perceived disinterest and/or suspicion on the part of Social Services prevented parents from seeking help. Three birth parents stressed that, irrespective of how impoverished or in need of support (e.g. respite care) they might be, they would never approach Social Services. On being asked to consider her child's future, Joseph's mother commented:

> *As long as they don't grow up to be social workers, I don't care.*

One of the most often cited manifestations of Social Services' lack of support was their perceived unwillingness to listen to what birth parents had to say, including their involvement in decision-making concerning their child. Lack of meaningful dialogue was thrown into particularly sharp relief with regards to LAC meetings: four parents described their experiences of these meetings as a waste of time, humiliating and distressing, convincing them that their presence made no material difference to decision-making as they were rarely, if ever, consulted. Such experiences had prompted Emma's parents to stop attending the LAC reviews, while Aidan and Alexandra's parents continued to attend in the midst of (sometimes acute) discomfort, embarrassment and frustration. Alexandra's mother described her experience of LAC review meetings, as:

Hard enough ... I don't know what to say there [at the reviews] ... I just think they're a bit sore on me at times ... They should be looking out for people ... They put it down as neglect ... Does she look like somebody who's neglected? I'm sitting crying usually.

Of those birth parents who talked specifically about their child's care order status, two knew with certainty that their child was under such an order, one that the order had definitely been lifted, and two remained unsure. The care order tended to be looked upon with ambivalence, with some aspects being adhered to more than others, depending on the parent's priorities. For example, Aidan's mother considered the order largely irrelevant in terms of Aidan's health care, but adhered closely to its provision in terms of consulting with Social Services over his contact with his father.

One aspect of Social Services' involvement that seemed to work well was the access to other services/support that they facilitated. The support made available varied according to individual parent/family needs and included respite care, family holidays, family counselling, and educational support. Where parents discussed such support, they were invariably complimentary and acknowledged the (often considerable) benefits for both themselves and their child.

Ashley's mother voiced considerable appreciation for the support Social Services had provided in the past – facilitation of her thrice-weekly extended visits to her daughter throughout Ashley's time in foster care was seen as crucial to the ease with which they had been able to establish family life, particularly in terms of the maintenance of a bond between the two. Irrespective of this, after an initial period of support immediately following her daughter's return, Ashley's mother deliberately sought to end all involvement with Social Services, as part of her efforts to lead what she considered to be a "normal" life with her daughter.

Foster adoptive parents

Seven out of the nine foster adoptive parents interviewed addressed this issue. Again, experience of Social Services' involvement varied, both within and between individual accounts. Laura's adoptive parents could identify positive and negative aspects of their relationship with Social Services, while three parents were more critical. Generally, irrespective of their assessment of the quality of Social Services support, involvement was limited, having diminished considerably after the adoption. For some parents, Social Services' involvement was reduced to dealing with contact with birth family members. Thus, Bridget's adoptive parents' current contact consisted only of the passing on of cards to their daughter sent by her birth father twice a year, and both Amy and Karl's adoptive parents dealt with Social Services specifically about their child's contact with birth relatives.

Laura's adoptive mother's assessment of her involvement with Social Services was that they were essentially "okay". Due to the recent deterioration in Laura's behaviour, her adoptive mother was in receipt of a number of different elements of support from Social Services. Some of these she considered to be very good / appropriate, including the respite care package that had been put in place, whereby Laura's care was shared with a foster carer. However, an aspect she considered to be lacking was the failure of Social Services to supply a counsellor with whom Laura could talk through and resolve her issues.

Of the three more critical parents, two directed criticism exclusively at actions impacting on their child/children. Thus, Joey's adoptive parents complained about Social Services' lack of responsiveness to their application for a post-adoption care package to help fund the purchase of specialist equipment for their son. Amy's adoptive mother criticised the lack of information provided concerning her daughter's early childhood, as she knew that her daughter had suffered physically/emotionally, but lacked specific information. She complained about feeling that they were being 'kept a bit in the dark' in terms of information, and that made her feel hampered in her ability to deal with emerging problems/issues. Justin's adoptive mother also commented on the fact that, prior to her son's adoption, she had been told nothing of the mental health problems within his birth family. Given her son's increasingly pronounced mental health difficulties over the recent past, she had committed much time and effort trying to secure appropriate Social Services help, but none had been forthcoming. In the meantime, her son's psychiatrist had been of considerable help, both in terms of helping her to understand the nature of his mental health problems and how best to manage and respond to them, as well as trying to secure other relevant health care for him:

> *The paediatrician had put in a referral to Social Services two years ago to get help . . . so a social worker from adoption came out and then said that this wasn't an adoption issue . . . Then a post-adoption team would have helped if it was over contact . . . but because it was a mental health problem it was nothing to do with them . . . So then we had to get referred back to Initial Assessment again who passed it to Disability. Disability said they weren't taking him because he wasn't severely disabled . . . So this is two years later and we're back with the assessment team again.*

Amy's adoptive mother was the only one who voiced criticism of Social Services relating to herself. Although she understood the rationale for Social Services' involvement in organising Amy's contact with birth siblings, she resented the fact that they had interfered in an arrangement made between her and the birth sibling's foster mother and which had worked to their mutual benefit. Consequently, they now had to adhere to a structure imposed by Social Services, something that she considered contravened her role and rights as a parent.

Five foster adoptive parents reflected on the role of Social Services post adoption, with four believing that support should be available, depending on the individual child/circumstances, and one advocating for no involvement whatsoever. Fundamentally, those parents in favour of a role for Social Services believed that involvement should occur only at the request of adoptive parents. Thus, they argued that it should be left up to the latter to approach Social Services, as and when they considered it appropriate; otherwise, Social Services should not intervene. For instance, Bridget's adoptive parents could envisage circumstances in which support would be necessary; in particular, they had considered the possibility of approaching Social Services in the future in relation to their daughter's wish to make contact with her birth family.

Amy's adoptive mother had recently been told by the foster carer of Amy's birth siblings that their birth mother had returned to Northern Ireland temporarily. She felt that she should have been given this information by Social Services as 'forearmed is forewarned':

> [Social Services] can't have it both ways. You can't sit down and dictate 'Right, this is the way you are sorting out your contacts', and then on the other hand, not let you know that the birth mother has suddenly appeared out of the blue.

Due to serious problems with her son in the past, during which time she tried to identify why his behaviour had deteriorated so badly and how he could be helped, Danny's adoptive mother had asked Social Services for support, but felt that she been totally sidelined. If not for the fact that she was fostering another child, and therefore had been able to access support from another Trust, she believed she would have received no help whatsoever. As a result of this and similar experiences, she was strongly of the opinion that post-adoption support should be available at all times. Conversely, Steve's adoptive mother stressed that she would avoid contact with Social Services if at all possible, believing that contact could cause her son to worry about the permanency of his placement with them.

Stranger adoptive parents

Five out of the nine stranger adoptive parents interviewed addressed this issue. Once again, there was a range of experiences both within and between individual accounts. Charlie's adoptive parents related only positive experiences, commenting on the excellent training and support provided by Social Services to themselves as prospective adoptive parents. Involvement had continued for a short time post-adoption, consisting essentially of telephone conversations about specific issues. As a way of reciprocating the commendable support shown to them, they were involved in prospective adoptive parents' groups facilitated by Social Services:

> *I thought that when we were getting ready to adopt that Social Services were very good . . . They had training sessions . . . and I thought those were very good . . . They need to be really highly commended for all the preparation that they did . . . and we reciprocated by going to groups for, you know, prospective adopters.*

Four stranger adoptive parents reported more ambivalent experiences. Siblings Morgan and Claire's adoptive mother had found Social Services to be supportive throughout the extended adoption process, but disinterested thereafter. Despite being told by Social Services that they were 'only at the end of the phone', she considered that attempts to communicate her concerns about one of her daughters had been basically ignored. Similarly, Abbie's adoptive mother reported both good and bad experiences. Those of their own social worker and wider adoption team with whom they had dealt throughout the extended adoption process were considered to be very supportive. However, she considered her daughter's social worker to have been disinterested, neglecting to investigate what turned out to be significant health issues, and adopting an otherwise 'typically lazy' approach to her daughter's care. Paul's adoptive mother wholeheartedly praised the support given to her son by a particular social worker, whom she described as always having her son's best interests at heart, working hard to ensure that contact with his birth mother did not upset him. However, the total withdrawal of Social Services post adoption had left her feeling isolated and vulnerable, something that she continued to experience:

> *A really, really lovely man . . . a terribly nice man and he really took Paul's interests to heart and things worked out well there,*

and apart from that, once the adoption went through, you know,
we felt as though we were on our own. There were times when I
thought, well, if we have a problem, who do we contact?

Despite the fact that she had been told by Social Services that they were only a phone call away, Paul's adoptive mother was never given a phone number/contact. Two other parents highlighted the need for involvement to continue post adoption, at least theoretically speaking. Claire and Morgan's adoptive mother considered that, although it was entirely appropriate that Social Services were no longer involved in relation to one of her daughters, involvement/support should have continued in relation to the other daughter, given her suspected cognitive/developmental limitations. Ciara's adoptive parents expressed concern over a discontinuity between the intense scrutiny of themselves in the run-up to adoption, and the total lack of Social Services' involvement thereafter. They stressed that involvement, however infrequent, should continue in the first few months/years of a child's adoption, to ensure that they were being properly looked after as well as to provide relevant support to the adoptive parents:

We sort of felt that once we took over the role nobody else
wanted to know ... We didn't question at the time the fact that
people came to our house and they had all these home visits.
Questions and questions, police checks, we had these checks
and those checks, and then all of a sudden a judge hands you a
child and you can do anything to them that you wanted to and
nobody is there to check up on you, maintain tabs on the child
and make sure that she is alright ... and that you are looking
after her and not abusing her ... It just seemed to me you could
bluff your way through the whole thing ... There have been no
checks whatsoever since, a small concern of mine.

Two adoptive parents commented negatively on post-adoption parents groups (typically facilitated by Adoption UK), seeing these as unnecessary and essentially demeaning, and thus avoiding involvement. The most frequently voiced argument was that they were "real" mothers and fathers, not "alternative carers", and as such, the idea of a specially designated adoptive parents group was insulting, because it singled them out as somehow different (i.e. not "normal" or "real" parents). A secondary argument, offered by Abbie's adoptive parents, focused on the "negativity" of the groups, whereby they were seen to emphasise the problems of being an adoptive parent. Notwithstanding these views, Morgan and Claire's adoptive mother had been involved in prospective adoptive parent groups, giving talks about their experiences. She considered this role to be important on the basis of her personal journey through the adoption process, being aware of how frustrating and upsetting it could be.

Foster carers

All the foster carers addressed this issue. As with the other groups, their experiences of involvement with Social Services ranged both within and between individual accounts. Dylan and Anna's carers reported a "mixed bag" so that their overall assessment of involvement was satisfactory. Dylan's foster carers' involvement centred on Dylan's son's cognitive and behavioural problems that, at times, had been so severe that they had contemplated relinquishing care of him. In that context, they complained strongly about a prolonged lack of respite care, which was eventually put in place, but which was extremely limited and had come to an abrupt halt after only a few months. However, this limited help, alongside substantial support from their foster son's paediatrician, had been enough for them to continue with the placement:

> *We were thinking if we didn't get respite or didn't get some help we would have to say we're very sorry but we have to put our family first . . . and we didn't want to do that.*

Otherwise, Dylan's foster carers considered support from Social Services, particularly from their appointed link worker, to be good. They described themselves as heavily reliant on this support, given their son's cognitive/behavioural issues. Training provided by Social Services over the years was also considered to have helped them be able to care for their foster son. In terms of Dylan's own involvement with Social Services, his foster carers described his very close emotional bond with his appointed social worker, how much he depended on and trusted her, and how good was her care and support of him:

> She's a great girl . . . He has a lot of faith in [name of social worker]. Dylan would not cry easily . . . and at one stage she was going to be over in another team and she told Dylan . . . and he just cried and sobbed. It was like losing a mummy . . . he was very attached to her. She's very good to him.

Daniel and Anna's foster mother was critical of Social Services in relation to their approach to Daniel, highlighting how their constant interaction (i.e. monthly visits/six-monthly LAC reviews) served only to remind him of the fact that he was in care, and that his birth parents were alcoholics. She knew these reminders upset him, reflecting that it would be better if social workers became involved as and when needed:

> We've got social workers and everything coming out of our ears, and health visitors . . . can get a wee bit tedious.

Conversely, she had nothing but praise for her own link worker, and considered that the training provided by Social Services had benefitted them enormously in terms of how they cared for and responded to their foster children's poor relationships with one another; having put their training into practice, they were aware of how it had helped the situation:

> Well, we have had no problem. I mean, our link worker is great. I mean, I think she is brilliant . . . She is very good at cheering me up, so you know what I mean. The likes of mileage . . . I keep forgetting to claim my mileage and she's going to me, 'Get it in before the end of the month or you're going to lose it all'.

Four foster carers focused on negative experiences. Mary's foster mother complained at some length about Social Services' reluctance to pay her what she considered to be an appropriate income to foster sibling sisters. Not only had she been denied appropriate financial support, but even that to which she was entitled had been subject to questioning and delay. Sally's foster mother bemoaned the number of changes in Social Services personnel throughout the extended period of her very troubled time with her foster daughter, considering that it led to disruption in support, frustration for all involved and, especially for Sally, a lack of security, as she had to continually form new relationships with yet another stranger. Although she acknowledged that individual social workers had tried hard to be supportive, she considered that they had fallen far short, particularly considering the issues she had been facing, which eventually led to the breakdown of the placement.

Tony had recently been removed from his foster mother's care because of uncontrollable and aggressive behaviour, and was currently in an assessment unit with a view to being returned to his birth family. Not only did Tony's foster mother believe that, despite her repeated requests, she had never been given adequate support by Social Services in order to prevent the breakdown of the placement, but she felt that, once involved, Social Services had totally failed to consult her and keep her informed of the decisions and action being taken by them:

> At that meeting they [Social Services] suggested to me that they were sending him back to his natural parents and that is the first I had heard of that . . . And I said, 'You obviously had that decision made before coming to this meeting and I am the last to know and I'm looking after him,' you know . . . Send him home was the cheaper option, wash their hands of him.

Martin's foster mother was critical of Social Services' approach to his behavioural problems. They had tried to prevent him from taking the Eleven Plus on the grounds that he was not academically able. She fought with all concerned and he sat the test, achieving a grade B1. More generally, she cited lack of involvement/communication from

Social Services concerning all aspects of Martin's welfare; a recent example of this was his birth mother's latest attempt to have contact, throughout which she (the foster mother) had been prevented from attending court sessions. Such attitudes and behaviour on the part of Social Services convinced her that she was not given sufficient acknowledgement as the person who knew and cared about her foster son better than anyone else:

> But what bothers me is when they are not working with you . . . you need a partnership.

Ten foster carers reported more positive involvement. Libby's foster mother found the monthly "check-up" visits by a social worker to be very helpful. Although she was fundamentally positive about the support received from Social Services, a minor complaint was the length of time taken to recover expenses incurred. In this context, she stressed her preference for not asking for help from Social Services on the grounds that she considered herself and her husband as responsible for raising their foster daughter (and her brother):

> They are our children and we took on responsibility with them and that's the way it is.

Four foster parents described the support they received from their link social workers as very good. Their visits were described as providing an opportunity for discussion and feedback and requests for help were typically met with a positive response, including requests for financial and other support. James and Pol's foster mother talked about the early difficulties she had experienced when trying to get James' ADHD diagnosed and educational resources put in place, but commended the regular respite care currently provided, as did Patrick and Jack's foster mother. In addition, she was particularly appreciative of the financial and other help received directly from Social Services, as well as regular help (e.g. provision of a laptop and outdoor play equipment) from the Fostering Network:

> They [Social Services] are very good . . . I have a link worker

there and she is very good, and I only have to tell her . . . I was laughing . . . I was down at a meeting this morning and I was saying about Patrick's trousers ... were all white ... and she said, 'Do you want us to get trousers?' ... I'm not that bad, I'm not going for a pair of trousers from Social Services!

Although Sue's foster mother considered that the social work system was generally too inflexible, adhering to rules and regulations to the detriment of listening and responding to the views and needs of foster carers, she acknowledged a high degree of support in terms of resources for her foster daughter, as well as responsiveness on the part of both her own and her foster daughter's social workers, as and when issues arose. Connor's foster mother described limited involvement with Social Services, consisting primarily of attendance at LAC reviews, as well as the monthly visits by her foster son's social worker. She considered that relevant support was potentially available should she ever need to avail of it.

Several of the foster carers (n = 9) discussed attendance at LAC reviews. Dylan and Sue's foster carers considered them of no real merit. Dylan's foster mother saw them as lacking consistency and unable to make meaningful decisions concerning his care/progress. She described the last three reviews as 'a complete farce', due to the fact that three different Chairs had been leading the review, none of whom had had any real knowledge of her foster son and the relevant circumstances/background. As a result of their experiences, Dylan's foster carers recommended that LAC reviews should involve only those individuals who had adequate knowledge of the circumstances, namely, that consistency of personnel should be maintained:

And you kind of felt with them [previous statutory representatives who had knowledge of Dylan] that they had the power to act on things to change things . . . Recently it's just been a formality . . . It has to be done so we'll do it and get it over as quickly as possible.

Sue's foster mother described LAC reviews as invariably ineffective because of a lack of meaningful dialogue between her foster daughter's birth parents and social workers, as typically the review would end in a row between the two.

Seven foster carers described their experiences of the LAC reviews more positively. Apart from Martin's foster mother, they all considered them to be of significant value, an opportunity to have their concerns listened to/dealt with, and to catch up with the range of professionals involved in their child's care. For example, Libby's foster mother felt that she and her husband were respected, their views were listened to, and they were treated as their foster daughter's "real" parents:

> Well, I find them good, I find that I need to get said what I need to say.

Although less enthusiastic, Martin's foster mother described the reviews as 'not too bad', in that she was able to make her points, and she felt that the current chairperson was willing to listen to her.

Kinship carers

Eleven of the 12 kinship carers interviewed addressed this issue. The majority (n = 8) were, overall, satisfied with the support they had received. Two carers were unreservedly complimentary, with Rebecca's carer describing the assigned social worker as being very supportive:

> She is a phone call away any time I need her. She is there at the other end of the phone and if anything was to happen, she would be here, no problem . . . We've got a great social worker.

However, most carers highlighted at least one problematic issue. Annie's grandmother praised the access her granddaughter had been given to out-of-school activities, but was critical of the pressure exerted by Social Services for Annie to return to counselling, which she had found upsetting and which her carer had withdrawn her from. Annie's carer commended Social Services for their timely payment of standard allowances, as well as additional expenses, such as school-related expenses and birthday presents. She also considered all contact/link workers assigned to them over the years to have been supportive. Her one complaint was that the allowances themselves were inadequate, contrasting these with what foster carers are paid for "working" for Social Services. Although Orlaith's aunt found the social worker's monthly visits to be personally supportive, she complained about the frequent changes in assigned social workers, as these adversely affected her niece, who would be gaining trust in one social worker only to have them replaced by another. The same complaint, regarding staff turnover, was raised by David's aunt, who considered this to militate against meaningful relationships between both her and her nephew and appointed social workers. Orlaith's aunt described her frustrations:

> *They [social workers] are fine regarding me, and they can be very supportive. It was a bit hard at the start that there were so many different social workers. I didn't like that change in social workers so often; it wasn't fair on the child, because you would only get to know one social worker and then the next minute, 'Oh, Orlaith has a new social worker' ... She had one for about two years who she got on so well with, and then chopping and changing social workers ... A child gets to know somebody, to confide in somebody ... and then next minute there is a stranger coming to the door. To me it's wrong, all wrong.*

Maggie's grandparents considered that, although their current link worker was supportive, on balance, the majority were more supportive of their granddaughter's mother than themselves. Nonetheless, they sought continuing Social Services involvement for two reasons: firstly, the financial support provided that they, as pensioners, were dependent on to raise their granddaughter and, secondly, the advocacy role assumed by Social Services when they experienced problems with their granddaughter's mother and her ongoing push for custody.

Only one kinship carer was exclusively critical of Social Services. Nathan's grandmother complained about the manner in which her grandson was initially placed with her. Rather than being asked if she could take her grandson and his sister, and be supported to do so, she was told that there was no other option:

> No other option. The children were dumped on us . . . That's honestly, I'm telling you nothing but the truth . . . and the social worker says you have to take them, didn't ask will you take them . . . just take them.

Similar to Marie's carers, Nathan's grandmother complained that they had received very little financial support in the first three or four years until the situation was formalised as kinship foster care.

Kinship carers' experiences of other services and support accessed through Social Services varied, with two carers describing this support in positive terms, and two in essentially negative terms. Maggie's grandparents talked about the respite care they received for their granddaughter approximately twice per year. Both Marie and Nathan's carers described the counselling provided to their children, as well as kinship care grants for a wide range of items. However, although Marie's carers considered the latter to be adequate, Nathan's grandmother was heavily critical, focusing on the appointed kinship care link worker whom she found totally unsupportive. The most recent example of such lack of support concerned her request for a grant to buy her grandson a shed for Christmas. Although the link worker stated that grants for such items were not available, the grandmother had subsequently discovered that a grant for a shed had been paid out previously.

Of those kinship carers who talked about LAC meetings specifically, the majority (n = 5) were, overall, positive. Accordingly, Annie's grandmother considered the LAC meetings to be "okay", in that she was able to update Social Services, as well as raise any concerns she might have. Three carers considered that they were allowed to meaningfully contribute to the meetings, and Nathan's grandmother commented that she wouldn't miss them, considering them to be an important opportunity to learn what Social Services and the link worker were planning concerning her grandson. However, Marie and

Áine's carers considered the meetings to be 'a waste of time' (described as such by both). For Marie's carer this was because, over the years of attending, they considered that their requests and concerns had not been taken into consideration.

Two carers talked explicitly about keeping their involvement with Social Services to a minimum. In particular, they did not seek any financial support, on the grounds that they wanted to care for the child in the same way as they did for their birth children. For Jessica's aunt, irrespective of her niece's special needs and concomitant expenses, she and her husband financed Jessica's care by themselves as much as possible. This included all aspects of her educational special needs and health care provision. In the same vein, David's aunt explained her motivation for looking after her nephew:

The way I look at it, I don't do it for the money . . . David is like my child.

Eoghan's grandmother's lack of involvement with Social Services was the result of previous negative experiences. She had stopped asking for help because of repeated experiences of being denied adequate financial support to care for her grandson, in the context of caring for her other (at the time, young) children. She described Social Services as "using" her, and contrasted the lack of support she received to that given to the foster carer who had briefly looked after her grandson, and who had been in receipt of full allowances.

Residence order carers

All residence order carers addressed this issue, with the majority citing either no involvement with Social Services or involvement consisting solely of financial support (n = 6). These carers stated that involvement consisted simply of statutory payment for their child's care. Both Jemma and Jo's carers talked about how they had taken out the residence order primarily to ensure that Social Services were no longer involved in their lives. Both stressed how its granting had enabled them to lead a more "normal" family life. Jemma's carers explained some of the challenges she faced before the order had been granted:

And she wanted to go and stay at other people's house, wee girls that she met in school and all and she wasn't allowed to go.

Similarly, Jo's carer did not want her to feel different from the other children at school, because of Social Services' involvement in her life:

But I didn't want them going to school and the Welfare going into the school and the kids getting them going and calling them "welfare baby" and all that.

A number of carers (n = 5) complained about what they saw as unfair discrimination against children cared for under a residence order, i.e. being denied funding and other resources from both core Social Service budgets, as well as the Fostering Network, which were routinely provided to fostered children. Thus, Conall's carer stressed how all such children were cared for under the same criteria/ arrangements, including those concerning contact with birth parents, and he therefore believed there should be equality in the provision of funding. Although pleased that they no longer needed to have any involvement with Social Services since the granting of the residence order, Kirsten's carer contrasted the availability of quite generous resources (e.g. sports equipment, laptops) for her foster children with the complete lack of any such resources for Kirsten under the residence order:

But what I do think is not fair is the Fostering Network. I find that very unfair . . . where the rest of the children in the house are getting things that they need and Kirsten gets nothing.

Luke's grandparents echoed these sentiments when discussing the fact that they had unintentionally forfeited a substantial amount of money by opting to care for their grandchildren as their designated "grand-parents" as distinct from "carers". They considered the system to have treated them very unfairly. Luke's grandmother had had to ask for extra help that year for the first time since assuming care of her four grandchildren, including money for school uniforms as well as school trips. Jonny's carers described their son as unfairly discriminated against as compared to another boy they fostered long-term, with the latter receiving both specific items (e.g. a laptop) as well as financial support (e.g. for training courses), none of which were available to Jonny.

Similarly, Megan's carers contrasted their personal benefit gained from the granting of the residence order (in that it provided them with security) with the disadvantage suffered by their daughter, in that she lost out on significant financial support that continued to be available to other children whom they fostered. As Megan's carers explained:

It helped us but they lost out ... we may have benefitted from the residence order but they lost, if that makes sense.

Although they received an allowance for Megan's care (which they argued was essential to their ability to care for her and two other children for whom they had been granted residence orders, given their limited household income), they stressed that continued access to funds, such as those provided through the Fostering Network, would have helped their children significantly, citing the example of laptops that would have benefitted them in their GCSE coursework.

Megan's carers offered suggestions regarding four other issues. First, they advocated the continuing involvement of Social Services, no matter how limited/infrequent, commenting that they had just disappeared three months after the residence order was granted. They suggested that the availability of such help and advice, even if it was never sought, could potentially help both carers and children cope with problematic issues as and when they arose. In addition, it would ensure continuity of care. Second, they advocated the extension of residence order authority to 18 years of age, describing their eldest child on a residence order (aged 16) as now "in limbo", being neither formally in nor out of a care situation. Third, they suggested that the number of training courses required to be completed was excessive. Despite the fact that they were considered suitable for the granting of a residence order, they still had to complete annual training. Fourth, they suggested that the current upper limit of three children under a residence order, as well as three children under foster care, per household was problematic. Not only did it mean that individual carers could become overloaded, it also had the potential to create resentment among children in that those under a foster care arrangement would be able to access financial help to buy specific things/undertake training, which was denied to those under a residence order.

Roisin, Caoimghin and Greg's grandfather as well as Ryan's carer also complained about the financial support available but, in contrast to those quoted above, it appeared that they received no financial allowances whatsoever. Thus, Roisin, Caoimghin and Greg's grandfather talked about the lack of support from Social Services, contrasting this to the much welcomed support he had previously received (e.g. respite care, equipment, household appliances) to help with his three grandchildren's care. He highlighted that he had not fully appreciated that all support would come to an end with the granting of the residence order, but believed that he had had little choice but to seek this for all three grandchildren, given his previous personal circumstances. He described the lack of respite care as curtailing his own activities and social life, and the lack of financial support as preventing him from being able to provide for his grandchildren optimally:

So, no, since I got the residence order, they [Social Services] won't have anything to do with the children.

Similarly, Ryan's carers focused on the lack of any support (financial or otherwise) from Social Services, commenting on how they had had to pay the full court fees of £2,000 when their son's birth mother had recently contested the residence order access arrangements.

Only two carers talked about any other type of involvement with Social Services. For Gary's carer, involvement was limited to infrequent requests for contact between her son and his birth family. She talked about applying for a residence order (as distinct from adoption) because of the financial support available:

I thought if we adopt him . . . that was that and times is hard enough to get through.

Julie's carers talked about the statutory allowance they received as their daughter's carers, as well as the four times per week home help support. They highlighted that, up until very recently, they had not been accorded their full rights as residence order carers. This had caused significant problems for them in relation to their daughter's health care. Julie needed frequent operations, some of which had had to be postponed or cancelled because the hospital authorities had not known that they were eligible to sign for health care procedures, and a social worker had failed to attend on the day.

Both Nicole and Sarah's carers had an entirely different attitude, stressing that they did not look for or need any support from Social Services. As stated by Sarah's carer:

Sarah wants for nothing. Anything she needs, she gets it.

Similarly, Nicole's aunt commented that she had accepted her niece 'as my own', so that any issues that emerged were dealt with within the family, as any other issues would be. She and her husband added that caring for their niece had been helped enormously by the fact that she had been accepted so readily by both sides of the family, responded to, and cared about the same as all the others.

Social support

Birth parents

Birth parents tended to mention similar sources of support, principally provided by family (n = 3) and friends (n = 4). Support from friends tended to be that which helped on a day-to-day or ad hoc basis (e.g. brief periods of looking after their child while they took care of time-limited chores, or to "sound off" to when feeling under stress). These friends were usually neighbours living locally and the child care provided was reciprocal, as described by Aidan's birth mother:

If I need to nip to the shop I'd say look, he doesn't want to come with me, is it alright if you keep an eye on him 'til I come back down again . . . and the same goes for them [neighbours].

Family support, when provided, tended to be more extensive. Even when such support decreased as circumstances changed over the years, and as children grew older and became more independent, the parents' strong sense of being able to rely on their family, if necessary, remained. For instance, Emma's birth father described the invaluable help he received from his sister:

The sister minded her for six weeks for me, see sometimes you don't know how lucky you are with family. Like, I feel sorry for young fellas or girls out there who have nobody.

However, the general sense conveyed within the birth parent group was of a lack of support, particularly from within family (n = 4). In such cases, the parents tended to see themselves as essentially "on their own" in terms of looking after their child and, irrespective of claiming they wished to rely on themselves, there could be a sense of isolation and loneliness. For example, Jim's mother talked about the fact that she was too preoccupied with looking after her five children to be able to maintain friendships. Given her particular circumstances, the lack of any respite care, particularly the lack of support from Social Services, was keenly felt. Ashley's mother stressed her and her daughter's isolation from others, including potential friends and especially her family, because of her determination not to have to ask for help from anyone. Although she talked about feeling proud of having raised her daughter alone, she acknowledged the limitations of relying entirely on social benefits, as well as the adverse social and emotional impact on herself, particularly as her daughter became older and closer to leaving home. Bronagh's parents considered themselves to have succeeded in reuniting their family in the face of little support from those they considered they should have been able to call on (i.e. support from father's previous employer), as well as the active opposition of Social Services:

As for my brothers and sisters, as I said, I never see them so they weren't supportive at all . . . so we were doing it by ourselves . . . I don't need anybody else I'd say . . . what I have got inside these four walls, that's all I need.

When support from statutory agencies other than Social Services was mentioned, it was usually in relation to their child (e.g. school or family counselling). However, birth parents had received help on a personal basis as well, such as counselling, family support worker, or housing authority help to access appropriate accommodation. Parents were generally appreciative of these services and co-operated with them, working together to advance their child's (and their own) development and prospects.

Foster adoptive parents

Foster adoptive parents tended to talk about the support provided from within their extended family (n = 6), as described by Bridget's adoptive parents:

We're quite fortunate in that we have a quite strong family unit in and around here, so you have a lot of support from the mother-in-law and the two sisters and the two brothers-in-law and then from my lot . . . you know, so it's a strong family unit, so any support you need is always there.

Family support was crucial for Laura's adoptive mother due to her ongoing health issues, which left her unable to do much housekeeping. An adult birth daughter had moved back into the home to help look after her, as well as her adoptive daughter. Amy's adoptive mother considered that raising her daughter, particularly concerning the issues with birth parents/birth family, would have been impossible had she not had the support of her wider family. Although Danny's adoptive mother tended not to look for any family help in looking after her son, on the rare occasions she did ask, it was always freely given, with both her adult son and one of her adult daughters taking Danny for occasional overnight stays.

Karl's adoptive father described extensive family support in looking after his son, as an adult birth daughter lived at home and was closely involved in Karl's care, and other adult children living elsewhere regularly took him for weekend stays and days out. Similarly, Justin's adoptive mother talked about wide-ranging help from family, particularly her adult birth children, who took Justin overnight, and at the weekends, to give her some respite. Steve's adoptive mother described the help she received from adult girls she had fostered some years ago and who had grown up with her son as, in effect, their younger brother. They continued to be very close to him, and he saw them as his sisters:

> Most of my support would come from the girls I fostered years ago. Three girls live quite close to me . . . and they would be very supportive, they have a great relationship with Steve and would be very close to him because he came here as a baby . . . and he would go to their houses, have my sister as well. She is a social worker and works in fostering and I would talk to her quite a bit, I can talk to her if I need to.

In Joey's case, no support was sought from either within or outside the family. Joey's adoptive mother commented that she and her husband took care of their son by themselves, partly because of his autism and consequent dependence on them. Two foster adoptive parents talked about support received from statutory/voluntary agencies. Laura was taken for days out by a Barnardo's service, during which time she was offered counselling. Steve's adoptive mother described the support of her foster care link worker as invaluable, less in the context of facilitating access to services for her son, and more as somebody who understood her circumstances, and thus to whom she could "sound off" or ask questions.

Stranger adoptive parents

Stranger adoptive parents tended to describe the need for only limited support from outside their own home. On occasions, specific help was sought, e.g. babysitting from a family member when going out for the evening, or the family looking after their child when they were going away for the day themselves. Adoptive parents who both worked full-time required the greatest amount of support. Ciara and Rory were frequently picked up from school by their adoptive grandparents and/or other parents of children at the school, and subsequently looked after by their grandparents, as Ciara's adoptive mother explained:

Well, we certainly would have been stuck without your mum and dad, wouldn't we? . . . even school . . . [my husband] works shifts and I work nine to five, so there are times he is here in the morning and not in the afternoon, and then the other way around . . . [friends] live around the corner too and are a big help with the school runs and what not.

Two stranger adoptive parents described support from statutory agencies other than Social Services. Claire's adoptive mother talked about her ongoing efforts to secure appropriate educational support for her daughter, now in first year of secondary school. She considered that she had had to 'plague the school to get help' when her daughter had been in primary school, eventually securing a dedicated classroom assistant. She considered that the secondary school had provided good educational support for her daughter, who was in a class of only 14, with a teacher and additional classroom assistant. Similarly, Abbie also had learning problems, and her adoptive mother had found the support at primary school level to be inadequate; at secondary level it was considered to be much better in that special needs support had been arranged and she felt that she had effective input. Morgan and Claire's (siblings) and Tracy's adoptive parents commented that they intentionally tried to ensure self-sufficiency. Morgan and Claire's adoptive parents stressed that they carved up their working lives, so that one or both of them would always be with their daughters, as stated by their adoptive mother: 'When we adopted the girls we didn't adopt them to farm them out'. Similarly, Tracy's adoptive parents talked about working through any problems themselves.

Foster carers

The majority of foster carers (n = 11) described extensive help received from members of their immediate and extended family. For Dylan's foster carers, the help given to them by their adult eldest daughter was considered invaluable in relieving the pressure of caring for Dylan. Similarly, Libby's foster mother described her extended family, in particular her mother, as being a constant source of help in terms of babysitting:

You would never have thought, like, you don't think to yourself I can't ask Mummy now or I can't ask our girls because the children aren't ours, you know, it was never like that ... you know, when people say to my mother, how many grandchildren do you have, she always includes them and it's not that she has to think about it ... If you needed a babysitter or if you had to go to your work and the child's sick, they just do what anybody else would do, you bring them down in their pyjamas ... and Mummy would put them on the sofa and put a blanket around them and look after them.

Mary's foster mother's grown-up birth children regularly babysat, and she and her sister (also a foster carer) took turns looking after each other's children for days and short breaks away:

Support in that if you were going somewhere you could call on them ... you always have that network of support, I never hardly need it, thank God, but it's always there and I know it's there ... we never ever felt trapped.

Both Ben and Trevor's foster carers' grown-up birth children looked after their foster sons when required, as described by Ben's foster carers:

As far as he's concerned when we go anywhere he's staying with his big brother.

Similar to Mary's foster carers, Ben's foster carers had two good friends who were also foster carers and they had developed a support network between themselves. Jack's foster mother described her three grown-up children as more than happy to look after her foster son, as and when required. All three were police vetted, and Jack regularly stayed with them for sleepovers, being considered part of the family. Similarly, Connor's foster mother talked about her grown-up children as close to her foster son(s) and consequently very happy to help out when necessary. Two of her grown-up children who lived close by were involved in their care, particularly a birth son who was very hands-on with both boys. Connor's foster mother commented on how much she valued their help:

> I think all foster carers need support as in . . . the rest of the family accepting them.

Martin's foster mother described a very integrated family network in which all of her foster children were involved. Her grown-up birth children were involved in the care of her foster children in that they were included in all family activities, taken everywhere they were going with their own families, as well as given special attention at times (e.g. one of her grown-up sons came every weekend to take them to the cinema).

For different reasons, James and Pol's (siblings), and Anna and Daniel's (siblings) foster carers did not receive any help from family. James and Pol's foster carers' family all lived too far away to provide support. For Anna and Daniel's foster mother, although she did receive help from her family, particularly one sister who helped out with looking after the children, this was relatively infrequent, as she did not like asking them to give up their time.

Five foster carers described support received from statutory agencies other than Social Services. For Dylan's foster carers, the help given to them by their son's paediatrician, who worked tirelessly to find an appropriate treatment regime to control his previous extremely aggressive and abusive behaviour, was considered invaluable. Patrick's foster mother listed the befriending scheme (Strength to Strength) from which her foster son received twice-weekly visits when he was taken out to different social activities, as well as the counselling service to which he had recently been referred, and was awaiting his first appointment at the time of interview. Mary was in receipt of social work therapy in the form of life story sessions with an independent social worker, who visited her once a fortnight. Mary's foster mother believed that this work was helpful to her foster daughter, who always appeared content when she returned from the session. Both Daniel and Martin's foster carers commented very positively on the help provided by the Fostering Network over the course of several years, and in relation to the provision of a range of resources, both material and practical.

Three foster carers talked about support from voluntary agencies other than Social Services, with quite different experiences. Jack's foster mother mentioned the items/finances provided by the Fostering Network, something she had found to be supportive over the years. Similarly, Liam's foster parents talked about the counselling provided to Liam by Barnardo's, which they considered to have been helpful, although he did register a low security of parental/carer attachment on the IPPA. Dylan's foster mother talked about her attempts to access help for him through the CAMHS service, and considered that he had been badly let down by this service, which, despite numerous meetings and consultations with their foster son, had resulted in them concluding that they could not help: 'They were a disgrace'. Only after considerable arguing on their part did CAMHS eventually recommend consultation with a psychotherapist, something that was due to happen shortly after the interview took place, funded by Social Services.

Kinship carers

The majority of kinship carers mentioned the usual sources of support, especially that provided by family. Such support was of varying degrees, from none/very little (n = 2), now and again (n = 2), to much more substantial (n = 3). For instance, Rebecca's carer sought occasional support from her family:

No, no they don't [provide support]. My own family is only a small family ... [name of mother-in-law] would take her now and again.

On the other hand, Annie's grandmother received considerable help from her adult birth son with whom her granddaughter stayed regularly, and who was currently applying to provide more formal respite care in order to allow the grandmother more time to herself. Joanne and Jessica's (siblings) carer talked about the help she received with all her children from her mother and father, as they lived next door and helped her out with all her children. Maggie's grandparents described their birth son (resident in the home) as being very supportive, always being there to look after their granddaughter, should they have to go out:

The only one around is my son ... God help him, he's sort of ... if something came up that I had to go out he'll say, 'Well, I'll stay here sure'. You know, I don't know what we'd do if he happened to be away.

Residence order carers

The vast majority of residence order carers (n = 8) received support from their extended family and, to a lesser extent, from friends. Thus, Greg, Caoimghin and Roisin's grandfather described himself as being in receipt of extensive support from both his ex-partner and ex-wife, as well as sisters, in terms of helping to look after them as and when needed:

I've got plenty of options there ... I don't really want for that sort of support.

Conall's carer talked about the help, primarily in the form of looking after him and taking him for overnight stays, given by her grown-up birth daughter. She described her grown-up children as regularly taking Conall out for the day and including him in their family activities. Similarly, both Ryan and Gary's carers described their birth grown-up children as very supportive, as Ryan's carer elaborated:

Especially my son and daughter-in-law are very, very supportive . . . they are really supportive . . . would babysit at the drop of a hat . . . and even my older daughter . . . it's very good . . . But as I say, if anything happened to me in the morning, my son would have Ryan at the drop of a hat, there would be no question about it.

Kirsten's carer described her as being looked after by her own grown-up children frequently and not only when she actively needed their support. Kirsten was never happier than when she got to stay with one particular grown-up daughter, whose own daughter was the same age, and to whom she was very close. Similarly, Gary's carer talked about how he had never had to go into respite care, including when she was in hospital for an extended period of time, because he always went to stay with one of her grown-up daughters. Sarah's carer described her grown-up birth son as particularly close to Sarah, as he and his girlfriend took her out very frequently, and there was an explicit understanding that should anything ever happen to her or her husband, Sarah would live with him. Luke's grandmother talked about the closeness of all of her family and how she could rely on any of her sons and daughters to help her; one son, in particular, was close to Luke and was more involved in his care. Megan's carer described very good support provided by family:

Very good . . . there's only so many certain ones that can take the two wee ones because they're police checked . . . my friend can take the three big ones . . . So if we were going out for a night . . . the two wee ones have to go down and stay with my niece . . . [husband]'s sister, she has been so good to us, she really has . . . when we started they came on board, big time.

Only Julie's carer did not mention any support received from family or friends. Jo and Julie's carers mentioned support received from statutory agencies other than Social Services. Jo's carer talked about the counselling Jo was currently receiving, which she considered to have been of significant benefit to him, although it should be noted that Jo received a low security of attachment to parents/carers rating for the IPPA–R, which suggests that the counselling had not assisted with his sense of attachment to his carers. Julie's carers received weekly respite care from the Cedar Foundation, as well as home help four evenings per week. They also accessed respite community care from the children's hospice as and when required, for example, if they needed to attend a hospital appointment.

Summary of main findings

- Comparing all six placement groups, it was birth parents who reported the most and, conversely, residence order carers who reported the least, involvement with Social Services. In terms of the perceived quality of the relationship, birth parents emerged as most critical of the support provided by Social Services. To an extent, this may be due to their greater involvement; however, they did talk more about feeling marginalised, undermined and distrusted by Social Services, relative to other carer groups.
- The comparative figures relating to carer group assessment of involvement with Social Services were:
- out of a total of 10 birth parents, three were solely complimentary about their relationship with Social Services, two identified positive and negative aspects, and five were solely critical;
- out of a total of seven foster adoptive parents, none were solely complimentary about their relationship with Social Services, one identified positive and negative aspects, and three were solely critical;
- out of a total of five stranger adoptive parents, one was solely complimentary about the relationship with Social Services, four identified positive and negative aspects, and none were solely critical;
- out of a total of 11 kinship carers, two were solely complimentary about their relationship with Social Services, seven identified positive and negative aspects, and one was solely critical;
- out of a total of 15 foster carers, nine were solely complimentary

about their relationship with Social Services, two identified positive and negative aspects, and four were solely critical;

– the accounts offered by the 13 residence order carers were qualitatively different in that they did not explicitly assess the quality of involvement with Social Services, save for those carers who commented on what they saw as the unfair lack of financial support available to children under a residence order.

• LAC reviews were relevant to three of the carer groups – birth parents, kinship carers and foster carers. Of these three groups, it was birth parents who were most critical of the reviews, with all those who commented highlighting problems, typically related to their sense of marginalisation. Amongst kinship carers, five were positive about the purpose and functions of the reviews, and two were critical. Amongst foster carers, seven were positive and two were critical.

• Given their particular circumstances, fewer adoptive parents were involved with Social Services, so there was, predictably, less talk amongst these groups concerning Social Service support. However, this very lack of involvement was, for some adoptive parents, at least, problematic.

• Amongst the five foster adoptive parents who commented on the issue of withdrawal of Social Services' involvement once the adoption process was completed, four advocated a continued role, albeit one that was essentially "hands-off" and reactive. Amongst stranger adoptive parents, all four who commented on this issue were of the same opinion. Indeed, there was a distinct sense of "abandonment" by Social Services post-adoption. Their descriptions highlight a sense of being "on their own", without access to support, and with a concomitant sense of offence and vulnerability. These experiences underpinned their recommendation that it should be possible for adoptive parents to contact Social Services at any time should anything arise in relation to the care/welfare of their child, about which they required guidance. To a much lesser degree, the same issue was evident within the residence order carer group.

- In addition to the above, carers' accounts highlighted the following issues (in no particular order of importance):
- some adoptive parents expressed awareness of being deliberately misinformed about aspects of their child's (birth) history/circumstances; typically, relevant information was withheld, leaving them feeling less equipped to deal with issues arising. Others felt undermined in their now legal role as parents when Social Services insisted on organising certain aspects of their child's lives, for example, in making contact arrangements, or in their treatment of them as somehow different from/less than "normal" or "real" (birth) parents;
- some kinship carers experienced a sense of disregard and concomitant lack of support regarding them taking on the care of a family child; and felt less valued/supported by Social Services precisely because they were relatives;
- some residence order carers viewed the granting of the residence order as an effective way of disengaging from involvement with Social Services. Such disengagement was seen as a way of furthering their ability to lead a normal family life. In contrast, other residence order carers advocated a continued role for Social Services in the lives of their children, specifically in terms of the provision of financial support; in this context the unfair difference between the treatment of foster care children (who received financial support provided through the Fostering Network, for example) and children under a residence order, who received no such support, was highlighted. The effects of this discrimination were magnified in cases where a participant was caring for children under a residence order as well as foster children.
- There was some evidence of inconsistency in payment to residence order carers, with some receiving some form of financial help, and others receiving nothing.
- Across all six groups, the most important source of support provided was by the family.
- The group in which family support appeared to count for least was that of birth parents. Not only did this group tend to talk more

about the support provided by friends, but, overall, this group of parents emerged as having access to the least extensive network of support, in relation to both family and friends.

- At the opposite end of the continuum, both foster carers and residence order carers appeared to have had access to the most extensive/comprehensive family support networks. The accounts offered by these carers suggest that their extended families were closely involved in the lives of their children. Support from extended family was also provided on an extensive basis for the majority of foster adoptive parents.

13   Discussion and conclusion

Introduction

The Care Pathways and Outcomes study had two main aims: firstly, to ascertain whether or not young children in care fared differently depending on the long-term placement provided for them, i.e. adoption, foster care, kinship care, on residence order, or with birth parents; and secondly, to identify differences (if any) within and between the various types of placement. Its primary focus was to highlight the perspectives of the children's themselves, in ways that captured their development, sense of family, and health and wellbeing; and to explore what appeared to be working well and not so well for these children, in order to help inform policymakers and practitioners, locally, nationally, and internationally, of their needs in long-term placements.

The findings presented in Chapters 3 to 12 have shown evidence of a placement effect, in that there were differences, sometimes significant, in performance on both quantitative and qualitative measures between the groups of children in the different placements. However, the over-riding finding in this study was the uniformity of experience that was apparent between the groups, with each group demonstrating internal variations in experience, but with these being quite similar across all groups. The remainder of this chapter draws together the key findings from each of these chapters, discusses these in the light of what we already know about the lives of these children, and draws out their implications for policy and practice regarding the long-term placement of young children in care.

Placement patterns

The significant number and proportion of children from the study population who were either adopted (42%) or placed for adoption

(3%) by 2007 is evidence of the growth of a "permanence movement" in Northern Ireland, which appeared to accelerate at the time the study commenced in 2000, with prior rates of adoption being relatively low (Kelly and Coulter, 1997; Kelly and McSherry, 2002). It is not clear why there was such a radical practice shift towards using adoption as a long-term placement option for children in care in Northern Ireland. However, four possible contributory factors can be suggested, with these being primarily related to a growing momentum towards adoption in the later part of the 1990s.

Firstly, when the current legislative framework that governs the placement of children in care was introduced, i.e. the Children (Northern Ireland) Order 1995, the regulations and guidance required that a plan for achieving permanency be considered at each statutory Looked After Child (LAC) review. Secondly, in 1996/97, the Northern Ireland Adoption Forum engaged with a range of relevant agencies in a consultation process on its discussion paper on adoption as a placement option for children in care (Kelly, 1999). In a follow-up to these discussions, in February 1998, a Department of Health and Social Services (DHSS) conference advocated the examination of adoption as a viable option in the family and child care programme, and to ensure that all the necessary systems were in place to support this.

Thirdly, social work academics based in Northern Ireland were beginning to promote the importance of permanence for children in care, and were advising the Trusts on how best this could be achieved (Kelly and Coulter, 1997; Kelly, 1999). Fourthly, a DHSS Circular, *Permanency Planning for Children: Adoption – Achieving the right balance* (May 1999), for the first time required Trusts to consider adoption as a long-term placement for children in care in their children's service plans.

The current study does appear to have mirrored this shift in long-term placement policy in Northern Ireland towards adoption. Similarly, the DHSSPS (2006, p. 61) noted that 'the sudden leap in the numbers of children placed for adoption in 2001–2002, and the increasing use of freeing during that year, may indicate that permanency policies are beginning to have an impact on the lives of children in care'.

Governmental statistical data from Northern Ireland indicate that the percentage of children being adopted from care between 2002 and 2008 has hovered at between two and three per cent (DHSSPS, 2009b). However, these statistics are based on an assessment of the number of children being adopted from the total care population on a biennial basis, and do not reflect the radical changes in placement practices that have been witnessed in this study. This highlights the importance of longitudinal design when conducting research relating to children in care.

The use of the percentage of children in care adopted annually, as a measure of the use of adoption from care, appears to be unsatisfactory, as it only provides a snapshot of the rates of adoption and because most children in care are never likely to be adopted. Most children and young people in care tend to be too old for adoption, have well-established links with their birth families that render adoption unsuitable, and may be well settled in foster care (Lowe and Murch, 2002). The current study, however, tracks a population of children who were under the age of five when the study commenced, with 90 per cent having spent longer than three months in care at that point in time and with an expectation that they would remain in care for a lengthy period (McSherry et al, 2010). Consequently, it is primarily focused on children who might be described as eligible for adoption and may thus provide a more accurate account of the use of adoption in Northern Ireland than the biennial statistics on adoption rates that are currently available.

Regional variations

In terms of the types of background factors that were related to care pathways, a key finding was the significant relationship that existed between the child's HSC Trust locality and their care pathway. Given that comparisons conducted across multiple background variables (reason for entry to care, parental problems, etc.) showed that the groups of children within each of the HSC Trusts were very similar, the findings suggest that within Northern Ireland, the type of care pathway that young children in care follow may depend on the HSC Trust area they live in, the all too familiar "postcode lottery". Findings from England and Wales highlight similar regional placement patterns (Department of Health, 1998, Biehal *et al*, 2010). The Department of Health (1998) flagged up the challenge associated with balancing the need for local solutions that matched situational need whilst also avoiding the pitfalls of the "postcode lottery", whereby variation between local authorities may result in poor care experiences and reduced opportunities for children. The issue was highlighted during the review of adoption services in Northern Ireland (DHSSPS, 2002), with plans made to regionalise some parts of the adoption service (DHSSPS, 2006), and in 2012, some aspects of the adoption and foster care services for the five HSC Trusts in Northern Ireland were reorganised into one regional service.

A key question remains: if the needs of the child are central to deciding on a long-term placement, and the children across the five HSC Trusts were very similar in their backgrounds and needs, why were regional variations found in professional decision-making regarding long-term placements for these children? The reform of public administration that took place in 2007, the development of regional policy and procedures in relation to adoption, and the Government's push to regionalise aspects of the adoption service, may promote greater consistency across the different HSC Trusts. However, consistency may not be improved if the reasons for the variations stem from the opinions and values of decision-makers regarding the appropriateness of different types of long-term placements. It is hoped that the findings of this study will help inform future professional decision making, both by Social Services and within the courts, in terms of highlighting the potential strengths and weaknesses of the different long-term placement options available, and how these placement options have the capacity to meet the child's individual needs.

Age at entry to care

An important finding that emerged from this study was the significant difference in age that the children first entered care across the pathway groups. In terms of the adoption pathway, as many as 69 per cent of these children first entered care at less than one year old, with a similar percentage for those children in the residence order (67%) pathway. In England, Sinclair *et al* (2005) also found that adoption tended to be restricted to very young children. They found that 75 per cent of their sample who were under two years old when their study began in 1997, had been adopted by 2000, in comparison with only 40 per cent of those aged between two and four. For children under one year old at the beginning of their study, they noted that 'adoption and birth family were essentially the only options for this age group' (p. 93).

While endorsing the spirit of Sinclair and colleagues' conclusions, the findings of the current study indicate that, whilst adoption within Northern Ireland is similarly heavily weighted towards children who come into care under the age of one, foster care also continues to be a sizeable placement option for these children, representing 38 per cent of those who followed both the kinship and foster care pathways. These findings reflect the variation in long-term placement options across different HSC Trusts highlighted earlier. For example, of all the children who entered care under one year old across the five HSC Trusts, no children from the Southern HSC Trust remained in care by 2004, whereas this figure was as high as 52 per cent in the Western HSC Trust. Furthermore, the finding that eight per cent of those children on the adoption pathway in 2007 were aged between three and four years old when they first entered care suggests that in Northern Ireland adoption is not the sole preserve of babies.

Length of time in care

The study findings indicated that the longer children were in care the less likely it was that they would return home. For example, 60 per cent of those on the birth parent pathway in 2007 had been in care for less than a year when the study commenced, compared with around

40 per cent for each of the other pathways. This would appear to reflect the fact that most children who return to their birth parents do so within three months of entering care (McSherry *et al*, 2010) and that the likelihood of returning home decreases as length of time in care increases (Biehal, 2006; Thoburn *et al*, 2012).

In the longer term, it was also found that there was a steady increase in the numbers of children living with birth parents between 2000 and 2002, but that this levelled out between 2002 and 2007. This provided further evidence that the likelihood of a child returning home from care decreases the longer they remain in care, and that there appeared to be a critical period for a return home, i.e. up to two years after the study commenced, beyond which a return home became highly unlikely.

Placement stability

It was found that this population of children had been provided with a very high level of stability in their placements. Adoptive placements provided the greatest degree of stability between 2000 and 2007 (99%), with kinship (95%) and birth parent (95%) placements also showing very high levels of long-term stability. Although extremely high even when compared with research findings in Great Britain (Sinclair *et al*, 2005; Biehal *et al*, 2010), the high levels of stability found for adoptive placements is what might have been expected, given the extent to which related research has highlighted stability as one of the main advantages of adoption over other types of long-term placements. However, the fact that birth parent placements were also found to have very high levels of stability (95%) was quite unexpected. Ward *et al* (2003) questioned the logic of describing birth parent placements as "permanent", as there tends to be frequent movement between family members for these children. Unfortunately, the current study was not designed to examine this aspect of the children's lives after they returned to live with birth parents.

Further, even though children in foster care had the lowest level of stability in their placements (87%), as might have been predicted considering similar research in Great Britain (Sinclair *et al*, 2005;

Biehal *et al*, 2010), the figure is still comparatively high, and could be described as a successful placement type in terms of providing stability. Literature widely reports that the risk of disruption or breakdown in long-term placements increases as the child gets older. The children in the current study were interviewed in 2009/10, when they were aged between nine and 14. Hence, this early adolescent stage may have been a contributing factor to placement stability. The next phase of this study, "the teenage years", will reflect on the impact that the middle and late adolescent phase may have upon these high levels of placement stability, particularly when comparing adoption and long-term foster care. Interestingly, the recruitment process which took place in 2009 indicated that some (n = 3) long-term foster placement disruptions/breakdowns had occurred since the placement profile for the study population was specified in 2007. In the next phase of the study, further analysis will explore more comprehensively the factors which lead to placement breakdown in long-term placements, particularly in respect of child development and placement needs.

Children's attachments

A primary concern when children enter the care system is on maintaining and preserving attachments with birth parents, so that a speedy return can be made with as little damage as possible done to these important relationships. Where rehabilitation is not likely, a delicate balance needs to be struck between maintaining existing attachments to non-resident birth parents, whilst also allowing these children to develop new attachments with new resident carers, and potentially new parents. This often requires complex negotiation and planning by professionals, but the greatest mental flexibility, and resolution of complexity, is required by the children themselves, a reconfiguration of their internal working models (Bowlby, 1958).

Most of the children in this study, irrespective of placement type, received high security of attachment ratings to their parents/carers. Although some non-significant variation in attachment score was evident within each of the placement groups, the pattern of distribution was very similar, suggesting that type of placement had little effect on the children's attachment relationships. What did appear to be important was the *length* of placement. Most of the children had remained in these placements from a very young age, and as evidenced by the interviews with children and their parents/ carers, had formed new and lasting attachments to their new parents/ carers, whilst also skilfully negotiating a new mental representation of the relationship, or lack of, with their birth parents. Similar to other related research findings (Rushton, 2003; Kaniuk *et al*, 2004; Biehal *et al*, 2010), it appeared that these new parents and carers had provided these children with the necessary security to progress through life, and handle the challenges that it presented, irrespective of the social or legal definition associated with the placement itself.

Triseliotis (2002) commented that adoption provides higher levels of emotional security and a stronger sense of belonging than long-term foster care, whilst Sinclair *et al* (2005) found that adopted children did better than children in long-term foster care on most outcome variables. The findings of the current study in relation to security of attachment to parents/carers, and the children's own depictions of family and their sense of connection to their birth and alternative families, did not concur with this view. The attachment profile for children in the foster care, kinship care, and residence order groups was equally positive, and on occasion more positive, when compared with children who had been adopted. In the kinship, foster care, and residence order groups, as in the adoption group, their carers were invariably specified as being the closest and most important to them. Rarely were their birth parents specified with the same degree of closeness or importance.

However, this perspective is nuanced, as almost all the children in foster and kinship care, on residence order, and with birth parents, stated that they wanted to live with their current parents/carers when aged 16 or older. In contrast, bearing in mind that these children were aged between nine and 14 years old, only a small proportion of children in either stranger or foster adoption held this desire. Does this difference tell us anything about the nature of attachment in adoption compared to other forms of long-term placement?

As this is not an aspect of the relationship with adoptive parents and other long-term carers that has been researched within this area to date, any interpretation of these findings is speculative at this stage. However, it might be argued that these findings suggest that adopted children have less of an attachment to their adoptive parents, or have a less well-defined sense of permanence within their current living arrangements than children in other long-term placements. It was also interesting to note that there did appear to be an association between children who had received low or medium IPPA-R scores, and their wish not to be living with their parents/carers at 16. It could also be argued that because adopted children tend to have relatively less knowledge and experience of their birth parents, they might consequently have greater ambivalence about the permanence of their placement with their adoptive parents.

Another interpretation is that, although only in early adolescence, the adopted children may have been beginning to negotiate the transition from dependence upon parents/carers, which epitomises early attachment relationships, to having the confidence to consider a world where they would be moving away from dependence on their adoptive parents to greater independence, which would be consistent with normal development (Bardwick, 1974; Rutter *et al*, 1976; Maier, 1986). The fact that most of the children in the other placement types wanted to remain living with their parents/carers might suggest that the functional/survival aspect of the attachments that they had with their parents/carers was still in the ascendency, in other words, there was still enough uncertainty in their lives for them to solely depend upon the secure base provided by their parents/carers, and to view this as still necessary when they were older.

It does appear ironic that the research evidence would suggest a contrary position regarding where these children would be living when 16 years old, with this being less likely to be with current carers for those children in foster and kinship care (contrary to what they desire), than those adopted (apparently contrary to what they desire). The next phase of the study will examine the lives of these children when they are aged between 14 and 18 years old, and it will be very interesting to see if the desire of the children in foster and kinship care to remain with their carers continues, and if the desire of the adopted children to live elsewhere wanes, and if changes in opinion do become evident, it will be interesting to understand why these changes have occurred.

Children's self-concept

The research literature suggests that children who have been abused and neglected are more likely to have overall poor self-esteem and self-concept because of feelings of incompetence, and lack of support and encouragement from their birth parents (Kim and Cicchetti, 2009). For many of the children in the current study, this would have been their experience of early life with their birth parents. Yet, the findings on the standardised children's self-concept scale did not portray a negative picture. On the contrary, the findings indicated that most of the children, irrespective of placement type, scored within the average or high range, across all dimensions. In terms of their development of self-concept, these children were doing as well as, and in some instances better than, their non-care peers.

This may be a profile that would have been expected for the adopted group, but perhaps not either of the care groups (foster and kinship), or the birth parents group, who are traditionally thought to have been more damaged by their care experiences. So, how can this be explained? It may be that the answer comes from other research that suggests that children who receive affection, acceptance, safety, and assistance from their parents/carers, are more likely to show high levels of self-esteem and self-concept (Kim and Cicchetti, 2003; DeHart et al, 2006). The vast majority of the children who were interviewed for the current study were in stable long-term placements since infancy. From the interviews that were conducted with the children and their parents/carers, it was clear that these relationships were mostly underpinned by mutual love and affection. It would appear, therefore, that the support, encouragement, love and affection that have been provided by the parents/carers have helped mitigate against any more negative and self-defeating early experiences they may have had with their birth parents.

These findings highlight two important points. First, that any discussion of the potential impact that being in care can have on children, the "outcome" debate, should be informed not only by cross-sectional reviews of populations, but also by longitudinal studies that have the capacity to reflect a more positive perspective of children who remain in stable long-term placements, and whose profile, as argued by Rushton (2004), tends to be very similar to that for adopted children. Second, as was the case with attachment to parent/carers, children's self-concept did not vary significantly with the type of placement. This suggests that at this point in their developmental trajectory, the critical issue for ensuring their positive self-concept has been the longevity of their placement, and their relationships therein, rather than the legal or social definition of the placement itself.

Children's health

In recent years, the Government has set out to address the poor health of children in care. *Every Child Matters* (DCSF, 2003) has served as an overarching framework from which subsequent policies have been developed. In Northern Ireland, *Our Children and Young People – Our Pledge* (OFMDFM, 2006) aimed for all children to be healthy, stay safe, enjoy and achieve, make a positive contribution, and achieve economic wellbeing. Other national policies specifically aimed at driving forward the children in care agenda, have included: *Care Matters: Time for change* (DfES, 2007); *Care Matters: Time to deliver for children in care* (DCSF, 2008); and *Healthy Lives, Brighter Futures: The strategy for children and young people's health* (DoH, 2009).

These policy and strategy documents identified the need to improve health outcomes for children in care, and set out what children and carers should be able to expect from services. The UK government also produced statutory guidance on promoting the health and well-being of children in care, aimed at removing inconsistencies in delivery, and promoting better co-ordinated care (DoH, 2009). However, the health of children adopted from care, or who return home from care, has remained largely ignored at policy level. This may be understood in terms of the lack of statutory duty that resides on the part of HSC Trusts, and de-facto government departments, when children are adopted or returned home. Furthermore, research has also lagged behind in these areas.

The findings that are presented in the current study, in terms of the level and degree of complex health problems for children who are adopted from care, relative to all other types of long-term placement, suggest that there needs to be a re-balancing of the policy focus. This would not necessarily be away from the in-care population, because it is clear that many of the children in foster care (less so in kinship care) had significant health issues, but would include greater consideration of those children who are adopted from care, particularly those adopted by former foster carers, where complex health conditions, such as FAS, predominate.

Where complex health issues are present for children in care, there are statutory provisions in place that, in principle, should facilitate appropriate supports being provided for children and carers. These do not exist for children adopted from care. Consequently, adoptive parents are required to access universal services to deal with these complex health problems, and to deal with the types of stresses that can be related to managing these, in the same way as any other parents in the community. Many of the adoptive parents interviewed felt that this position was untenable, and argued that there was a need for ongoing support for adoptive families post-adoption, particularly where this was deemed necessary by the adoptive parents. One possible mechanism for ensuring that adoptive parents can access services is presented later, in the section on Social services' involvement.

Children's behaviour

Contrary to the belief that adoption by-passes all the problems that children might experience if they were to remain in care, many children who have been adopted from care have been found to experience persistent impairments in their socio-emotional development (Thoburn, 1991; Howe, 1997, 1998; Quinton et al, 1998; McSherry et al, 2008). For example, compared to children placed as babies, older children who were adopted from Romanian orphanages were much more likely to present to mental health services with a range of behavioural problems and psychological needs (Rutter and the ERA Study Team, 1998). Persistent hyperactivity and inattention have also been found for adoptive cohorts. For example, Rees and Selwyn (2009) asked parents and teachers of 130 children adopted beyond infancy (aged between 3 and 11 years) to complete the SDQ. They found that hyperactivity and inattention frequently persisted, despite the adoptions being stable. It was suggested that these persistent difficulties may be linked to dysfunctional hypothalamus-pituitary-adrenal axis programming, associated with adverse early attachment experiences.

The current study highlighted that there were no significant differences between means scores on the different dimensions of the SDQ across the pathway groups. Essentially, the adopted children were viewed by their parents as just as problematic as the children in the other groups. Furthermore, it was the children in kinship care or subject to a residence order who were rated as having fewer behavioural problems by their parents/carers, not the adopted children. Additionally, the parent interviews highlighted a difference between the two adopted groups, with only foster adoptive parents, and not stranger adopters, flagging up concerns regarding the child's behaviour. However, this is not unexpected given the high level of complex health needs highlighted within the adopted group, particularly those children who had been adopted by foster carers.

These findings provide further evidence, if this were needed, that adoption is not a panacea, and that a large minority of these children, as is the case with children who remain in long-term foster or kinship care, on residence order, or living with their birth parents, have behavioural problems that can be related to a range of cognitive/developmental deficits that these children may have (Biehal *et al*, 2010). It could be argued that, as rates of adoption disruption in Northern Ireland are extremely low (only two adopted children out of 170 in the current study), these adoptive parents do not require any additional supports. However, the findings that have been presented here in terms of the health and behavioural challenges faced by adoptive parents, particularly those who were previous foster carers, suggest that many are struggling to maintain these placements, and that the love and commitment they have for their children can be sorely tested. It is worrying to think how these challenges may impact upon the children and parents' relationships as they enter the more challenging teenage years. Clearly, there is a need for those adoptive parents who are facing significant challenges to be afforded the opportunity to avail of support, be that for the children in the form of therapeutic support, or for themselves in the form of additional training or counselling/support services.

Although the degree of behavioural problems was much less for residence order carers, which may be an indicator of the type of children who go on to have their care order superseded by a residence order by their foster or kinship carers, there were still a proportion of carers who were struggling with their child's behaviour. These carers should also be able to avail of support services from Social Services. These could be specified as "placement protection" services, and could also be available to birth parents whose child has returned home from care. Even where the Trust has no statutory obligation to pro-actively provide support, these services could be created to allow for a re-engagement with families where a placement has continued for a specified length of time, for example, an initial three-year period. This would allow the Trust to re-engage with these families and identify any supports that may be required to help sustain the placement in the long term. The alternative is to allow problems to go unchecked, which may result in a placement breakdown, and the child needing placement back in the care system, with the associated interpersonal and financial costs that would involve.

The importance of collecting quantitative and qualitative data was also evidenced in the current study, as some of the parents/carers of the children scoring high in the SDQ had no concerns regarding the children's behaviour, as they knew how to manage it and minimised their problems, while highlighting the strengths and positive aspects of their children's conduct. If only quantitative data had been collected, these complexities would not have been revealed.

In terms of the capacity of the current study to reflect behavioural change for these children across time, comparative analysis between the SDQ data collected from parents/carers in 2003/4 and 2009/10 indicated that there was an increase in mean scores for the adopted children, and a decrease for the children in foster care. Similar findings were found by Biehal *et al* (2010) in their longitudinal study of children in the care system in England. These findings suggest that adoptive parents may be less inclined than foster carers to describe their children as problematic in the early stages of the placement, but that a more realistic appraisal may develop over time. Conversely, the early reflections of foster carers regarding the behaviour of the children may reflect the harsh realities of caring for these children, but that over time and as relationships develop, these challenges may become less pronounced, and certainly this was reflected by the comments made by foster carers regarding the developmental progress that was being made by some of the children.

Children's education

All the groups of children appeared to be performing below average in terms of their scholastic aptitude as measured by the BPVS-II. However, the children who seemed to struggle the most were those living with their birth parents, followed by those in kinship and foster care. This confirms previous research findings that children in care are more likely to experience a range of educational difficulties and have poor educational outcomes (Decheneau, 2011; Flynn *et al*, 2013; DHSSPS, 2012). However, it also shows that children living with birth parents can be educationally more disadvantaged than children in care.

Although adopted children did not seem to perform exceptionally well, they did appear to be doing considerably better than children living with their birth families, confirming Juffer *et al*'s (2005) meta-analytic findings. It is also striking that, although children living with their birth families were finding it hardest to cope at school, they were the group that received fewer supports, whereas foster and adoptive families seemed to better be able to obtain educational support for their children. This suggests that there is a need for statutory services, such as Social Services and schools, to work better with these parents to ensure that appropriate educational support provided to children when they return home from care, perhaps by reviewing their educational needs and access to support at the point of rehabilitation. This would be important for helping these children attain improved educational outcomes, and it would provide them with a better opportunity and chance to improve their lives.

It was also evident from some cases in this study that professionals (social workers and teachers) involved with these children had low expectations of them. This highlights the need for professionals to be cognisant of the influence of their attitudes on their practice. Despite the children's limitations and their background, they have a right to an effective and inclusive education. Helping these children achieve their potential, and understanding how to enhance their strengths and supporting them with their limitations, will safeguard their placement at school and at home, and will give them the opportunity to develop positive life chances and outcomes.

On a more positive note, despite their obvious educational difficulties, it was also found that the majority of children across all pathway groups were able to identify areas of school that they liked, particularly social aspects and practical/active subjects, such as physical education or home economics. Interestingly, teachers emerged as crucial for children liking or disliking particular subjects, and were also viewed as people who were important in their lives and were a source of support. Many parents/carers believed that their children were faring well at school, which suggests that there are positive aspects of school that can be built on to support these children to achieve their educational potential.

Parent/carer stress

The findings from the current study regarding parent/carer stress demonstrated that a significant proportion was experiencing clinical levels of parental stress, albeit at differing levels, across the five pathway groups. This is unsurprising given the reasons the children come into care and their associated difficulties. These findings have important clinical and practical implications, and highlight the need to assist parents and carers with supportive interventions, in order to promote sensitive and nurturing care for these children.

Birth parents in this study seemed to fare worst of all, with higher clinical levels of parental stress than parents/carers from the other pathway groups. However, this differs from other studies of parental stress, as the children of birth parents have experienced care due to childhood adversity, and have returned to their care. Evidently, their children were returned to their care because it was deemed safe to do so. Yet, findings indicated that half of the birth parents were clinically stressed and were more likely to experience clinical levels of distress than parents/carers in the other groups. They also had higher clinical scores in the child difficulty domain and parent–child dysfunctional interaction domain than the other groups.

This would suggest that birth parents faced greater challenges than the other parents/carers in their parenting role. This may be related to their self-efficacy, difficulty coping with their child's behaviour, fear of having their child removed from their care again, their own personal difficulties and its impact on parenting, or their lack of resources and supports. Such levels of parental stress and distress may have an impact on placement stability and on parent and child wellbeing, if unsupported. It is important that research unravels these complexities in order to understand better the situations that birth parents are coping with, so that support that is unstigmatising is accessible for these, at times, "hard to reach" parents.

Adoptive parents had the lowest levels of clinical stress in this study which is consistent with other research evidence (Palacios and Sanchez-Sandoval, 2006; Judge, 2003, 2004) and earlier findings from Phase 2 of the current study (McSherry et al, 2008). A number of explanations for this may be postulated. Firstly, adopters tend to be older couples in stable relationships; they will often have gone through infertility treatment, and may have already had to overcome conflict and stress prior to adopting their long sought child (Ceballo et al, 2004). Secondly, the majority of children in the adopted group came into care under the age of one, and therefore would have experienced less early childhood adversity.

Within the PSI/SF measure, findings on the child difficulty domain showed a more consistent level of clinical scores across the pathway groups than the other domains. Research evidence consistently shows parental stress and children's challenging behaviour to be inextricably linked. Further research investigating the relationship between parental stress and children's challenging behaviour would help identify parents'/carers' needs, and how sensitive parenting and placement stability may be achieved. A longitudinal study such as this one has the opportunity to identify the behavioural difficulties in children and associated parenting stress over time. The next phase of this study may help unravel the cause and effect relationship between these two critical coping indicators.

Previous research suggests that parent wellbeing affects parenting style. Given the significant levels of parent/carer stress in this study, it would be valuable for future research to examine this characteristic using a more clinically sensitive tool. Such a tool would include investigation of parents/carer psychological distress, anxiety and depression, as well as their life satisfaction, wellbeing, efficacy, resilience and coping styles. Research evidence that develops a deeper understanding of how parents/carers internalise and externalise their stress, and which identifies factors that mediate these characteristics within and across different types of long-term placement, will assist in ensuring that these parents/carers are appropriately supported, and consequently that their children's welfare is further promoted.

Children's contact

Recent research evidence shows that contact with birth family members can have both positive and negative consequences for children in care, depending on a range of interrelated factors (Schofield and Beek, 2005). The findings of the current study support the view that contact cannot be governed by a simple rule of thumb, or a "one size-fits-all" approach (Wilson and Sinclair, 2004). The findings indicated that contact can be either detrimental or beneficial depending on the circumstances of the placement. Thus, children reacted in different ways to contact; and while some were upset or angry and refused to go to visits, others seemed happy about the level of contact with particular birth family members, and some longed for more contact. In particular, residence order and foster carers commented that negative reactions were relatively common when the children were younger, but as contact arrangements changed over time, so did children's reactions, mostly for the better.

The concept of "ambiguous loss" (Boss, 1980) has been used to make sense of the experiences of foster children (Lee and Whiting, 2007). However, in the current study it was usefully applied across the different pathway groups to understand the children's experiences of contact with their birth families. Thus, a considerable number of children across the pathway groups considered their birth parents and/or birth siblings to be part of their family (psychologically present), but either had no contact with them or were longing for more (physically absent). Children in foster care and on residence orders were more likely to want more contact with birth relatives, although a few adopted children also wanted more contact with birth family, with their adoptive parents often not being aware of this. These findings suggest that more needs to be done in order to uncover and act upon children's feelings and wishes regarding contact, and this needs to be facilitated appropriately in adoptive placements.

On a practical level, children need to be listened to and consulted about the progress of their contact, and its impact on their wellbeing assessed, monitored, evaluated and adapted to meet their needs when necessary. At a strategic level, robust assessment frameworks need to be developed that focus on the meaningful purpose of contact, detect issues and highlight concerns that need to be addressed if contact is to advance the child's development and wellbeing in a positive way.

Children's communication

While the literature has focused on openness and communication within adoptive placements, this issue has not been sufficiently dealt with in relation to other forms of long-term placement. This is substantiated by the findings from the current study, which highlight the importance of effective communication between children and their parents/carers across the pathway groups. Most parents/carers across the placement groups described communication with their child as easy, and believed that they would disclose their feelings and any problems/worries to them, either immediately or after some encouragement on their part, although some acknowledged that their children would sometimes rather talk with somebody else in the family about certain issues. Some children across the different placement types mentioned talking with their parents/carers about "everyday" issues, but a few also revealed that they shared their secrets and feelings with their parents/carers.

However, despite this natural and positive level of openness between parents/carers and their children, difficulties in communication were identified. Adoptive parents, and some foster and kinship carers, found it hard to talk to their children about their birth families and past history, particularly when dealing with sensitive subjects, such as the birth parents' mental illness; alcohol and drug abuse; or rejection of the children. Furthermore, there were a few contradictions between the parents' and the children's accounts regarding this issue, as some children were curious about their birth family but their parents/carers appeared unaware of this and thought that they were not interested.

It was apparent that out of all the parent/carers, birth parents seemed to struggle the most in terms of communicating with their children, and the majority never talked about or discussed their children's past in care. This suggests that all the groups of parents/carers, but particularly the birth parents, require additional support and/or training to assist them to develop effective communication strategies with their children with regards to their life story. This will help the children to feel cared for and supported and will also support the development of their self-esteem, self-concept, identity, and mental wellbeing (Kernis *et al*, 2000; Levin and Currie, 2010).

Social Services' involvement and social support

Children who are adopted and in other forms of long-term placement often require extensive help and support to assist their developmental recovery (Quinton, 2012). They will likely have experienced separation from attachment figures; lost significant relationships in their lives; experienced some form of maltreatment; been exposed to pre-natal drug and/or alcohol abuse, poor maternal health and/or nutrition; and inherited a predisposition to mental health problems. Consequently, the parents/carers may require the support of a range of routine and specialist services to help them cope, whilst the children themselves may need some form of help (psychological, health, educational, practical or financial) beyond that which their immediate family can offer (Thomas, 2013). The findings of the current study would substantiate this perspective.

The findings concerning the extent to which the parents/carers believed that they were adequately supported by Social Services, and the extent of additional informal supports they were able to avail of, across the pathway groups, point to major differences in parent/carer experiences both within and between the groups. Birth parents presented an overall negative perception of Social Services and highlighted reluctance on their part to approach them for support. Their vulnerability was exacerbated by their being the least able/willing to call on informal supports from family, often relying on friends and neighbours in deprived neighbourhoods.

This presents Social Services with a familiar difficulty. How to provide supports to those who may be unwilling to avail of them? The birth parents in this study made some suggestions to help improve their relationship with Social Services. They viewed that Social Services should ensure that the relationship with the birth parents prior to returning the child was relatively positive by effectively engaging and actively listening to them. This could be achieved in two ways: firstly, by trying to facilitate their contact with their child in care, and when it occurs, ensuring that it takes place in an environment that facilitates normal communication and interaction between parent and child; and secondly, by ensuring that birth parents have their views listened to at LAC reviews.

Both foster and kinship carers, but particularly foster carers, appeared to have relatively positive views of the support that was provided by Social Services, and of the informal network of friends and family that they were able to call upon if needed. Examples were provided of support to carers and children that did appear to help hem with the challenges they were facing. Some carers, however, highlighted concerns in relation to support services that were not provided, even when requested, particularly in relation to educational and therapeutic support for children.

It would be important that HSC Trusts take cognisance of these concerns, given the task facing these carers in terms of providing a stable and supportive environment for these children. Given the financial pressures that HSC Trusts are under, it might be argued that it would be difficult to respond to every request for support from a foster or kinship carer. However, bearing in mind that these carers are ensuring that these vulnerable children have a stable and loving home, where they are being nurtured and encouraged to achieve their full potential, and where a placement disruption could inevitably lead to an extremely expensive residential placement, it would appear sensible to try and meet as many of these requests as possible. One particular concern raised by kinship carers was that they were not being paid the same amount as foster carers for doing the same job, and some residence order carers appeared to be receiving an allowance, whilst others received nothing. These financial discrepancies are evidence that there can at times be an inequitable approach to properly compensating these carers for their important work, and bearing in mind the costs that can be incurred when placements breakdown, it would appear sensible that HSC Trusts try and ensure that they are adequately and equitably funded.

Both groups of adoptive parents felt that the support they had been provided by Social Services prior to their child's adoption was generally adequate, but most did not appear to be prepared for the way that the HSC Trust stepped out of their lives post adoption. Many felt that, given the challenges they faced in terms of the children's complex behavioural and health needs, and early experiences of trauma, adoptive families should be able to avail of post-adoption support, if and when they felt this was needed. One possible idea would be for HSC Trusts to have an additional duty to facilitate an annual or biennial review of adoptions from care. This may take the form of a discussion with the adoptive parents regarding how the placement has been progressing, and identifying any potential areas where particular support could be provided by the HSC Trust, i.e. educational or therapeutic support for children, or counselling and bespoke training for adoptive parents.

For residence order carers, the greatest frustration was not being able to avail of the excellent and often commented upon support provided to children in care by the Fostering Network. It was commonly the case that these carers were caring for children in foster care and well as on residence order, which often compounded the sense of injustice felt, particularly by the children. One carer commented that these children all have the same background, and subsequent challenges, so why should any distinction be made between being in care or on residence order? This is an issue that the Fostering Network and the HSC Trusts may want to consider further. It was interesting, though, that this inequality of opportunity argument was not made by any of the adoptive parents. However, this may be a reflection of their lack of knowledge of the types of additional support provided to children in care, or their view of their children as being distinctly different from children in care.

Of course, the main point of a residence order is to move children out of care. As reflected by the residence order carers who were interviewed in this study, there were positive aspects to this, such as increased carer independence. However, moving to residence order clearly had negative aspects also, such as the removal of Social Services input, and the inability to access support for the child through the Fostering Network. This has implications for social workers working with these families. If foster or kinship carers are considering having the child's care order superseded by a residence order, then the full implications of this needs to be explained to carers by the social worker, particularly the removal of Social Services support that would follow such a change in the child's legal status, and the requirement for carers to manage future relationships with birth parents without recourse to such support. Where requirements for Social Services support for the child are high, then carers may need to be advised that this may not be a course of action that would be beneficial to themselves or the children in the longer term.

Conclusion

The findings presented in this book tell a very positive story about the lives of most of the children who were interviewed as part of the third phase of the Care Pathways and Outcomes study. Irrespective of whether they were adopted, living in long-term foster and kinship care, subject to a residence order, or living with their birth parents, most appeared to be securely attached to their parents/carers, and were happy and content with life. They appeared to be living fulfilling lives and dealing effectively with the problems that life throws up from time to time. Despite their difficult start in life, their prospects for developing into productive and successful adults appeared as realistic as might be expected for many other children in the community. Credit for these positive outcomes must go first and foremost to the children themselves, but their parents/carers also deserve recognition for the commitment that they have made to these children, and the associated sacrifices that this has involved, to support and encourage them through life's journey. Credit also needs to be given to the professionals who have worked with these families, particularly social workers, who were often highly valued and appreciated by parents/carers in this study.

The findings also present a relatively unexpected story. As mentioned in Chapter 1, the main thrust of outcomes research, and media commentary, regarding children in care is often negative. Commenting on this issue, Hare and Bullock (2006, p. 26) noted that 'portrayals of looked after children often rely on misconceptions about their needs, experiences and development. While their disadvantaged status should not be ignored, poor outcomes are often emphasised at the expense of good ones and pejorative stereotypes can prevail'.

Much of the problem appears to stem from the characterisation of the care population as a homogenous group, with little effort to make distinctions between different sub-groups whose experiences in care can be very different. The children in care in the current study were in what Biehal *et al* (2010) defined as "stable" care. Most had been with their carers since infancy, and it appeared that it was this longevity, and the associated capacity of this type of placement to support the development of secure attachments and a strong sense of belonging and family, that was of critical importance in determining the children's positive profiles.

These findings highlight how important it is for researchers and academics in this field to ensure that they describe research on the care population in ways that allow for the different sub-groups to be described discretely, and for accurate comparisons to be drawn between groups, and with children who have been adopted from care. Again, research predominantly continues to specify adoption as providing better outcomes for children than foster care. However, the findings of the current study, and those of Biehal *et al* (2010), illustrate that these differences become less apparent when adoption is compared with long-term stable and secure foster placements, where the carers have long since assumed the parenting role, and this has been accepted and desired by the children themselves.

Of course, it is also important to note that not all the children were doing well. A small minority across the different pathway groups appeared to struggle in terms of their sense of identify within their current placement, were not securely attached to their parents/carers, and consequently struggled with their behaviour at home and in school. This is not unexpected, given the difficult early experiences that they faced, and the types of lingering insecurities that can persist in such circumstances. The point has already been made that there needs to be some mechanism for all the different types of long-term placement to be reviewed at some point in a manner that is less about scrutiny and more about identifying additional support to ensure stability for the placement, where its continuation is considered to be in the child's best interests. These reviews exist in principle for children in foster and kinship care, but none exist at present for children who are adopted, on residence orders, or living with birth parents.

The level of stress being experienced by some parents/carers, often exacerbated by the children's behavioural problems, is a cause for concern. Certainly, the fact that, despite these difficulties, these placements had not disrupted by the time the children were aged between nine and 14, is a welcome sign of placement stability. However, some of the carers commented that they have at times been on the brink of ending the placement due to these problems, and one wonders how they will cope during the child's teenage years. Clearly, there is an onus on policy makers, service managers, and practitioners to take cognisance of these findings, and more importantly to take action to make sure that appropriate supports are provided where necessary to ensure the continuation of these placements, for the long-term health and wellbeing of these children.

References

Abidin R. (1990) *Parenting Stress Index / Short Form*, Lutz, FL: Psychological Assessment Resources, Inc

Abidin R. (1992) 'The determinants of parenting behaviour', *Journal of Clinical Child Psychology*, 21, pp. 407–412

Abidin R. (1995) *The Parenting Stress Index Short Form*, (third edition), Odessa, FL: Psychological Assessment Resources

Achenbach T. M. (1992) *Manual for the Child Behaviour Checklist/2-3 and 1992 Profile*, Burlington: University of Vermont, Department of Psychiatry

Ackerman J. P., and Dozier M. (2005) 'The influence of foster parent investment on children's representations of self and attachment figures', *Applied Developmental Psychology*, 26, pp. 507–520

Ainsworth M. D. S. (1989) 'Attachments beyond infancy', *American Psychologist*, 44:4, pp. 709–716

Ainsworth M. D. S., Blehar M. C., Waters E., and Wall S. (1978) *Patterns of Attachment: A Psychological Study of the Strange Situation*, Hillsdale, NJ: Erlbaum

Aldgate J. (2009) 'Living in kinship care: a child-centred view', *Adoption & Fostering*, 33, pp. 51–63

Aldgate J. and Bradley M. (1999) *Supporting Families through Short Term Fostering*, London: The Stationery Office

Aldgate J. and Jones D. (2005) 'The place of attachment in children's development', in Aldgate J., Jones D., Rose W., and Jeffery C. (eds) *The Developing World of the Child*, London: Jessica Kingsley Publishers

Aldgate J. and McIntosh M. (2006) *Looking After the Family: A Study of Children Looked After in Kinship Care in Scotland*, Edinburgh: Social Work Inspection Agency

Allen M. (2003) *Into the Mainstream: Care leavers entering work, education and training*, York: Joseph Rowntree Foundation

Andersson G. (1999) 'Children in residential and foster care: A Swedish example', *International Journal of Social Welfare*, 8, pp. 253–266

Anderson L., Spencer N. and Vostanis P. (2004) 'The health needs of children aged 6–12 years in foster care', *Adoption & Fostering*, 28, pp. 31–40

Armsden G.C. and Greenberg M.T. (1987) 'The inventory of parent and peer attachment: individual differences and their relationship to psychological well-being in adolescence', *Journal of Youth and Adolescence*, 16, pp. 427–454

Bamford F. and Wolkind S. (1988) *The Physical and Mental Health of Children in Care: Research needs*, London: ESRC

Bardwick J. M. (1974) 'Evolution and parenting', *Journal of Social Issues*, 30:4, pp. 39–62

Barnes G. M. and Farrell M. P. (1992) 'Parental support and control as predictors of adolescent drinking, delinquency, and related problem behaviors', *Journal of Marriage and the Family*, 54, pp. 763–776

Beckett C., Castle J., Groothues C., Hawkins A., Sonuga-Barke E., Colvert E., Kreppner J., Stevens S. and Rutter M. (2008) 'The experience of adoption (2): the association between communicative openness and self-esteem in adoption', *Adoption & Fostering*, 32, pp. 29–39

Belsky J. and Cassidy J. (1994) 'Attachment: theory and evidence', in Rutter M.L., Hay D. F., and Baron-Cohen S. (eds), *Development Through Life: A Handbook for Clinicians*, Oxford: Blackwell

Berrick J. D., Barth R. P. and Needell B. (1994) 'A comparison of kinship foster homes and foster family homes: implications for kinship foster care as family preservation', *Children and Youth Services Review*, 16:1–2, pp. 33–63

Berridge D. and Cleaver H. (1987) *Foster Home Breakdown*, Oxford: Blackwell

Biehal N. (2006) *Reuniting Looked After Children With Their Families:. A review of the research*, London: National Children's Bureau

Biehal N., Ellison S., Baker C. and Sinclair I. (2010) *Belonging and Permanence: Outcomes in long-term foster care and adoption*, London: BAAF

Bilson A. and Barker R. (1995) 'Parental contact with children fostered and in residential care after the Children Act 1989', *British Journal of Social Work*, 25, pp. 367–381

Bird G. W., Peterson R. and Miller S. H. (2002) 'Factors associated with distress among support-seeking adoptive parents', *Family Relations*, 51, pp. 215–220

Bowlby J. (1958) 'The nature of the child's ties to his mother', *International Journal of Psychoanalysis*, 39, pp. 350–373

Boss P.G. (1980) 'Normative family stress: family boundary changes across the life-span', *Family Relations*, 29:4, pp. 445–450

Bowlby J. (1951) *Maternal Care and Mental Health*, World Health Organisation Monograph (Serial No. 2), London: WHO

Bowlby J. (1969) *Attachment and Loss: Vol. 1. Attachment*, New York, NY: Basic Books

Bowlby J. (1973) *Attachment and Loss: Vol. 2. Separation: Anxiety and anger*, New York: Basic Books

Bradshaw J. and Millar J. (1991) *Lone Parent Families in the UK*, Department for Social Security Research Report No. 6, London: HMSO

Brodzinsky D. M. (2005) 'Reconceptualizing openness in adoption: implications for theory, research, and practice', in Brodzinsky D. M. and Palacios J. (eds), *Psychological Issues in Adoption: Research and practice*, Westport, CA: Praeguer

Brodzinsky D. M. (2008) *Adoptive Parent Preparation Project. Phase 1: Meeting the mental health and developmental needs of adopted children. Final policy and practice report*, available at www.adoptioninstitute.org

Brown D. and Moloney A. (2002) 'Contact irregular: a qualitative analysis of the impact of visiting patterns of natural parents on foster placements', *Child & Family Social Work*, 7, pp. 35–45

Bullock R., Gooch D. and Little M. (1998) *Children Going Home: The reunification of families*, Aldershot: Ashgate

Burgess C., Rossvoll F., Wallace B. and Daniel B. (2010) '"It's just like another home, just another family, so it's nae different": children's voices in kinship care: a research study about the experience of children in kinship care in Scotland', *Child & Family Social Work*, 15, pp. 297–306

Carbone J. A., Sawyer M. G., Searle A. K. and Robinson P. J. (2007) 'The health-related quality of life of children and adolescents in home-based foster care', *Quality of Life Research: An international journal of quality of life aspects of treatment, care & rehabilitation*, 16:7, pp. 1157–1166

Casey Family Services (2005) *A Call to Action: An integrated approach to youth permanency and preparation for adulthood*, New Haven, CT: Casey Family Services

Ceballo R., Lansford J. E., Abbey A. and Stewart A.J. (2004) 'Gaining a child: comparing the experiences of biological parents, adoptive parents, and step-parents', *Family Relations*, 53, pp. 38–49

Centre for Social Justice (2008) *Couldn't Care Less*, London: Centre for Social Justice

Clark A. (2005) 'Listening to and involving young children: a review of research and practice', *Early Child Development and Care*, 175:6, pp. 489–505

Cleaver H. (2000) *Fostering Family Contact*, London: TSO

Coakley T. M., Cuddeback G., Buehler C. and Cox M. E. (2007) 'Kinship foster parents' perceptions of factors that promote or inhibit successful fostering', *Children and Youth Services Review*, 29, pp. 92–109

Cole S. A. (2005) 'Infants in foster care: relational and environmental factors affecting attachment', *Journal of Reproductive and Infant Psychology*, 23:1, pp. 43-61

Coleman P. K. and Karraker K. H. (1997) 'Self-efficacy and parenting quality: Findings and future applications', *Developmental Review*, 18:1, pp. 47–85

Courtney M. E. and Barth R. P. (1996) 'Pathways of older adolescents out of foster care: Implications for independent living services, *Social Work*, 41, pp. 75–83

Courtney M. E., Piliavin I., Grogan K. and Nesmith A. (2001) 'Foster youth transitions to adulthood: a longitudinal view of youth leaving care', *Child Welfare*, 80, pp. 685–717

Courtney M. E, Terao S. and Bost N. (2004) *Midwest Evaluation of the Adult Functioning of Former Foster Youth: Conditions of the youth preparing to leave state care*, Chicago: Chapin Hall at the University of Chicago

Crozier J. And Barth R. (2005) 'Cognitive and academic functioning in maltreated children', *Children and Schools*, 27, pp. 197–206

Dance C and Rushton A. (2005) 'Joining a new family: the views and experiences of adopted and fostered young people', *Adoption & Fostering*, 29:2, pp. 18–28

Darbyshire P., MacDougall C. and Schiller W. (2005) 'Multiple methods in qualitative research with children: more insight or just more?', *Qualitative Research*, 5:4, pp. 417–36

DeHart T., Pelham B. W. and Tennen H. (2006) 'What lies beneath: parenting style and implicit self-esteem', *Journal of Experimental Social Psychology*, 42, pp. 1–17

del Valle J. F., López M., Montserrat C. and Bravo A. (2009) 'Twenty years of foster care in Spain: profiles, patterns and outcomes', *Children and Youth Services Review*, 31, pp. 847–853

Denecheau B. (2011) 'Children in residential care and school engagement or school dropout: what makes the difference in terms of policies and practices in England and France?', *Emotional and Behavioural Difficulties*, 16:3, pp. 277–287

Denuwelaere M. and Bracke P. (2007) 'Support and conflict in the foster family and children's well-being: a comparison between foster and birth children', *Family Relations*, 56, pp. 67–79

Department for Children, Schools, and Families (2003) *Every Child Matters*, London: TSO

Department for Children, Schools, and Families (2008) *Care Matters: Time to deliver for children in care*, London: TSO

Department for Education and Skills (2007) *Care Matters: Time for change*, London: TSO

Department of Health (1998) *Modernising Social Services: Promoting independence, improving protection, raising standards*, London: TSO

Department of Health (2009) *Statutory Guidance on Promoting the Health and Wellbeing of Looked After Children*, London: Department of Health

Department of Health and Social Services (1999) *Permanency Planning for Children: Adoption – achieving the right balance*, Belfast: DHSS

Department of Health, Social Services and Public Safety (2002) *Adopting Best Care: Inspection of statutory adoption services in Northern Ireland*, Belfast: DHSSPS (An Roinn Sláinte, Seirbhísí Sóisialta agus Sábháilteachta Poiblí)

Department of Health, Social Services and Public Safety (2006) *Adopting the Future*, Belfast: DHSSPS (An Roinn Sláinte, Seirbhísí Sóisialta agus Sábháilteachta Poiblí)

Department for Health, Social Services and Public Safety (2009a) *Children in Care in Northern Ireland 2008/09: Statistical bulletin*, Belfast: DHSSPS (An Roinn Sláinte, Seirbhísí Sóisialta agus Sábháilteachta Poiblí)

Department for Health, Social Services and Public Safety (2009b) *Adoption of Looked After Children in Northern Ireland 2007/08*, Belfast: DHSSPS (An Roinn Sláinte, Seirbhísí Sóisialta agus Sábháilteachta Poiblí)

Department of Health, Social Services and Public Safety (2012) *Children in Care in Northern Ireland 2009/10: Statistical Bulletin*, Belfast: DHSSPS (An Roinn Sláinte, Seirbhísí Sóisialta agus Sábháilteachta Poiblí)

Dimigen C., Del Priore C., Butler S., Evans S., Ferguson L. and Swan M. (1999) 'Psychiatric disorder among children at time of entering local authority care: questionnaire survey', *British Medical Journal*, 319: 7211, p. 675

Dixon J. (2007) 'Young people leaving care: health, well-being and outcomes', *Child and Family Social Work*, 13, pp. 207–217

Dumaret A. C., Coppel-Batsch M. and Couraud S. (1997) 'Adult outcome of children reared for long-term periods in foster families', *Child Abuse and Neglect*, 21, pp. 911–927

Dunn L., Dunn L.M., Whetton C. and Burley J. (1997) *The British Picture Vocabulary Scale*, Second Edition, London: NFER Nelson

Dunne E.G. and Kettler L.J. (2008) 'Grandparents raising grandchildren in Australia: exploring psychological health and grandparents' experience of providing kinship care', *International Journal of Social Welfare*, 17, pp. 333–345

Egelund T. and Lausten M. (2009) *Prevalence of Mental Health Problems among Children Placed in Out-of-Home Care in Denmark*, Oxford: Blackwell Publishing Ltd

Fargas M., McSherry D., Larkin E., Kelly G., Robinson C. and Schubotz D. (2010) 'Young children returning home from care: the birth parents' perspective', *Child and Family Social Work*, 15:1, pp. 77–86

Farmer E. (2010) 'What factors relate to good placement outcomes in kinship care?', *British Journal of Social Work*, 40, pp. 426–444

Farmer E., Sturgess, W., O'Neill, T. and Wijedasa D. (2011) *Achieving Successful Returns From Care: What makes a difference?*, London: BAAF

Fernandez E. (2008) 'Unraveling emotional, behavioural and educational outcomes in a longitudinal study of children in foster care', *British Journal of Social Work*, 38, pp. 1283–1301

Festinger T. (1983) *No One Ever Asked Us: A postscript to foster care*, New York, NY: Columbia University Press

Fischer K. and Ayoub C. (1994) 'Affective splitting and dissociation in normal and maltreated children: developmental pathways for self in relationships', in Cicchetti D. and Toth S. (eds) *Rochester Symposium on Development and Psychopathology: Vol. 5. Disorders and dysfunctions of the self*, Rochester, NY: University of Rochester Press

Flynn R.J., Ghazal H., Legault L., Vandermeulen G. and Petrick S. (2004) 'Use of population measures and norms to identify resilient outcomes in young people in care: an exploratory study', *Child and Family Social Work*, 9, pp. 65–79

Flynn R. J., Tessier N. G. and Coulombe D. (2013) 'Placement, protective and risk factors in the educational success of young people in care: cross-sectional and longitudinal analyses', *European Journal of Social Work*, 16:1, pp. 70–87

Ford T., Vostanis P., Meltzer H. and Goodman R. (2007) 'Psychiatric disorder among British children looked after by local authorities: Comparison with children living in private households', *The British Journal of Psychiatry*, 190, pp. 319–325

Fratter J., Rowe J., Sapsford D. and Thoburn J. (1991) *Permanent Family Placement: A decade of experience*, London: BAAF

Freeark K., Rosenblum K.L., Hus V.H. and Root B.L. (2008) 'Fathers, mothers and marriages: what shapes adoption conversations in families with young adopted children?', *Adoption Quarterly*, 11:1, pp. 1–23

Fulker D.W., DeFries J.C. and Plomin R. (1988) 'Genetic influence on general mental ability increases between infancy and middle childhood', *Nature*, 336, pp. 767–769

Gallagher B. (1999) 'The abuse of children in public care', *Child Abuse Review*, 8, pp. 357–65

Gil E. and Bogart K. (1982) 'Foster children speak out: a study of children's perceptions of foster care', *Children Today*, Jan–Feb, pp. 7–9

Gilbertson R. and Barber J. (2002) 'Obstacles to involving children and young people in foster care research', *Child and Family Social Work*, 7, pp. 253–258

Gilligan R. (2000) 'Adversity, resilience and young people: the protective value of positive school and spare time experiences', *Children and Society*, 14:1, pp. 37–47

Goodman R. (1997) 'The Strengths and Difficulties Questionnaire: a research note', *Journal of Child Psychology and Psychiatry*, 38, pp. 581–586

Goodman R. (2001) 'Psychometric properties of the Strengths and Difficulties Questionnaire (SDQ)', *Journal of the American Academy of Child and Adolescent Psychiatry*, 40, pp. 1337–1345

Goodman R. and Scott S. (1999) 'Comparing the Strengths and Difficulties Questionnaire and the Child Behaviour Checklist: Is small beautiful?', *Journal of Abnormal Child Psychology*, 27, pp. 17–24

Grotevant H.D. (2000) 'Openness in adoption', *Adoption Quarterly*, 4:1, pp. 45–65

Groze V. and Rosenthal J. (1993) 'Attachment theory and the adoption of children with special needs', *Social Work Research and Abstracts*, 29:2, pp. 5–12

Gullone E. and Robinson K. (2005) 'The Inventory of Parent and Peer Attachment – Revised (IPPA-R) for children: A psychometric evaluation investigation', *Clinical Psychology and Psychotherapy*, 12, pp. 67–79

Hare A.D. and Bullock R. (2006) 'Dispelling misconceptions about looked after children', *Adoption & Fostering*, 30, pp. 26–35

Harris R. and Lindsey C. (2002) 'How professionals think about contact between children and their birth parents', *Clinical Child Psychology and Psychiatry*, 7, pp. 147–161

Harter S. (1998) 'The development of self-representations', in Damon W. and Eisenberg N. (eds) *Handbook of Child Psychology*, New York, NY: Wiley

Hastings R.P. and Brown T. (2002) 'Coping strategies and the impact of challenging behaviors on special educators' burnout', *Mental Retardation*, 40:2, pp. 148–156

Hess P. and Proch P. (1988) *Family Visiting in Out-of-Home Care: A guide to practice*, Washington, DC: Child Welfare League of America

Hicks C. and Nixon S. (1989) 'Allegations of child abuse: foster carers as victims', *Foster Care*, 58, pp. 14–15

Hill C. and Thompson M. (2003) 'Mental and physical health co-morbidity in looked after children', *Clinical Child Psychology and Psychiatry*, 8, pp. 315–321

Hill C. and Watkins J. (2003) 'Statutory health assessments for looked after children: what do they achieve?', *Child: Care, Health and Development*, 29, pp. 3–13

Hodges J. and Tizard B. (1989) 'Social and family relationships of ex-institutional adolescents', *Journal of Child Psychology and Psychiatry*, 30, pp. 77–97

Howe D. (1997) 'Parent reported problems in 211 adopted children: some risk and protective factors', *Journal of Child Psychology and Psychiatry*, 37, pp. 401–412

Howe D. (1998) *Patterns of Adoption: Nature, Nurture, and Psychosocial Development*, Oxford: Blackwell Science

Howe D. and Fearnley S. (2003) 'Disorders of attachment in adopted and fostered children: recognition and treatment', *Clinical Child Psychology and Psychiatry*, 8, pp. 369–387

Humphreys C. and Kiraly M. (2011) 'High-frequency family contact: a road to nowhere for infants', *Child and Family Social Work*, 16, pp. 1–11

Iwaniec D. (1995) *The Emotionally Abused and Neglected Child*, Chichester: Wiley

Jackson S. (2010) 'Reconnecting care and education: from the Children Act 1989 to Care Matters', *Journal of Children's Services*, 5:3, pp. 48–60

Jackson S., Ajayi S. and Quigley M. (2005) *Going to University from Care: Final report of the By Degrees Project*, London: Institute of Education

James A. and Prout A. (1990) *Constructing and Reconstructing Childhood*, London: Falmer

Jeske P.J. (1985) 'Piers Harris Children's Self-concept Scale', in Mitchell I. V. Jr. (ed) *Ninth Mental Measurement Yearbook, Lincoln: University of Nebraska*, Lincoln, NE: Buros Institute of Mental Measurement

Jones C. and Hackett S. (2008) 'Communicative openness within adoptive families: adoptive parents' narrative accounts of the challenges of adoption talk and the approaches used to manage these challenges', *Adoption Quarterly*, 10:3–4, pp. 157–178

Judge S. (2003) 'Determinants of parental stress in families adopting children from Eastern Europe', *Family Relations*, 52, pp. 241–248

Judge S. (2004) 'Adoptive families: the effects of early relational deprivation in children adopted from Eastern European orphanages', *Journal of Family Nursing*, 10:3, pp. 338–356

Juffer F., Bakermans-Kranenburg M. J. and Van Ijzendoorn M. H. (2005) 'Enhancing children's socio-emotional development: a review of intervention studies', in Teti D. M. (ed) *Handbook of Research Methods in Developmental Science*, Oxford: Blackwell

Juffer F. and Van Ijzendoorn M. H. (2007) 'A longitudinal study of Korean adoptees in the Netherlands: infancy to middle childhood', in Bergquist K. J. S., Vonk M. E., Kim D. S. and Feit M. D. (eds) *International Korean Adoption: A fifty-year history of policy and practice*, Binghamton, NY: Haworth Press

Kaniuk, J., Steele M. and Hodges J. (2004) 'Report on a longitudinal research project, exploring the development of attachments between older, hard-to-place children and their adopters over the first two years of placement', *Adoption & Fostering*, 28:2, pp. 61–67

Kaufman J. and Cicchetti D. (1989) 'The effects of maltreatment on school-aged children's socioemotional development: assessments in a day camp setting', *Developmental Psychology*, 25, pp. 516–524

Kelly G. (1995) 'Foster parents and long-term placements: key findings from a Northern Ireland study', *Children and Society*, 9, pp. 19–29

Kelly G. (1999) 'Freeing for adoption: the Northern Ireland social care context', *Child Care in Practice*, 5:3, pp. 243–50

Kelly G. and Coulter J. (1997) 'The Children (Northern Ireland) Order 1995: a new era for fostering and adoption services?', *Adoption & Fostering*, 21, pp. 5–13

Kelly G. and McSherry D. (2002) 'Adoption from care in Northern Ireland: Problems in the process', *Child and Family Social Work*, 7, pp. 297–309

Kelly G. and McSherry D. (2003) *Report on the Freeing Order Processes in Northern Ireland*, Belfast: Department of Health, Social Services & Public Safety (An Roinn Sláinte, Seirbhísí Sóisialta agus Sábháilteachta Poiblí)

Kenrick J. (2009) 'Concurrent planning: a retrospective study of the continuities and discontinuities of care, and their impact on the development of infants and young children placed for adoption by the Coram Concurrent Planning Project', *Adoption & Fostering*, 33, pp. 5–18

Kernis M. H., Paradise A. W., Whitaker D., Wheatman S. and Goldman B. (2000) 'Master of one's psychological domain? Not likely if one's self-esteem is unstable', *Personality and Social Psychology Bulletin*, 26, pp. 1297–1305

Kim J. and Cicchetti D. (2003) 'Social self-efficacy and behaviour problems in maltreated and nonmaltreated children', *Journal of Clinical Child and Adolescent Psychology*, 32, pp. 106–117

Kim J. and Cicchetti D. (2009) 'Mean-level change and intraindividual variability in self-esteem and depression among high-risk children', *International Journal of Behavioral Development*, 33, pp. 202–214

Kufeldt K., Armstrong J. and Dorosh M. (1995) 'How children in care view their own and their foster families: a research study', *Child Welfare*, 74, pp. 695–715

Kuhn J. C. and Carter A. S. (2006) 'Maternal self-efficacy and associated parenting cognitions among mothers of children with autism', *American Journal of Orthopsychiatry*, 76, pp. 564–575

Laible D. J., Carlo G. and Roesch S. C. (2004) 'Pathways to self-esteem in late adolescence: the role of parent and peer attachment, empathy, and social behaviours', *Journal of Adolescence*, 27:6, pp. 703–716

Leathers S. (2003) 'Parental visiting, conflicting allegiances, and emotional and behavioural problems among foster children', *Family Relations*, 52, pp. 53–63

Lee R. and Whiting J. B. (2007) 'Foster children's expressions of ambiguous loss', *The American Journal of Family Therapy*, 35:5, pp. 417–428

Leon D. and Walt G. (2001) *Poverty, Inequality and Health: An international perspective*, Oxford: Oxford University Press

Leslie L. K., Hurlburt M. S., Landsverk J., Rolls J. A., Wood P. A. and Kelleher K. J. (2003) 'Comprehensive assessments for children entering foster care: a national perspective', *Pediatrics: Official journal of the American Academy of Pediatrics*, 112, pp. 134–142

Levin K. A. and Currie C. (2010) 'Family structure, mother–child communication, father-child communication, and adolescent life satisfaction: a cross-sectional multilevel analysis', *Health Education*, 110:3, pp. 152–158

Lindsey C. (1995) 'Systemic and developmental aspects of contact, in Argent H. (ed) *See you Soon: Contact with children looked after by local authorities*, London: BAAF

Lipscombe J., Moyers S. and Farmer E. (2004) 'What changes in "parenting" approaches occur over the course of adolescent foster care placements?', *Child and Family Social Work*, 9, pp. 347–357

Logan J. and Smith C. (1999) 'Adoption and direct post-adoption contact', *Adoption & Fostering*, 23, pp. 58–59

Lowe N. and Murch M. (2002) *The Plan for the Child: Adoption or long-term fostering*, London: BAAF

Loxterkamp L. (2009) 'Contact and Truth: The unfolding predicament in adoption and fostering', *Clinical Child Psychology and Psychiatry*, 14, pp. 423–435

Luckock B. and Hart A. (2005) 'Adoptive family life and adoption support: policy ambivalence and the development of effective services', *Child and Family Social Work*, 10, pp. 125–134

Luke N. and Coyne S. M. (2008) 'Fostering self-esteem: exploring adult recollections on the influence of foster parents', *Child and Family Social Work*, 13, pp. 402–410

Lyman S. B. and Bird G. W. (1996) 'A closer look at self-image in male foster care adolescents', *Social Work*, 41, pp. 85–96

Macaskill C. (2002) *Safe Contact? Children in permanent placements and contact with their relatives*, Dorset: Russell House Publishing

MacDonald M. and McSherry D. (2011) 'Open adoption: adoptive parents' experiences of birth family contact and talking to their child about adoption', *Adoption & Fostering*, 35, pp. 4–16

MacDonald M. and McSherry D. (2013) 'Constrained adoptive parenthood and family transition: adopters' experience of unplanned birth family contact in adolescence', *Child and Family Social Work*, 18:1, pp. 87–96

Maier H. W. (1986) *Dependence and Independence Development Throughout the Human Life Span: Implications for the helping professions*, Seattle, WA: University of Washington

Marmot M. (2010) *Fair Society, Healthy Lives: The Marmot Review*, London: The Marmot Review

Martin P. Y. and Jackson S. (2002) 'Educational success for children in public care: advice from a group of high achievers', *Child and Family Social Work*, 7, pp 121–130

Masson J. (1997) 'Maintaining contact between parents and children in the public care', *Children and Society*, 11, pp. 222–230

Mather M. (2010) '30 years of childcare practice and research: an overview', *Adoption & Fostering*, 34, 54–58

Matthews H. and Limb M. (1999) 'Defining an agenda for the geography of children: review and prospect', *Progress in Human Geography*, 23:1, pp. 61–90

Mayall B. (2000) 'Conversations with children: working with generational issues', in Christensen P. and James A. (eds) *Research with Children: Perspectives and practices*, London: Routledge Falmer

McCann J., James A., Wilson S. and Dunn G. (1996) 'Prevalence of psychiatric disorders in young people in the care system', *British Medical Journal*, 313, pp. 1529–1530

McCarthy G., Janeway J. and Geddes A. (2003) 'The impact of emotional and behavioural problems on the lives of children growing up in the care system', *Adoption & Fostering*, 27, pp. 14–19

McGlone K., Santos L., Kazama L., Fong R. and Mueller C. (2002) 'Psychological stress in adoptive parents of special needs children', *Child Welfare*, 81, pp. 151–171

McGue M., Bouchard T. J., Iacono W.G. and Lykken D.T. (1993) 'Behavioural genetics of cognitive ability: a life-span perspective', in Plomin R. and McClearn G.E. (eds) *Nature, Nurture and Psychology*, Washington DC: American Psychological Association

McSherry D., Larkin E., Fargas M., Kelly G., Robinson C., Macdonald G., Schubotz D., and Kilpatrick R. (2008) *From Care to Where? A Care Pathways and Outcomes report for practitioners*, Belfast: Institute of Child Care Research, Queen's University

McSherry D., Weatherall K., Larkin E., Fargas Malet M. and Kelly G. (2010) 'Who goes where? Young children's pathways through care in Northern Ireland', *Adoption & Fostering*, 34:2, pp. 23–37

Meltzer H., Corbin T., Gatward R., Goodman R. and Ford T. (2003) *The Mental Health of Young People Looked After by Local Authorities in England*, London: Office of National Statistics

Meltzer H., Lader D., Corbin T., Goodman, R. and Ford, T. (2004a) *The Mental Health of Young People Looked After by Local Authorities in Scotland*, Edinburgh: TSO

Meltzer H., Lader D., Corbin T., Goodman R. and Ford T. (2004b) *The Mental Health of Young People Looked After by Local Authorities in Wales*, London: TSO

Mendenhall T. J., Berge J. M., Wrobel G. M., Grotevant H.D. and McRoy R. G. (2004) 'Adolescents' satisfaction with contact in adoption', *Child and Adolescent Social Work*, 21, pp 275–290

Milburn N.L., Lynch M. and Jackson J. (2008) 'Early identification of mental health needs for children in care: a therapeutic assessment programme for statutory clients of child protection', *Clinical Child Psychology and Psychiatry*, 13:1, pp. 31–47

Millham S., Bullock R., Hosie K. and Little M. (1986) *Lost in Care: The problems of maintaining links between children in care and their families*, Aldershot: Gower

Millward R., Kennedy E., Towlson K. and Minnis H. (2006) 'Reactive attachment disorder in looked after children', *Emotional and Behavioural Difficulties*, 11, pp. 273–279

Minty B. (1999) 'Annotation: outcomes in long-term foster family care', *Journal of Child Psychology and Psychiatry*, 40, pp. 991–999

Mooney A., Statham J. and Monck E. (2009) *Promoting the Health of Looked After Children: A study to inform revision of the 2002 Guidance*, London: Institute of Education, University of London

Morgan J., Robinson D. and Aldridge J. (2002) 'Parenting stress and externalising behaviour: research review', *Child and Family Social Work*, 7, pp. 219–225

Morgan K. and Baron R. (2011) 'Challenging behaviour in looked after young people; feelings of parental self-efficacy and psychological well-being in foster carers', *Adoption & Fostering*, 35, pp. 18–32

Moyers S., Farmer E. and Lipscombe J. (2006) 'Contact with family members and its impact on adolescents and their foster placements', *British Journal of Social Work*, 36, 541–559

Mullan C., McAlister S., Rollock F. and Fitzsimons L. (2007) 'Care just changes your life: factors impacting upon the mental health of children and young people with experiences of care in Northern Ireland', *Child Care in Practice*, 13, pp. 417–434

Neil E. (2002) 'Contact after adoption: the roles of agencies in making and supporting plans', *Adoption & Fostering*, 26, pp. 25–38

Neil E. (2010) 'The benefits and challenges of direct post-adoption contact: perspectives from adoptive parents and birth relatives', *Aloma*, 27, pp. 89–115

Neil E., Beek M. and Schofield G. (2003) 'Thinking about and managing contact in permanent placements: the differences and similarities between adoptive parents and foster carers', *Clinical Child Psychology and Psychiatry*, 8, pp. 401–418

Neil E. and Howe D. (2004) *Contact in Adoption and Permanent Foster Care: Research theory and practice*, London: BAAF

Nelis S. M. and Rae G. (2009) 'Brief report: peer attachment in adolescents', *Journal of Adolescence*, 32:2, pp. 443–447

Nomaguchi K. M. and Milkie M. (2003) 'Costs and rewards of children: the effects of becoming a parent on adults' lives', *Journal of Marriage and Family*, 66, pp. 413–430

Office of First Minister and Deputy First Minister (2006) *Our Children and Young People – Our Pledge: A ten year strategy for children and young people in Northern Ireland 2006–2016*, Belfast: OFMDFM

O'Kane C. (2000) 'The development of participatory techniques: facilitating children's views about decisions which affect them', in Christensen P. and James A. (eds) *Research with Children: Perspectives and practices*, London: Routledge Falmer

Oke N., Rostill-Brookes H. and Larkin M. (2011) 'Against the odds: foster carers' perceptions of family, commitment and belonging in successful placements', *Clinical Child Psychology and Psychiatry*, doi: 10.1177/1359104511426398

Oyserman D., Bybee D., Terry K. and Hart-Johnson T. (2004) 'Possible selves as roadmaps', *Journal of Research in Personality*, 38, pp. 130–149

Palacios J. and Jiménez J. (2009) 'Kinship foster care: protection or risk?', *Adoption & Fostering*, 33, pp. 64–75

Palacios J. and Sanchez-Sandoval Y. (2006) 'Stress in parents of adopted children', *International Journal of Behavioural Development*, 30, pp. 481–487

Pecora P., Williams J., Kessler R. C., Downs A. C., O'Brien K., Hiripi E. and Morello S. (2003) *Assessing the Effects of Foster Care: Early results from the Casey National Alumni Study*, Seattle, WA: Casey Family Programmes

Peterson G. W., Southworth L. E. and Peters D. F. (1983) 'Children's self-esteem and maternal behavior in three low-income samples', *Psychological Reports*, 52, pp. 603–609

Piers E. V. (1984) *Manual for the Piers-Harris Children's Self-Concept Scale*, Los Angeles, CA: Western Psychological Services

Piers E. V. and Herzberg D.S. (2002) *Piers-Harris 2: Piers-Harris Children's Self-Concept Scale*, (second edition), Los Angeles, CA: Western Psychological Services

Pithouse A., Lowe K. and Hill-Tout J. (2004) 'Foster carers who care for children with challenging behaviour: a total population study', *Adoption & Fostering*, 28, pp. 20–30

Plomin R., Fulker D.W. and Corley R. (1997) 'Nature, nurture and cognitive development from 1 to 16 years: a parent–offspring adoption study', *Psychological Science*, 8, pp. 442–447

Punch S. (2002) 'Research with children: the same or different from research with adults?', *Childhood*, 9:3, pp. 321–41

Quinton D. (2012) *Rethinking Matching in Adoptions from Care*, London: BAAF

Quinton D., Rushton A., Dance C. and Mayers D. (1997) 'Contact between children placed away from home and their birth parents: research issues and evidence', *Clinical Child Psychology and Psychiatry*, 2, pp. 393–413

Quinton D., Rushton A., Dance C. and Mayers D. (1998) *Joining New Families: A study of adoption and fostering in middle childhood*, London: Wiley

Quinton D., Selwyn J., Rushton A. and Dance C. (1999) 'Contact between children placed away from home and their birth parents: Ryburn's "reanalysis" analysed', *Clinical Child Psychology and Psychiatry*, 4, pp. 519–531

Raikes H. A. and Thompson R. A. (2005) 'Efficacy and social support as predictors of parenting stress among families in poverty', *Infant Mental Health Journal*, 26, pp. 177–190

Rees C. A. and Selwyn J. (2009) 'Non-infant adoption from care: lessons for safeguarding children', *Child: Care, Health and Development*, 35:4, pp. 561–567

Richards L., Wood N. and Ruiz-Calzada L. (2006) 'The mental health needs of looked after children in a local authority permanent placement team and the value of the Goodman SDQ', *Adoption & Fostering*, 30, pp. 43–52

Ritchie J. and Spencer L. (1994) 'Qualitative data analysis for applied policy research', in Bryman A. and Burgess R.G. (eds) *Analysing Qualitative Data*, London: Routledge

Roberts E. L. and Bengtson V. L. (1993) 'Relationships with parents, self-esteem and psychological well-being in young adulthood', *Social Psychology Quarterly*, 56:4, pp. 263–277

Rowe J., Hundleby M. and Garnett L. (1989) *Child Care Now: A survey of placement patterns*, London: BAAF

Rowe J. and Lambert L. (1973) *Children who Wait*, London: Association of British Fostering Agencies

Rowe J., Cain H., Hundleby M. and Keane A. (1984) *Long Term Foster Care*, London: Batsford

Rushton A. (2003) *The Adoption of Looked After Children: A scoping review of research*, London: Social Care Institute for Excellence (SCIE)

Rushton A. (2004) 'A scoping and scanning review of research on the adoption of children placed from public care', *Clinical Child Psychology and Psychiatry*, 9, pp. 89–106

Rutter M. (1995) 'Clinical implications of attachment concepts: retrospect and prospect', *Journal of Child Psychology and Psychiatry, and Allied Disciplines*, 36:4, pp. 549–571

Rutter M. and the ERA study team (1998) 'Developmental catch-up, and deficit, following adoption after severe global early privation', *Journal of Child Psychiatry*, 39:4, pp. 465–476

Rutter M., Graham O., Chadwick O. and Yule W. (1976) 'Adolescent turmoil: fact or fiction?', *Child Psychology & Psychiatry*, 17, pp. 35–56

Ryburn M. (1998) 'In whose best interests?: Post-adoption contact with the birth family', *Child and Family Law Quarterly*, 10, pp. 1–21

Schofield G. (2002) 'The significance of a secure base: a psychosocial model of long-term foster care', *Child and Family Social Work*, 7, pp. 259–272

Schofield G. and Beek M. (2005) 'Providing a secure base: parenting children in long-term foster family care', *Attachment & Human Development*, 7, pp. 3–25

Schofield G., Beek M., Sargent K. and Thoburn J. (2000) *Growing up in Foster Care*, London: BAAF

Schofield G. and Simmonds J. (2011) 'Contact for infants subject to care proceedings', *Adoption & Fostering*, 35, pp. 70–74

Sellick C., Thoburn J. and Philpot T. (2004) *What Works in Adoption and Foster Care?*, London: Barnardo's/BAAF

Selman P. (2010) 'Intercountry adoption in Europe 1998-2008: patterns, trends and issues', *Adoption & Fostering*, 34:1, pp. 4–19

Selwyn J. (2004) 'Placing older children in new families: changing patterns of contact', in Neil E. and Howe D. (eds) *Contact in Adoption and Permanent Foster Care: Research, theory and practice*, London: BAAF

Selwyn J. and Quinton D. (2004) 'Stability, permanence, outcomes and support: foster care and adoption compared', *Adoption & Fostering*, 28, pp. 6–15

Selwyn J., Sturgess W., Quinton D. and Baxter C. (2003) *Costs and Outcomes of Non-Infant Adoptions*, Bristol: Hadley Centre for Adoption and Foster Care Studies, University of Bristol

Sempik J., Ward H. and Darker I. (2008) 'Emotional and behavioural difficulties of children and young people at entry into care', *Clinical Child Psychology and Psychiatry*, 13, pp. 221–233

Sen R. (2010) 'Managing contact in Scotland for children in non-permanent out-of-home placement', *Child Abuse Review*, 19, pp. 423–437

Sen R. and Broadhurst K. (2011) 'Contact between children in out-of-home placements and their family and friends networks: a research review', *Child and Family Social Work*, 16, pp. 298–309

Sinclair I. (2005) *Fostering Now: Messages from research*, London: Jessica Kingsley Publishers

Sinclair I., Baker C., Wilson K. and Gibbs, I. (2005) *Foster Children: Where they go and how they get on*, London: Jessica Kingsley Publishers

Sinclair I., Wilson K. and Gibbs I. (2004) *Foster Placements: Why they succeed and why they fail*, London: Jessica Kingsley Publishers

Skuse T. and Ward H. (2003) *Outcomes for Looked After Children: Listening to children's views of care and accommodation*, Interim Report to the Department of Health, Loughborough: Center for Child and Family Research, Loughborough University

Social Exclusion Unit (2003) *A Better Education for Children in Care*, London: SEU

Social Services Inspectorate (1998) *Circular on Adoption*, London: TSO

Spratt E., Saylor C. and Marcias M. M. (2007) 'Assessing parenting stress in multiple samples of children with special needs (CSN)', *Families, Systems and Health*, 25, pp. 435–449

Sykes J., Sinclair I., Gibbs I. and Wilson K. (2002) 'Kinship and stranger foster carers: how do they compare?', *Adoption & Fostering*, 26:2, pp. 38–48

Tabak I., Mazur J., Granado Alcón M. C. and Orkenyi A. (2012) 'Examining trends in parent–child communication in Europe over 12 years', *Journal of Early Adolescence*, 32:1, pp. 26–54

Tanner K. and Turney D. (2003) 'What do we know about child neglect? A critical review of the literature and its application to social work practice', *Child and Family Social Work*, 8:1, pp. 25–34

Teggart T. and Menary J. (2005) 'An investigation of the mental health needs of children looked after by Craigavon and Banbridge Health and Social Services Trust', *Child Care in Practice*, 11, pp. 39–49

Thoburn J. (1991) 'Evaluating placement: an overview of 1,165 placements and some methodological issues', in Fratter J., Rowe J., Sapsford D. and Thoburn J. (eds) *Permanent Family Placement: A decade of experience*, London: BAAF

Thoburn J. (2007) *Globalisation and Child Welfare: Some lessons from a cross-national study of children in out-of-home care*, Norwich: School of Social Work and Psychosocial Studies, University of East Anglia

Thoburn J., Robinson J. and Anderson B. (2012) *Returning Children Home From Public Care: Research Briefing 42*, London: Social Care Institute for Excellence (SCIE)

Thoburn J. and Rowe J. (1991) 'Survey findings and conclusions', in Fratter J., Rowe J., Sapsford D. and Thoburn J. (eds) *Permanent Family Placement: A decade of experience*, London: BAAF

Thomas C. (2013) *Adoption for Looked After Children: Messages from research*, London: BAAF

Thomas C., Beckford V., Murch M. and Lowe N. (1999) *Adopted Children Speaking*, London: BAAF

Thompson R. (1998) 'Early sociopersonality development', in Damon W (ed) and Eisenberg N (vol ed) *Handbook of Child Psychology (Vol 3), Social, Emotional, and Personality Development*, New York, NY: Wiley

Triseliotis J. (2002) 'Long-term foster care or adoption? The evidence examined', *Child and Family Social Work*, 7, pp. 23–33

Triseliotis J., Borland M. and Hill M. (2000) *Delivering Foster Care*, London: BAAF

Trout A. L., Hagaman J., Casey K., Reid R. and Epstein M. (2007) 'The academic status of children and youth in out-of-home care: a review of the literature', *Children and Youth Services Review*, 30, pp. 979–994

Trout A. L., Nordness P. D., Pierce C. D. and Epstein M. H. (2003) 'Research on the academic status of children with emotional and behavioral disorders: a review of the literature from 1961 to 2000', *Journal of Emotional and Behavioral Disorders*, 11:4, pp. 198–210

Turner W. and Macdonald G. (2011) 'Treatment foster care for improving outcomes in children and young people: a systematic review', *Research on Social Work Practice*, 2, pp. 501–527

UK Joint Working Party on Foster Care (1999) *UK National Standards for Foster Care*, London: National Foster Care Association

United States Department of Health and Human Services (2011) *Adoption USA: A chartbook based on the 2007 National Survey of Adoptive Parents*, Washington: USDHSS

Utting W. (1997) *People Like Us: The report on the review of safeguards for children living away from home*, London: TSO

Valentine G. (1997) 'A safe place to grow up? Parenting, perceptions of children's safety and the rural idyll', *Journal of Rural Studies*, 13:2, pp. 137–148

Vinnerljung B., Lindblad F., Hjern A., Rasmussen F. and Dalen M. (2010) 'School performance at age 16 among international adoptees: a Swedish national cohort study', *International Social Work*, 53:4, pp. 510–527

Von Korff L. and Grotevant H. D. (2011) 'Contact in adoption and adoptive identity formation: the mediating role of family conversation', *Journal of Family Psychology*, 25, pp. 393–401

Ward H., Jones H., Lynch M. and Skuse T. (2002) 'Issues concerning the health of looked after children', *Adoption & Fostering*, 26, pp. 8–18

Ward H., Munro E. R., Dearden C. and Nicholson D. (2003) *Outcomes for Looked After Children: Life pathways and decision-making for very young children in care or accommodation*, Loughborough: Centre for Child and Family Research

Webster-Stratton C. (1990) 'Stress: a potential disruptor of parent perceptions and family interactions', *Journal of Clinical Child Psychology*, 19:4, pp. 302–312

Whelan D. J. (2003) 'Using attachment theory when placing siblings in foster care', *Child and Adolescent Social Work*, 20:1, pp. 21–36

Whyte M. S. and Campbell A. (2008) 'The Strengths and Difficulties Questionnaire: a useful screening tool to identify mental health strengths and needs in looked after children and inform care plans at looked after children reviews?', *Child Care in Practice*, 14:2, pp. 193–206

Wilkinson R. and Pickett K. (2006) 'Income inequality and population health: a review and explanation of the evidence', *Social Science and Medicine*, 62, pp. 1768–84

Williams J., Jackson S., Maddocks A., Cheung W., Love A. and Hutchings H. (2001) 'Case–control study of the health of those looked after by local authorities', *Archive of Disease in Childhood*, 85, pp. 280–285

Wilson K. (2006) 'Can foster carers help children resolve their emotional and behavioural difficulties?', *Clinical Child Psychology and Psychiatry*, 11, pp. 495–511

Wilson K. and Sinclair I. (2004) 'Contact in foster care: some dilemmas and opportunities', in Neil E. and Howe D. (eds) *Contact in Adoption and Permanent Foster Care: Research, theory and practice*, London: BAAF

Wilson K., Sinclair I. and Gibbs I. (2000) 'The trouble with foster care: The impact of stressful events on foster carers', *British Journal of Social Work*, 30:2, pp. 193–209

Wilson K., Sinclair I., Taylor C., Pithouse A. and Sellick C. (2004) *Fostering Success: An exploration of the research literature in foster care*, London: Social Care Institute for Excellence (SCIE)

Index